The Inner Planets

THE
Inner
Planets

Building Blocks of Personal Reality

Liz Greene & Howard Sasportas

SEMINARS IN
PSYCHOLOGICAL ASTROLOGY
VOLUME 4

SAMUEL WEISER, INC.

York Beach, Maine

To Howard, in loving memory
1948-1992

First published in 1993 by
Samuel Weiser, Inc.
Box 612
York Beach, Maine 03910-0612

99 98
10 9 8 7 6 5 4

Library of Congress Cataloging-in-Publication Data
Greene, Liz.
        The inner planets : building blocks of personal reality / by
Liz Greene & Howard Sasportas.
                p.   cm.   --(Seminars in psychological astrology : v. 4)
                1. Astrology.   2. Inner planets--Miscellanea.
3. Individual differences--Miscellanea.
        I. Sasportas, Howard.   II. Title.   III. Series
        BF1724.G74   1993
133.5'3--dc20   91-34557
                                                                CIP
ISBN 0-87728-741-4
EB

Cover illustration is "The Birth of Venus" by Odilon Redon, Paris,
Petit Palais. Giraudon Art Resource, NY. Used by kind permission.

Printed in the United States of America

The paper used in this publication meets the minimum requirements of the American National Standard for Permanence of Paper
for Printed Library Materials Z39.48-1984.

CONTENTS

PREFACE

At the bar of history, contemporary judgements seldom prove reliable. Yet if one can be certain of anything it must be that Howard Sasportas will feature prominently in any list of the key figures involved in the reemergence of astrology as a major formative force in Western culture. It is no small tribute to the impact of the man and his work that at his death in London, England, at 17:11 BST, May 12, 1992 (as Pluto crossed his MC and the Sun his IC), Howard Sasportas became the very first astrologer in the history of the British Press to be honoured by a full length obituary. On the day of his funeral, this appeared on the Gazette page of *The Independent*[1], complete with his smiling face. It was published alongside the Court Circular together with celebrations of the lives of two other outstanding souls: Marshal Nie Rongzhen, the last of Mao Tse-Tung's generals, and Sylvia Syms, described by Frank Sinatra as "the world's greatest saloon singer"; a juxtaposition of diverse human greatness that Howard's Venus in Gemini humour and his Mars with Saturn and Pluto in Leo aspirations would have richly appreciated.

Howard's claim to fame and honour—beyond the relatively closed world of professional astrology—lies in the very fact that he was not content to let astrology blush unseen, unused and unconsidered by the larger world. He was determined to put astrology on the map of human consciousness in the service of humanity, and for the self-realization of individual souls. He was to give himself totally to this task with a zest, vitality, courage, wit, love, compassion, and wisdom that none who met him will ever forget. That today around the world a growing number of psychologists, therapists, counsellors, and others in the helping professions take

---

[1]*The Independent*, May 18, 1992, p. 15.

astrology seriously as a diagnostic and therapeutic tool is in no small measure due to the labours, enthusiasm, and concern of Howard Sasportas.

In this work, Howard's pivotal achievement was his visionary founding, together with Liz Greene, of the Centre for Psychological Astrology, at the time of the Saturn-Pluto and Jupiter-Uranus conjunctions of 1983. Their centre set out a rigorous professional training program designed to cross-fertilise the fields of astrology and depth, humanistic, and transpersonal psychology, with students being expected to undergo their own personal therapy as an integral part of their training (for further details, see About the Centre, p. 330). From the outset, the curriculum also included a deep concern with mythology and the study of the principles of kabbala and the tarot. With this potent combination, Howard and Liz created a crucial aquaduct between the rivers of depth and height psychology and the already swelling stream of renascent astrology. The riches that have flowed from and through this confluence are now apparent for all to see. Under Howard and Liz's inspired direction, the Centre for Psychological Astrology has gone from strength to strength, attracting to it some of the finest and most enquiring and imaginative minds in both fields. In the process it has generated directly, and indirectly, an incomparable wealth of astro-psychological literature, one precious volume of which you are now holding.

The present transcripts, like the three preceding volumes in this Seminars series, give a taste of the breadth and depth of understanding that Howard brought to his work as a teacher, and the fiery vitality and enthusiasm of his presentations and dialogues with the Centre's students. As always, here we see his probing, lively, intuitive mind ever eager to bring out the inner life of the planetary gods, bringing new and profound insights to the commonplaces of astrology, and yet at one and the same time educing and drawing out the students' own inner understanding.

So where, we may ask, was Howard coming from? He was born in Hartford, Connecticut, USA at 1.46 A.M. EST on April 12, 1948. Students will find endless instruction in the contemplation of his birth chart with the sheer power and vitality of all of its Fire and Earth which he lived and enjoyed to the full as pioneer, consolidator, and nourisher. But, as always, we can learn much from placing the man and his chart in its family context. Howard's parents, Max and Edith Sasportas, were from a long line of devout orthodox Sephardic Jews; and though he was later to become open to all dimensions of the spiritual life, these primary roots were undoubtedly of great significance to him. The Sephardim, the Jews of Spain, have always been noted for their cultural and intellectual achievements, and some, like Maimonides (1135–1204), played central parts in the return of the ancient wisdom tradition to Europe. It was, for example, Arab and Sephardic Jewish astronomer-astrologers who were engaged by Alfonso X of Spain in the 1250s to prepare the *Alfonsine Tables* of planetary movement that were so crucial to the development of astrology in Europe. When the Jews were expelled from Spain in 1492, they dispersed throughout Europe and North Africa. One of these Sephardim, Jacob Sasportas (born in Oran, Morocco 1610, died 1698), a direct ancestor of Howard's, was to become London's first Rabbi in 1664. The Sasportases later moved on to Amsterdam and, in due course, to the USA.

Whether it was consciously or unconsciously, this great creative Sephardic tradition undoubtedly informed an important level of Howard's life. In 1973, Howard moved to London, England, perhaps subliminally drawn back to Europe by these ancient and illustrious roots. Here he was soon to become involved in the emerging astrology movement that was focused around the independent Faculty of Astrological Studies. The FAS had been founded in London in 1948 by the great Charles Carter, Edmund Casselli, Margaret Hone, and Lorenz von Sommaruga for the purpose of advancing the understanding of the astrological tradition and producing practicing astrologers of integrity. In 1979, Sasportas was awarded the Gold Medal for the Faculty of Astrological Studies' Diploma Exam, its highest honour, and the same year became a tutor for the Faculty and began to establish himself as an immensely popular teacher and speaker there and with the Astrological Association.

As someone who believed that education is a way of life, Howard continued his exploration of psychology and spiritual studies, as well as astrology over the following years. He was a graduate of the London based Psychosynthesis and Education Trust, which focuses on the very broadly based psychological theories and methods of the Italian psychologist Roberto Assagioli and also of the highly influential Centre for Transpersonal Psychology founded by Ian Gordon-Brown and Barbara Somers. The ever-growing breadth and certitude of Howard's inner spiritual vision was undoubtedly also assisted by his lifelong practice of Transcendental Meditation which he had taken up while still at college.

Sasportas was not only a superb teacher and counsellor but also, when he could find time from his endlessly active teaching and therapeutic practice, a fine writer. In addition to the transcripts of his seminars at the Centre, his books, such as *The Gods of Change* and *The Twelve Houses*, are models of clarity and have all the freshness and humour of his brilliant and engaging lectures. *The Gods of Change*, like most of his writing, is a classic in its field. It illuminates the profound transformative significance of the cycles of the planets Uranus, Neptune, and Pluto in the unfoldment of a human life. In it, his own wealth of personal experience, study, and client work shines through as he teaches us how we can learn to collaborate with the inevitability of change and find the deeper meaning and significance behind the periods of pain and crisis in our lives.[2]

Just as he constantly encouraged students to grow and fulfill their own unique potential, so too as series editor of Viking-Penguin's Arkana Contemporary Astrology Series from 1987 to 1991, he seized an opportunity to bring real astrology to a much larger audience and was responsible for encouraging his fellow astrology writers to give of their very best for astrology, as I was myself privileged to discover. In that series, he put together a superb collection of books by some of the world's leading astrologers, such as Liz Greene, Judy Hall, Michael Harding, Melanie

---

[2]For those readers who wish to read more by this key figure in twentieth-century astrology, Howard Sasportas's main opus is contained in seven books, including *The Twelve Houses* (1985); the Seminars in Psychological Astrology Series with Liz Greene containing *The Development of the Personality* (1987), *The Dynamics of the Unconscious* (1988), *The Luminaries* (1992), and *The Inner Planets* (1993); *The Gods of Change—Pain, Crisis and the Transits of Uranus, Neptune and Pluto* (1989); and *The Sun Sign Career Guide*, with Robert Walker (1989). Howard wrote few essays, but three were published in *The Astrological Journal* of the Astrological Association of Great Britain. Copies of recordings of his UAC lectures are available through AFAN, ISAR, or NCGR. Finally, for additional appreciations of the man and his work by colleagues and students, please see *The Astrological Journal*, vol. XXXIV, no. 5, September/October 1992.

Reinhart, and Jane Ridder-Patrick. This widely available series has perhaps done as much as anything to transform the public's perception of astrology and to show it to be a subject worthy of serious study by all those concerned with better understanding the human psyche and the profound mysteries of our intimate relationship with the Cosmos.

Howard was full of vibrant fun, a warm, eloquent, loving soul, radiating light, who was both vital and dynamic, and even at times wildly outrageous—yet always humble, human, and ever ready to make himself available to anyone who sought his help and counsel. Like many of the finest teachers, Howard was a man who was in touch equally with his femininity and his masculinity; he was able to bring both qualities to his work, thereby sensitively educing the inner wisdom from his students, that personal wisdom which he knew was the essential prerequisite of every real psychologist and astrologer.

In many ways Howard was the archetypal Hero Soul depicted by Joseph Campbell. He was the Seeker who journeys ever onward, overcoming all obstacles in the quest for self-discovery and self-realisation. Howard's triumphs are for all to see. What will be unknown to those who did not have the privilege of meeting him in his later years was his constant battle with chronic ill health. During his last years, he bravely endured two major back operations undergone in an attempt to correct a congenital spinal disorder. These operations were to virtually cripple him, while, at the same time, he had to face the remorseless progress of AIDS to which he finally succumbed. Yet none of these trials prevented him continuing to live life to the utmost, not only with his Centre and therapeutic work, but voluntarily giving much of his time and energy at the Oasis Centre in North London for AIDS sufferers. Although wheelchair bound in his last year, he continued to travel and lecture worldwide to fulfill his vocation of showing how the ancient planetary and mundane gods are still alive and well and working in each one of us. His final triumphant lectures at the Easter 1992 UAC Conference in Washington, DC, which he gave from his wheelchair between blood transfusions and nights in hospital, marked a fitting culmination to his noble and truly heroic life. His enthusiastic committment to life and self-realization against all odds was endlessly uplifting for his many friends and students.

Howard's work lives on through his books and tapes and will continue to inspire and enthuse generations of astrologers yet unborn. Read and study his life and work and you will have an example, friend, companion, and wise counsellor for life.

Charles Harvey
August 11, 1992

INTRODUCTION

Man's main task in life is to give birth to himself, to become what he potentially is.

—Erich Fromm

When I say "I," I mean a thing absolutely unique, not to be confused with any other.

—Ugo Betti

The inner or personal planets—Mercury, Venus, and Mars—are understood by many astrological students and practitioners to be somehow superficial or "lightweight" in nature. They may appear less powerful than their bigger fellows; they are often dismissed with a few simple phrases such as "the aggressive urge" or "the urge for relationship"; and they are apparently not as relevant to inner development as are, for example, Saturn or Pluto. They are so *personal*, after all, and not concerned with serious issues like unconscious complexes and individuation and spiritual evolution. It might even seem as if they are not really very important in an in-depth psychological birth-chart analysis, except in terms of self-gratification—which, as we are perpetually being told by our more evolved colleagues, is such a very selfish motivation.

This is a very curious view of what is important. Yet those in the helping professions, of which psychological astrology is one, are sometimes prone to adopt it unthinkingly. If a human need is too intimate, too concerned with subjective pleasure and happiness, then it cannot be cosmically meaningful in this dawning

Aquarian Age. Personal fulfillment, especially if it means refusing to put others "first," may not accord with what many of us would like to believe is the higher or deeper purpose of our lives. Statements like that of Erich Fromm—"Man's main task in life is to give birth to himself, to become what he potentially is"—are generally understood as applicable to core identity and purpose, not to personal tastes and needs. Yet this is a great misinterpretation of the value of the whole individual.

The three inner planets, and the very human motivations which they symbolise, are no less important than the other, meatier denizens of the solar system. Ultimately it is the individual personality in its entirety—not just the "significant" bits—which must mediate the deeper, more universal forces that operate within life and within ourselves. The creative and destructive potentials of the larger collective energies must pass through the lens of ordinary old you and me, if they are to be handled with any degree of intelligent choice. The common or garden variety little self constitutes the vessel which contains—or is overwhelmed by—the archaic and daemonic elements of the collective psyche. And the strength and authenticity of this little self, whose essential characteristics are portrayed most succinctly in the birth chart by the Sun, Moon, and Ascendant, can only take root in the solid ground of our capacity to know what makes us feel good, happy, and at peace with ourselves on any ordinary Saturday afternoon.

The sense of unhappiness or "wrongness" that so many clients bring to an astrological consultation is not always a reflection of profound disturbances in the family psychic inheritance, nor of global configurations such as the Uranus-Neptune conjunction, which is currently playing havoc with our collective political and economic structures. Sometimes what makes us unhappy may also, or even primarily, reflect insufficient value and time given to those apparently unimportant building blocks of personal reality that the three inner planets symbolise. We are not always brought up to respect our ordinary feelings, desires, and perceptions. "Self-indulgent" is a term often heard when we do try to establish such personal boundaries in the face of others' needs. This in part reflects a larger dilemma, for we are just leaving two thousand years of what Richard Idemon called a "universal" sign—Pisces—

and are entering two thousand years of the equally universal Aquarius.

These two signs, being the last of the zodiac, are intrinsically more concerned with the group than with the happiness and personal unfoldment of one individual. In fact, the value-systems which these signs embody in their different ways can sometimes be downright antagonistic to any effort at individual expression. Within the helping professions, this dilemma may show a particularly poignant face. While by their nature such professions are concerned with growth, healing and the alleviation of suffering in the individual, many of the more ordinary aspects of life – particularly those reflected by the inner planets – may of necessity be ignored in the face of more apparently significant problems. Ostensibly one does not pay one's analyst to discuss the finer points of one's wardrobe and hairstyle.

We are also brought up to think of society first. In principle, this reflects a positive civilising instinct, which makes the quality of human life far safer, happier, and more productive. In practise, this dictum, followed with too much rigidity, sometimes backfires. We must adjust and adapt to the larger world in which we live; we must be loyal to the family unit as the cornerstone of social cohesion; we must look after our children, our aging parents, our partners, the starving in Ethiopia, and the oppressed in South Africa. We must be modest in our ambitions, restrained in our material desires, self-sacrificing in our expressions of love, and "politically correct" at all times; for if we are not, then we are selfish, antisocial, greedy, egocentric, or even fascist.

So powerful and pervasive is this argument that a great many people grow up without the vaguest idea of what colours they like wearing, or what music makes them feel happy, or which friends they really enjoy, or what books they like to read – largely because nobody has considered it important enough to help them find out, let alone affirm them in their choices. To a great extent our capacity to express what the three inner planets symbolise within us determines whether we are victims of life or creative individuals with the power of choice. The inner planets serve what psychology calls the ego, the sense of a personal self. In astrological terms, they serve the Sun and Moon. Mercury, Venus, and Mars provide the ways and means through which the Sun and Moon discover and express their fundamental natures.

An example might be relevant here. A woman with natal Venus in Cancer in square to Neptune may have had one or two disappointing love affairs in early adulthood, a period of psychotherapy that has apparently resolved early problems, and then a relatively contented marriage and family life for many years afterward. Then transiting Uranus arrives, moving into opposition with natal Venus and into square with natal Neptune. Lo and behold, her husband betrays her with his secretary, her daughter announces that she has been taking cocaine, her mother dies, and she is suddenly in the midst of a close Uranian encounter of the worst kind. If the lady is psychologically inclined, she may spend a great deal of time trying to track down the complex that previous efforts at psychotherapy have failed to reveal. And indeed, it is likely that she will find unconscious conflicts that have helped to create the challenge she is now facing. This deeper inward-looking procedure may be essential at a time of crisis if one is to avoid the bitter blaming of all and sundry while ignoring one's own emotional contribution to the chaos. But there is an equally important factor that can allow one to cope with what one cannot change in a way that preserves one's loyalty to oneself.

Whatever this woman's family background, psychological inheritance, or social and economic situation, natal Venus in Cancer makes a statement about her own personal tastes—what she finds beautiful, what makes her happy and contented, what she values most in her relationships with others, and what she needs to learn to value most in herself. Venus in Cancer is an irreducible absolute, and makes a fundamental statement about what this woman requires to be happy—and an ongoing requirement for emotional closeness, romance, and fantasy is an aspect of that statement. The less she recognises this, and the less she values it, the more likely she will be to martyr herself to please husband and daughter—a sure recipe for a cumulative resentment that alienates partners and children through unconscious destructiveness. Moreover, if she continues to betray these very personal tastes and values, she will not cope at all well with her current disillusionment—for such a self-betrayal will drive her into living a further lie in order to prevent such a catastrophe from happening to her again. In fact, her betrayal of Venus may be a large part of why she herself has been betrayed, and the transit of Uranus serves as the trigger to reveal—as Uranus generally does—a situation that badly needs changing but that no one wants to face.

Thus, we must live what we are in order to be happy, for we cannot control or bind others through the dubious weapon of "sacrifice." But what are we really? The inner planets tell us more about this ordinary everyday self than anything else in the birth chart. If one has Venus in Cancer and is flailing about trying to pretend that it is in Aquarius because he or she has partners and friends who dislike too much intimacy in their relationships, then perhaps one is choosing the wrong people. Or, perhaps, more might be achieved by expressing what one is and what one values plainly and honestly, rather than manipulatively; for then others could respond with equal directness; and some genuine adjustment and mutual respect might be possible.

Whatever our complexes and however deeply we delve into them, we are left with the task of living as ourselves. Our complexes may have dictated why we have betrayed our essential personal needs and nature. But understanding complexes will not relieve us of the responsibility of living what we are if we want our lives to feel like our own rather than a constantly repeating performance of the third act of *Tosca*.

Sometimes "inner work" requires an act of loyalty rather than an effort at transformation. Knowing what makes us happy (Venus), expressing this to others (Mercury), and standing firm in the face of opposition (Mars) may seem very petty against the more profound concerns of the outer world. Yet in their own way, these things are equally profound, for it is these small acts of self-affirmation that define the ego and ultimately the capacity to mediate the heavy planets with their destructive and transformative potentials. If we cannot express Mercury, how can we hear another person? If we do not have our own thoughts and attitudes, how can we listen? If we cannot express Venus and do not value ourselves, how can we find beauty or value in another person? If we cannot express Mars, how can we recognise and respect other people's right to be themselves? Or, put another way, why should we assume that another person—or God, for that matter—should want our noble self-sacrifice when we ourselves do not value the self we are offering up?

It has been said that life imitates art. Sometimes it also imitates television. We can view life through different channels; and according to the channel to which we are attuned, we may see some very different pictures of what reality is all about. We may get the news on BBC1, while on BBC2 there is a football match being broadcast. On ITV, we may encounter *Neighbours* or *Coronation Street* or some other daily soap, while on Channel 4, we can enjoy an old film. Just as people's tastes differ, so too do their perceptions of reality and the things they value most in life. An individual's perceptions can shift as well, depending upon the stage of life at which he or she has arrived. On one level or another, all these programmes are valid, even if one person finds *Neighbours* abhorrent and another cannot face yet another showing of *Casablanca*.

We can also view a horoscope through the perspective of different channels. Put simplistically, Channel One is the cosmic channel. When we are viewing the "blueprint of life" through this lens, we perceive the deeper meaning, the myths which underpin behaviour, the connectedness with a larger reality. This is the channel of the outer planets, and of Jupiter and Saturn which condition our faith in life and our vision of the future and the past. Here the inner planets may at first viewing seem to fade into insignificance beside the greater plan, the higher order of things. A sense of rightness and destiny permeates Channel One, and pain and suffering carry with them an attendant sense of meaning and potential for growth and evolution. Most of us cannot tune in to Channel One for any length of time—hence the popularity of consciousness-altering drugs, which appear to reproduce the sense of oneness that this perception of reality generates in us. Those individuals throughout history who seem to be permanently attuned to this channel are viewed either as avatars or lunatics, or both.

The alternative channel is the one to which we are most often attuned—that of ordinary life. This is the channel of immediate reality. Here we are made aware of our differentness from each other, our separateness, our "me-ness." While perception of Channel One lifts us out of our bodies, Channel Two opens up an acute perception of material reality, and this means recognition of the corporeal vessel in which we are incarnated. This is the channel of the Sun and Moon, and the three inner planets which serve them. Our bodies are different, our emotional needs are different, our values and abilities and perceptions and skills are different. On Channel Two, we are not One, we are many; and the inner planets are, to use Dane Rudhyar's words, our "celestial instructions" for the truest and most natural way through which we can form a distinct and separate individuality.

Joy is not limited to one channel or the other; it is available on both. But the joy differs: the joy of Channel One is ecstatic, universal and ego-dissolving; the joy of Channel Two is that of personal fulfillment. There is perhaps more pain and suffering on Channel Two, and there may not always be a readily available sense of meaning when we confront frustration, unhappiness, and loneliness. On Channel One, death is a rite of passage. On Channel Two, death is simply death, frightening and potentially painful. The unfairness of life is most evident on this channel, and we feel and perceive that unfairness most acutely during our efforts to express the inner planets in our personal lives.

The inner planets are very vulnerable to the pressures of family and society. It may not be easy for a family or collective to suppress our essential individuality as reflected by the Sun; and it is virtually impossible to block the erupting energies of the heavy planets when they are triggered by transits or progressions. But it is not difficult for an envious mother to crush her young daughter's nascent Venus or a dictatorial father to psychologically cast ate his young son's developing Mars; and an educational system that devalues effort and excellence in the name of giving everybody an easy run may play havoc with even the most lively Mercury, rendering it clumsy and mute. More than anything else in the birth chart the inner planets—those highly personal statements about who we are—need our loyalty and our willingness to stand by our specialness in the face of even the cosmic messages of Channel One. The spirit itself may demand too much, and it is up to us to say so, for no one will defend us if we cannot defend ourselves.

It is the inner planets that describe our ground as unique personalities, and we cannot express these without being separate enough to define our own values. Separation is the most basic and painful of all human dilemmas, and it is inevitably included in the programme schedule of Channel Two. Incarnating, whether one interprets this spiritually or psychologically, seems a pretty rough deal compared with life in the Paradise Garden where we were at one with Mother/God. The moment we express the inner planets, we assert our separateness. It is not surprising that some astrologers consider them "unimportant," for they are so important that they pose a permanent threat to our fantasies of fusion. It is not possible to be loved unconditionally by everybody if one is oneself, for as Abraham Lincoln once said, we cannot please all of the people all of the time. It is possible to view both channels at once, and enjoy the pleasures of the inner planets while remembering the greater life of which we are a part. This seems a sane and balanced attitude toward working with the horoscope. But a building cannot be built from the top downwards. It must start with its foundations on the earth, and move upward toward its ultimate design. The inner planets are the building blocks of our personal reality, and the foundations upon which we can raise our eyes and our hearts to glimpse distant horizons and the unending vault of the sky.

Liz Greene
Howard Sasportas
London, April 1992

PART ONE

MERCURY

We are not troubled by things, but by the opinions we have of things.

—Epictetus

The greatest discovery of any generation is that human beings can alter their lives by altering their attitudes of mind.

—Albert Schweitzer

TRICKSTERS, THIEVES, AND MAGICIANS

THE MANY FACES OF MERCURY IN MYTHOLOGY

BY HOWARD SASPORTAS

Back in the late 60s and early 70s I studied astrology in Boston with Isabel Hickey. She taught me something which has always stayed in my mind: if a person or situation is bothering you, try changing your attitude toward it. By doing this, she said one of two things will follow. Either the problem will alter in such a way that it no longer bothers you or feels like a problem, or it will just go away and disappear entirely. So if a person is getting on your nerves, maybe you have to try changing your attitude toward that person, holding them in a more positive light or new perspective. According to Isabel, the person will then change in such a way that he or she doesn't aggravate you as much; or, in some cases, the person will vanish from the scene so that you no longer have to deal with the culprit. The rule is that if you alter your attitude, you alter the whole situation. Such is the power of the mind, the power of the mental plane. As the Rosicrucians are fond of saying, "Thoughts have wings."

Over the years, I've followed Isabel's advice on numerous occasions, and I was amazed to see how frequently it works. You should try it yourself with something in your life which is bothering you. But I do have one condition, one stipulation to add. I'm not sure if it is always appropriate to try too quickly to get rid of things that are worrying or upsetting you. This smacks of running away from a situation that could offer you valuable lessons or insights; it might be more useful to your psychological growth and development if you first took the time to explore why a person or situation is "pushing your buttons" or triggering off your complexes. So rather than immediately trying to do away with the source of your irritation, you ought to go inside and ask yourself questions such as, "Why am I reacting in this manner? Does the person represent a facet of my nature which I find loathesome or embarrassing, and therefore I'm irked to see him or her behaving in that way?" These questions help you to probe into what Jung would call your *shadow*; by honestly examining your reactions to a problematic person or situation, you can learn a great deal about repressed or denied aspects of your nature which need to be brought into the light of consciousness and worked on. In this sense, the person or circumstances which are bothering you have something important to teach you.

To alter your attitude too quickly as a ploy to rid yourself of the problem could be seen as a psychological cop-out. Nevertheless, I still believe there are times it is right and useful to apply Isabel's suggestions, but try fulfilling the previously mentioned condition first. Later in the day, we'll do an exercise which involves taking something which is a problem for you and seeing if it can be altered or alchemised by a change of attitude. In the meantime you can be thinking about which of your problems you want to use for this exercise. If you can't come up with any, I'd be very happy to lend you one of mine to work on. In fact, I'm such a nice guy that you don't even have to give it back to me. You'd be more than welcome to keep it for yourself.

One of my problems is where to begin with Mercury. This planet has so many faces and manifestations, it's hard to know where to start. For the first part of the morning, we'll be discussing the myths associated with the Greek Hermes, which serve to illustrate and amplify how the Mercurial principle manifests astrologically and psychologically. Since I'm most familiar with the Greek myths, I'll be focussing on Hermes, although equivalent archetypes show up in many different cultures. Besides the Roman Mercury, we have Thoth in Egypt, who was known as the Lord of Holy Words. A Mercurial, Hermes-like figure is found in Nordic mythology in the guise of Loki. Coyote is the North American trickster equivalent to Hermes, and the Eskimos called him Raven.

Hermes has a bewildering number of roles in Greek mythology: he is the thief, the magician, the craftsman, the messenger of the gods, the god of boundaries, commerce, merchants, words and language to name a few. In order to better understand these epithets, I'd like to tell you a few stories about what Hermes got up to in his life, elaborating on these in terms of the psychological and astrological principles they illustrate. As you know, Zeus had numerous extramarital affairs, and one of these was with the wood nymph Maia. He used to sneak off and visit her while Hera was sleeping. In fact, Zeus's affair with Maia was the only one of which the jealous Hera was unaware—otherwise she would have caused trouble and used one of her tricks to break it up. The fruit of this clandestine romance was Hermes, so you can say that he was born of deceit, trickery and cunning on the part of Zeus. We have learned something already: astrologically (and this is one of the less pleasant faces of Mercury), wherever Mercury is in the chart is where we might be deceitful and prone to trickery or cunning, where we may slightly bend the truth to suit ourselves.

Hermes' birthplace was a cave at Mount Cyllene in the region of Arcadia. As soon as he was born, he immediately felt bored and restless. According to the Homeric hymn, Hermes was anxious to find something to do besides just idly lying around in his cradle wrapped in tight swaddling clothes. Again, this fits well with our astrological understanding of Mercury, especially its association with the sign of Gemini. Wherever Mercury shows up in the chart is where we are prone to restlessness, where we need variety, change and room to move. The god Hermes was only one day old, but he went off in search of adventure: not knowing precisely where he was heading or what was going to happen, he just set off and took things as they came. Mercury can thus be associated with the unexpected, with coincidence and synchronicity or with events which seem accidental but may later have meaning or prove to serve a greater purpose. This is especially true if you are under a Uranus transit to your Mercury: it can mark a phase when books fall off the shelf with just the information you need, or you turn on the television and there is a show you didn't know was on which is about something you are currently involved in or about which you have been curious. Even the fast-moving transit of Mercury over your Ascendant or Venus can give you the kind of day when you are out buying groceries and you run into someone you didn't expect to see, and the two of you pop into the coffee shop for a chat—these kinds of diversions or unexpected encounters are hallmarks of Mercury.

Anyway, Hermes followed his impulse to get out of his cradle, went to the front door of his home, and unexpectedly encountered a tortoise. Admiring its beautiful shell, Hermes said to the tortoise, "You are very nice as you are, but I can think of better things to do with you than just look at you."[1] Already he was displaying his inventiveness, his need to get his hands into something. Mercury's house position in a chart indicates the area of life where we are meant to be inventive, playful and willing to try new things rather than just being satisfied with the status quo of that domain. I've used the phrase "meant to be" on purpose. I agree with Dane Rudhyar's theory that the house placements of planets and signs in your chart are actually "celestial instructions" on how you can most naturally unfold your life-plan in that domain of existence.[2] To put it another way, the placements of your planets by sign and house indicate the most authentic way to fulfil your intrinsic potentialities, the most natural way to grow into what you are meant to become. So in order to realise your *dharma* (it is the *dharma* of a fly to buzz; it is the *dharma* of a lion to roar; it is the *dharma* of an artistic person to create), you are *meant* to be curious and inventive in the sphere of life associated with the house in which your Mercury is placed, and this also applies to the houses Mercury rules in your chart. It is an area of life where you are meant to keep an open mind, where you ought to be flexible and young at heart. Obviously this may vary somewhat if Mercury is in a fixed sign, for instance, or is obstructed in some way by Saturn — or if you were overly conditioned as a child to sit still, behave and be a nice, quiet good little boy or girl.

We left Hermes face-to-face with a tortoise. In a flash of inspiration, he killed the poor creature, chiselled out its shell, stretched oxhide around it, added a few strings and came up with the first lyre. He did this on impulse, not knowing that the musical instrument would prove itself very useful when he had to deal with Apollo later on. Here we can also detect Mercury as the craftsperson, someone who is ingenious, skilful or adept with his hands. This side of Mercury correlates with Gemini but perhaps even more so with Virgo. Mercury's house may show an area of life where we have natural craft, or where we can be quite crafty, to

---

[1] All quotations from the Homeric hymn are cited in Norman Brown, *Hermes the Thief* (New York, Vintage Books, 1969).

[2] Dane Rudhyar, *The Astrological Houses* (Sebastopol, CA: CRCS, 1986), p. 38.

use the word in a slightly different sense. Hermes also exhibits a certain degree of ruthlessness in this episode—he doesn't think twice about killing the tortoise. I've met some people who are strongly mercurial who may behave quite nastily or unkindly, and yet they do it with such charm and finesse, you're almost prepared to overlook their misdemeanours.

Hermes played with the lyre for a short time, got bored, threw it in his cradle, and went in search of something else with which to occupy himself. He was feeling hungry when he happened upon a herd of cattle belonging to Apollo, his older brother. You probably know the story. Hermes decided to steal the cattle by leading them backwards away from the meadow in which they were grazing. In other words, their footprints pointed the other way from where they were being led. Then he designed and made special sandals for himself so that they covered his own footprints, leaving no trace behind. (Like some mercurial types I've met, you don't know whether they're coming or going. And very often they themselves aren't sure if they're coming or going!) After stealing the cattle, Hermes lit a fire by rubbing two sticks together—in fact, some sources say this is the first time fire had been made that way. He then chose two of the cows to cook, divided them into twelve portions, and used each portion to make a sacrifice to one of the Olympian gods . . . including himself of course.

It's worth pausing a moment here to reflect on the significance of this last act. By making a separate sacrifice to each of the twelve gods, Hermes demonstrated that he was prepared to honour and partake of all of them, no matter how different one god may be from another. Likewise, the astrological Mercury symbolises a part of us which is able to identify almost at random with the varying principles represented by the other planets. So Mercury may partake of Saturn one day, extolling the virtues of discipline, patience and thrift, and then honour Jupiter the next by rushing enthusiastically into something new and untried, or by going berserk with the plastic on a shopping spree. If you are predominantly influenced by the planet Saturn, you'll mainly be like Saturn on Monday, on Tuesday, on Wednesday, etc. Even if you slip up over the weekend, let your hair down and act more like Venus or Neptune on Saturday night, Saturn will quickly take over again and remind you of its rules and regulations. If you're a Jupiterian by nature, you'll live out that archetype on one level or another throughout the week. But if you are strongly influenced by Mercury, your gift (and it may also be your curse) is your adaptability, a talent for mimicking the archetypal nature of the other planets. Mercury represents the archetype that can be any of the other archetypes. Mercury is Mercury and not Venus, Jupiter or Saturn, but he can take on the attributes of these or the other planets if it suits him to do so, and sometimes even when it isn't that appropriate. He is *not* any of them but he can temporarily *be* any of them. Mercury is a mimic, reminiscent of an impersonator on television who can "do" former President Reagan in one sketch and then be Michael Jackson or Sylvester Stallone in the following sketch. I wouldn't be surprised if famous impersonators have Mercury or Gemini prominent in their charts.

Besides displaying his allegiance to all twelve gods of Olympus, Hermes eventually managed to steal something from each of the other gods: Apollo's cattle is not his only theft. He absconded one day with Zeus's thunderbolts, he robbed Athene of her helmet for awhile, and he even borrowed Aphrodite's girdle without asking her. (I wonder what he did with that—a little bit of cross-dressing maybe? It wouldn't surprise me, since it suggests the hermaphroditic quality also part of his mythology, which I'll discuss later.) Stealing from each of the gods is another way of saying he possesses certain attributes of them all. But you can also see how this can be a curse, how strongly mercurial people can be all over the place, one way one day, another way the next. And you can also see how infuriating Mercury types can be to other people. You think you know where they're at, or where they're coming from, but just wait . . .

When he had finished sacrificing the cattle and satisfying his hunger, Hermes meandered back home and, according to the Homeric hymn, he entered his house through the keyhole, "like a wisp of cloud"; he climbed back into his cradle, tucking the tortoise-shell lyre under his arm as if it were a toy and slept like an innocent baby. Turning himself into smoke was another one of his tricks. Anyway, what happened is that his mother came home and saw him sleeping there so innocently, but she was not fooled. She was wise to him, and let him know it: "Alas, when your father begot you, he begot a deal of trouble for mortal men and the

immortal gods." That's what his own mother thought about him.
By the way, if you have the karma to give birth to a child predominantly influenced by the Hermes archetype, you should accept
him for what he is, but you also need to set some limits on him.
Hermes needs a strong, guiding parent who can say "You're going
too far this time, cool it." Similarly, in Mercury's house we may
need to learn to discipline the mind or contain some of our
thoughts and actions rather than acting these out indiscriminately.
Mercury ultimately functions most positively if he has a set of
guidelines to go by, or if he has moral or ethical standards to which
he tries to adhere. After his mother accused him of being a big pain
in the neck, Hermes was not short of a reply:

> Why do you try to scare me as if I were nothing but a silly
> child? I shall follow the career that offers the best opportuni-
> ties, for I must look after my own interests and yours. It is
> intolerable that we alone of the immortals should have to live
> in this dreary cave, receiving neither offerings nor prayers.
> Would it not be better to spend our days in ease and afflu-
> ence like the rest of the gods? I am going to get the same
> status in cult as Apollo. If my father does not give it to me, I
> will become the prince of thieves. If Apollo hunts me down, I
> will go plunder his shrine at Delphi. There is plenty of gold
> there—just you see!

Hermes' aspiration to equal Apollo deserves further consideration.
First, we can see this simply in terms of sibling rivalry. Apollo is
Hermes' older brother, and one of the archetypes Hermes is associated with is that of the younger brother. Apollo was Zeus's
favourite son, the golden-haired boy. Zeus respected Apollo's
rationality, intellect and organisational ability. As we'll soon see,
Zeus also liked Hermes, especially his cleverness, his capacity for
wheeling and dealing, and the adept way he was able to wriggle
himself out of tight corners. While we're on the subject, Zeus did
not care for his son Ares at all. According to Homer, Zeus once told
Ares that of all the gods on Olympus, he was the one he most
detested. He actually accused Ares of having the same intolerable
disposition as Hera; in other words, Zeus berated Ares for being
too much like his mother. Ares was simply too crass, too bloodthirsty, too pushy and too emotional for the likes of Zeus. Zeus

was ambivalent about Dionysus, another one of his sons. While he had himself provided a second womb for Dionysus and in that way was nurturing toward him, he found Dionysus a little too feminine to suit his taste.

Hermes' determination to equal Apollo also can be viewed from a political or social perspective. In Athens during the 5th century B.C., Apollo represented the aristocracy, while Hermes became the patron of the newly emerging merchant classes and the *nouveau riche* in general. Hermes symbolised their desire to gain as much respectability as the landed aristocracy. The conflict between the commercial classes and the upper-class gentry was projected onto the rivalry between Apollo and Hermes.

Back to our story. It didn't take long for Apollo to discover that his cattle were missing, and he immediately suspected Hermes as the culprit. But when Apollo challenged his younger brother on this matter, Hermes (curled up in his cradle) protested his innocence:

> Why, Apollo, what means this rough language? I never even saw your cattle. Do I look like a cattle-raider? I am only two days old, and all I am interested in is sleep and warm baths and my mother's milk. You had better make sure that no one hears you scolding me in this way. No one would believe that a newborn child would steal cows. I was only born yesterday. My feet are tender and the ground is hard. But if you want I shall swear to thee on the head of my father that I am not guilty and that I haven't seen anyone else steal your cows—whatever cows these might have been. This is the first time I have even heard of them!

He's outrageous, isn't he? After delivering this pack of lies, Hermes blinked earnestly, raised his eyebrows and emitted a long whistle to try to cover the falsity of his words. Hermes was the god of humour, and the Homeric hymn relating his exploits is really very funny to read.

Apollo is nobody's fool:

> You cunning deceiver, you speak like a trained thief. Many herdsmen shall suffer at thy hands in the mountains, when, lusting after meat, you come upon their herds. But if it is thy

wish that this slumber shall not be thy last, then leap from thy cradle, thou companion of black night. For this shall be your special glory among the immortal gods: Thou shalt be the prince of thieves for all eternity.

Apollo snatched Hermes from his cradle and took him to Zeus to settle the matter once and for all. Hermes, just to further irritate Apollo, let out a loud fart, which one translation poetically referred to as "an evil messenger of the stomach." Apollo claimed he could find the cattle by their droppings. He went on his way with Hermes trailing along, behaving like a brat, grimacing and putting his thumbs in his ears and wriggling his hands behind Apollo's back, at the same time as protesting his innocence and cursing all the cows in the world. Hermes reminds me of a child who will do anything to get attention, even if this means behaving badly. When Zeus spied the two of them he smiled and asked, "What is this fine prize you have carried off?" Apollo defended himself: "It's not me who is the thief. He [Hermes] is the thief and a most cunning one too," and explained the situation to Zeus. An earnest Hermes then appealed to his father for understanding:

> Father, you know that I cannot tell a lie. He [Apollo] came to our house looking for some cattle and began threatening me—and he is a grown-up whereas I was only born yesterday. I swear by the gates of heaven that I never drove the cattle to our house, and that I never stepped across our threshold. I will get even with this fellow for so violently arresting me. Dear Father, you must defend the cause of the weak and helpless.

One can only marvel at Hermes' bold-faced capacity to tell such whopping great lies. As I said before, Mercury's house position could be an area of life where we are prone to distorting the truth, or where we can be very persuasive, to the point of resorting to devious tactics to win over others. In the myth we're told that Zeus found the whole episode highly amusing, and he ordered the brothers to make up and be friends, at which point Hermes gave in and offered to take Apollo to where the cattle were hidden. Even so, he was still intent on giving Apollo a hard time, and used his magic powers to make the cows take root into the ground. Apollo was now truly flustered. Meanwhile, Hermes took up his lyre and began to sing about the origin of the gods and the offices assigned to each. Here we see Hermes' more serious and learned side. Apollo was fascinated by the lyre and the beautiful, sweet sounds it produced: "What you have there is worth fifty cattle! Tell me the secret of your instrument and I will see to it that you get a position of wealth and honour among the gods." Hermes answered back, "I am not selfish. It would be a pleasure to teach you the secret of my instrument. In return you must allow me to share your patronage of cattle." So a bargain was struck.

In the same way, Mercury's house placement will show where you are good at making deals, and anyone with the Hermes or Mercury archetype strong in the chart is a born deal-maker, a born trader. In this way, Apollo and Hermes became friends, although the older brother was still somewhat suspicious of his younger sibling: "I'm afraid you may steal my lyre back again, for Zeus has put you in charge of establishing the art of exchange on earth. I won't feel secure until you have taken a solemn oath." Hermes agreed, and was made the patron of oaths, and solemn pledges in the bargain. When Hermes swore he wouldn't steal the cattle or the instrument back again, Apollo offered him a gift—the caduceus, a magic wand with two ribbons or snakes wrapped around it—which becomes one of Hermes' most famous symbols.

I've gone into this myth in depth not just because I find it amusing, but because it casts so much light on the Hermes archetype and the way in which Mercury operates in the chart. I must add that Hermes is a thief and not a robber. The Greeks distinguished between the two: a robber assaults, he is open and forceful like a mugger, whereas a thief is more subtle or stealthy. Hermes is not a thug or mugger, but he is the patron of stealthy action. Zeus often used him to rescue others from danger. In one story, the young Ares was captured by two giants and kept in a jar, and Hermes was assigned the task of freeing Ares, which involved quite a lot of sneaking around. It also fell upon Hermes to rescue the child Dionysus from the clutches of Hera and the Titans. And it was Hermes who escorted the young Persephone back from the Underworld. Can you see a pattern here? Hermes is the one chosen when divine children need rescuing or saving.

There's one story along these lines I'd briefly like to tell, because it is a good example of how Hermes used trickery to come to the aid of the infant Herakles, and also serves to illustrate some of his other functions. Herakles was the son of Zeus and Semele, a mortal woman; therefore he was not wholly divine. For him to become divine, he would have had to suckle the milk from the breast of a goddess. Hermes wanted to help him, so he devised a rather good scheme: he placed the baby Herakles on a path in a wood, and then asked Hera, the Queen of the Heavens, if she would like to go for a walk. While Hermes and Hera were strolling along, Hermes casually commented on what great breasts Hera had. She was very flattered. Then, as Hermes had planned, they came across a crying infant abandoned on the road. The baby was wrapped in such a way as to conceal its identity—if Hera had recognised the baby to be a mortal or to be one of her husband's illegitimate sons, she would have done nothing for it. When they stumbled upon the child, Hermes appealed to Hera, "The poor infant looks very hungry. You, with your beautiful full breasts, could give this baby such fine milk." Hera consented and started to feed Herakles, until she realised he was not a divine child. Having no interest in raising mortals to the level of the divine, she quickly withdrew the breast. Herakles, however, had swallowed enough milk to become godlike and to follow a hero's path. You see how clever Hermes is? Through his trickery, he is able to transform a mortal into someone divine, which is an important point we'll be discussing in more detail shortly. There's an aside here. When Hera removed her breast, a lot of the milk spurted out into the air and this was supposed to have created the Milky Way. So indirectly, Hermes is responsible for the stars which guide travellers and give people direction in life.

Likewise, one of the functions of the astrological Mercury is to keep "the divine child" alive in us. We all have a divine child inside us—a part of us which is forever young and open to life no matter what our age. (And if you recall my lecture on the Moon, we also have "a hurt and angry child" in us, but that's not our concern right now.) Again, I would refer to Mercury's house as an area of life in which we are meant to stay young, open and childlike in the best sense of the word. So to be true to Mercury in the 3rd, you need to keep your mind open and up to date, to take up a study, to keep up with the world around you even if your contemporaries have long closed their minds to anything new. If you have Mercury in the 5th, taking up a creative outlet, even if you are seventy years old, it will revitalise you and help you to stay young and interested in life. Mercury rescues the divine child in us; use this planet well and you'll be young at heart no matter how wrinkled you are, or how bent your body is. Have you noticed that many people with Gemini or Virgo rising often look younger than their actual years? If your mind is open, your spirit remains young and fresh. To tell you the truth, I have a real admiration for some older Mercurians. In their youth and early adulthood, they may have been all over the place, too unsettled, coming and going, trying one thing, dropping it and then trying another. That kind of behaviour can get on one's nerves. But as Hermes types grow older, slow down and become more settled, many of them still retain their openness to life, their curiousity and interest in people and things, without the often infuriating restlessness and skittishness of their younger years.

I have a few more things to say concerning Hermes the Magician. We've heard about some of the magic he performs: he changes himself into a cloud of smoke to get through a keyhole; he makes Apollo's cattle root to the ground; he charms Cerberus to sleep so that he can slip in and out of the Underworld unnoticed; he has the power to make things invisible. He is a master of magic words and magic formulas. We shouldn't underestimate the power of words. Mantras, prayers, and chants, whether spoken silently to the self or aloud, can affect one's physiology and one's life, perhaps even affecting the consciousness of the entire planet. In the beginning was the Word. Words have power, but so do thoughts. Maharishi Mahesh Yogi used to say that "thought is the basis of action." You might be familiar with Alice Bailey's system of esoteric astrology, which when compared with traditional or what she calls exoteric astrology, attributes different rulerships to many of the signs. According to esoteric astrology, Mercury, not Mars, is the ruler of Aries. I always found this interesting.

From some cosmic point of view, Mars is not the ruler of the sign of action; instead we find Mercury (the planet associated with thinking) assigned to Aries—which is a very concise way of saying that thought is the basis of action, or in the beginning is the word. I believe that if there is something you wish to achieve or master, it helps to sit down first and have an image of yourself already there. For instance, if you want to be better at the piano, picture yourself performing as a virtuoso, just imagine with your whole mind and all your feelings that you are the master or mistress of that instrument. Feel your virtuosity in every cell of your body. Obviously you'll still need to practice and develop technical skill, but if you take the time to visualise as I have suggested, you will find that you do improve. Psychologists call this kinesthetic thinking: imagining how you would like to be, not only in your mind's eye, but also feeling it in your body and with all your senses. Psychosynthesis has referred to this as "mental rehearsal" or the constructive use of the imagination. Many of us waste a lot of time and energy worrying about how something will turn out, but we can redirect that energy more constructively by using kinesthetic imagination in the way I've been telling you. Instead of endlessly fretting about a performance or lecture you're due to give, or an important interview, meeting or exam which is coming up, you can prepare yourself through mental rehearsal. Sportspeople use it to improve their game, artists use it to improve their work, I try to use it to calm prelecture nerves and whenever I have a book to write, and you can try it too.

I came across kinesthetic thinking when I was just starting *The Twelve Houses*,[3] my first book. Even though I have times when I enjoy the creative process, I often find writing a struggle, especially the early stages of a manuscript. I don't wake up in the morning and think, "Great, today I have to write." Sitting down at the word processor to work on a book feels as enticing to me as diving into ice water. Once or twice I came very close to ringing the publisher and breaking the contract, but my Capricorn rising is too dutiful—it just wouldn't let me. I felt as if I was stuck in the birth canal: I had to produce the book, but I couldn't get moving. Then I attended a weekend seminar in which the American psychologist Jean Houston gave a talk on the work she was doing in the States using kinesthetic thinking with various groups. I decided to give it a go. First thing each morning and at different times during the

3Howard Sasportas, *The Twelve Houses: An Introduction to the Houses in Astrological Interpretation* (London: The Aquarian Press, 1985; and San Bernardino, CA: Borgo Press, 1988).

day, I would sit on my sofa and picture myself at the typewriter (I didn't have a word processor then) really enjoying writing and being creative. Or I would imagine myself gleefully handing the completed manuscript into the publisher, or even picture the finished book on the shelves of a bookshop. The more I practiced this technique, the stronger the images became. As I see it, these images became so powerful that they propelled me into getting the book done. Occult philosophy has long stated that energy follows thought. Hermes-Mercury has magical powers, and so do words, images and thoughts. Nonetheless, finishing the book still demanded enormous persistence and stamina — whoever said that creativity requires 1 percent inspiration and 99 percent perspiration was right as far as I'm concerned.

Of course, there could be a problem with the use of kinesthetic thinking. One part of us may consciously want something, but if we unconsciously are afraid of achieving or realising that goal, or if for whatever reasons we unconsciously believe we don't deserve what we are wishing for, then we will run into trouble. When there is a conflict between conscious goals and the unconscious, we are sending double or mixed messages out to the cosmos, which is not the best way to achieve results. Also, in any contest between the conscious and the unconscious, it is the unconscious which usually wins. Unconscious aims and urges are more powerful than conscious ones, because they operate surreptitiously, so we unwittingly find ourselves at their mercy. I'll share a personal example with you. After my neck operation in January, I healed fairly quickly around the region on which they operated — so after eight or nine days I didn't feel pain in my neck and could have gone home. However, I suffered from complications due to the side effects of all the medication I needed after the surgery. I ended up with pretty bad inflammation of the liver and gall bladder, which upset my digestion and other gastric functions, and on this account I was kept in hospital longer. Consciously I wanted to get better and back home, but my condition just didn't improve. I tried imagining myself healthy and robust, I tried visualising my liver and gall bladder back to their normal size, but I still felt unwell. Then, in the middle of one night, Hermes woke me quite suddenly with a kind of revelation: the reason I wasn't improving was that I equated getting better and going back home with having to start working again, and deep inside I really didn't feel like returning to work, with all the responsibility and tension it involves. What I really wanted was a chance to relax and more time just for myself. I realised I was using illness as a way of justifying these desires. So I changed my way of thinking to "I can get better and still take time off work," and it helped to foster the healing process. You see why we need to probe the unconscious to discover urges and aims that might conflict with what we consciously desire. If you can successfully do this, you won't have other aspects of your psyche undermining conscious goals.

There is a relationship between Hermes the Magician and Hermes the Craftsman. In primitive times, the craftsperson reputedly supplemented his techniques with magical practices. I guess I was suggesting something similar just now: using the power of the mind and techniques like kinesthetic thinking is a form of magic. Mercury's house (and the houses it rules in your chart) could be the area of life through which you discover the value of imaging as an aid to craft and achievement. In ancient Greece, a craftsman was said to owe his proficiency to Hermes who bestowed joy and glory on the works of all mankind. In the Greek language, the word for trick is interchangeable with the word for technical skill. This reminds me of the English word "stealthy": if we say a man is stealthy with a bow, we mean that he is adept at archery or whatever. Stealthy also has connotations of being secretive, tricky, crafty or sly.

It's time to elaborate on Hermes as the messenger and herald of the gods, and on his role as the god of boundaries, the god of the threshold, and the god of borders and crossroads. Compared with the other Olympian deities, Hermes is the one who covered the most territory. He was Zeus' personal messenger, but all the gods employed him in this capacity as well. A distributor of information, he delivered messages from one god to another, from a god to a mortal, or from one mortal to another mortal. He served as a go-between, just as Mercury in the chart indicates communication, travel and exchange of information and ideas. In fulfilling his missions, Hermes crossed borders—he travelled up to the heights of Olympus and back down to earth; he even had access to the Underworld in the guise of Hermes Psychopompos, something of great psychological importance which I'll be discussing in more detail quite soon. The name Hermes actually means "he of the stone-heap."

That reminds me, in the summer of 1988 I went trekking with a small group of people around Ladakh, a Buddhist region of the Himalayas. It's hard to believe now, when getting up the stairs to this lecture hall is a major achievement, but I walked seven or eight miles a day, sporting a pretty hefty backpack. Transiting Neptune (the planet of delusion) was squaring my Mercury around that time, and I thought how healthy all this walking must be for me, while in actual fact, I'm pretty sure it helped bring on my neck troubles. Anyway, while climbing up passes as high as 16,000 feet, we'd occasionally come upon a cairn or stone-heap, and the tradition was to add a stone to it. You couldn't resist stopping at these stone-heaps, milling around with the other people, waiting for those behind to catch up. Many of the stones had *Om Mane Padme Hum* inscribed on them. The Greek cairns were different; they were shaped in a square block with either a phallus or the face of Hermes on the top. Called *herms*, they marked places where travellers would stop and talk. Herms functioned as points of communication between strangers, and eventually became places where business transactions took place. It's easy to see how the god of the boundary stone evolved into the god of trade, another epithet ascribed to Hermes. The Greek word for doing business is derived from a word which means "to go across." Magic and rituals were also performed at these herms.

What really interests me is the psychological significance of Hermes as the god of boundaries and as a boundary crosser. I believe that the planet Mercury symbolises that part of the psyche which is able to move from one level, plane or dimension of existence to another. I've already mentioned that Hermes travelled up to Olympus, back down to earth, and even further down into the Underworld. I would equate Olympus and the heavens with the superconscious, spiritual or transpersonal realms; the earth plane with the conscious, everyday, linear level of life – mundane things like going to the shops, paying the gas bill, chatting with friends, and so on; and I think of the Underworld as the unconscious, where unintegrated positive and negative psychic contents are buried and repressed. Later, when we discuss Mercury by sign, house and aspect, you'll see how this applies. For instance, if you have Mercury in aspect to Pluto, it means that Pluto is beckoning your Mercury into the Underworld—you will need to explore and delve into the unconscious to root out complexes and untapped potentials. If you are born with Mercury in aspect to Jupiter or Uranus, your mind probably is drawn up to the starry heights of heaven, seeking philosophical or spiritual truth and wisdom. I'll be elaborating on all this later. The point I'm stressing now is that Hermes, unlike the other gods, had free access to all three of these levels or realms. In any case, most of the other deities much preferred to bask in the rarified air of Mount Olympus, rather than mixing with lowly mortals—but not Hermes, who apparently relished his role as an intermediary between the gods and ordinary folk. Hermes-Mercury is an adept channel-switcher. Let's look at this more closely.

The fact that Hermes was Zeus' personal fax machine or messenger boy is significant from both a psychological and spiritual point of view. Eagle-eyed Zeus lived high on a mountain, so he could see things from a distance and had a very broad perspective on life. Hermes was employed to bring Zeus' wisdom and understanding to people on earth. Similarly, Mercury equips us with the capacity to take any "higher" insights or spiritual visions we have and apply them in everyday life. Or to put it another way, Mercury (which rules the nervous system) mediates Jupiter's superconscious vision, wisdom and higher understanding and makes it accessible to our conscious minds. If we didn't have a nervous system, we couldn't connect with and channel spirit. Just as if we didn't have language and words (Hermes was reputed to have invented the alphabet), we couldn't give concrete expression to Jupiterian ideals and concepts. Consider the United States Constitution as an example. I would equate the ideals and concepts contained within something like the Constitution with the vision of Jupiter; but visions, ideals and concepts are pretty useless unless we have words to embody them, to give them form and a voice. Just as Hermes helped Herakles to attain a godlike state, the principle represented by Mercury enables us to learn and express—both in action and in words—our spiritual or philosophical beliefs, inspirations and insights. The Japanese have a saying, "To know and not to act is not to know at all." It's no coincidence that *hermeneutics* is the name given to the art and science of interpreting the Scriptures, and all that is considered sacred and divine.

Hermes ran missions for Zeus and the other gods, but he also delivered messages from one mortal to another. Besides acting as a bridge between superconscious and ego, Mercury is the link between ego and environment. Without Mercury, I couldn't waffle on as I do. And right now I want to waffle on about a very important and serious function Hermes also served: his role as Hermes Psychopompos, Hermes as the guide of souls into and out of the Underworld. I would highly recommend the chapter on Mercury by Erin Sullivan in a book called *Planets*, a compilation by different astrologers writing about each planet.[4] She points out that Hermes was the only god who could travel *at will* to Hades. He escorted both the dead and the living into the Underworld, some of whom stayed, some of whom returned to the upper world again. She equates this with the mercurial ability of the mind to descend into the depths of the unconscious in order to retrieve repressed or buried material, which can then be examined in the light of consciousness. Have you noticed how certain astrology books cast Geminis as light and a little superficial, labelling this sign as the butterfly of the zodiac, good at parties and small talk, but not the kind of person who explores anything in great depth? While some Geminis may fit this description, I've met many who do not. When Geminis (and more obviously, Virgos, the other Mercury-ruled people) do decide to explore the unconscious through psychotherapy or some other means, they are as adept at it as any Scorpio or Plutonian can be. Sometimes they are actually more thorough than Scorpio in this respect, because when detail-minded Geminis or Virgos commit themselves to an inward journey, they end up exploring little nooks and crannies of the psyche which even the most astute Scorpio might miss or overlook. For this reason, Hermes Psychopompos correlates with the field of psychotherapy, and some of the best and most successful psychotherapists I know are born under a Mercury-ruled sign.

Mercury governs reflective self-consciousness, the peculiarly human ability to reflect consciously on the self and what one is

---

[4]Erin Sullivan, "Mercury," in *Planets*, edited by Joan McEvers (St. Paul, MN: Llewellyn Publications, 1989).

doing. As humans, we are equipped with a highly evolved cerebral cortex which endows us with the capacity to examine ourselves, to weigh our actions against ideals and principles we might hold about the "right" way to behave or act. So we may want to unleash our anger on someone, but we think about it and decide to handle the situation differently. Animals don't have this capacity: they are guided solely by stereotyped instinctive urges and prepro-grammed behaviour (although some domesticated pets might learn about good or bad from their human owners). We have more alternatives from which to choose—a mixed blessing, as anyone knows who has agonised over an important decision or who has experienced the conflict and tension created when we are torn between responding instinctively to circumstances or coming from a more "civilised" place.

There is a figure in alchemy named *Mercurius*, who was referred to in two very contrasting ways. He was called "the world-creating spirit" (the spirit that created the world), but he was also referred to as "the spirit imprisoned and concealed in matter."[5] Somehow he creates the world and then finds himself trapped in the world he himself has created. Let's dwell a while on this, because many psychologists and philosophers believe that we are similar to Mercurius in this way: we shape our lives according to our beliefs, precepts and perception of "reality," and then we get stuck in our own creation: we are limited by our own perceptions. This is what I was on about when I said if you wish to change something, you first have to alter your attitude and beliefs, your way of looking at it. You've probably heard of Heisenberg's uncer-tainty principle, which states that the act of observation itself affects that which is being observed. Our mind (Mercury) plays a major part in determining what the world is like for us. For example, let's say you are someone who is very overweight or obese, and you work hard to slim down. That's great, but if you still have an inner image of yourself as fat, you'll eventually just put the weight back on again.

Here's another concept for you—*mental set*. Our mental set is the way in which we evaluate the world. If you have the mental set that the planet Earth is heading for major disaster and might even

[5]Sallie Nichols, *Jung and Tarot* (York Beach, ME: Samuel Weiser, 1980), p. 52.

be facing total destruction, you will be predisposed to notice any-thing going on which supports or fits your expectations or mental set, and you'll probably ignore, discredit or not even know about those things which might augur otherwise. Our mental set deter-mines how we interpret sensory data. If I have the mental set that I am an inadequate and useless person, then I'll interpret events to fit this belief or life statement. Even if people tell me how great I am or how good I am at something, I'll think how I could have done better or convince myself they are stupid for liking me or that they are just being nice. (What was it Groucho Marx once said? Something like "I wouldn't want to join a club that would have me as a member.") If I think I'm no good, I'll dwell on what I don't do well or where I am lacking rather than on my positive points, and I'll believe the people who criticise me and not really register what-ever praise or compliments I receive. Our minds are like Mercu-rius: our thoughts, our beliefs, our mental sets, our life statements are what limit us or land us in trouble, and yet it is through the mind and our thinking that we can free ourselves from many of our difficulties by perceiving new ways of looking at things.

There is a very simple exercise which will bring this home to you. I'd like you to keep your eyes open and turn your head as far as it can go and then note how far it turned—mark a mental spot on the wall, or wherever, which is the farthest point your head has revolved. Now, return your head to its normal position and spend one minute imagining that you are able to turn your head a full 360 degrees—just picture this in your mind, just see your head making a full circle. Okay, time is up, stop. Now open your eyes and repeat what you first did, try turning your head around as far as it can go. You see what happens—your head is able to turn farther than before. It's true, it really works. To repeat: Mercury governs our thoughts and perceptions and these can limit us; but Mercury also gives us the ability to have new thoughts and perceptions which free or expand us; and to top it off, Mercury is that part of us capable of becoming aware that we can change our perceptions in this way. That's the general idea anyway. In alchemy, Mercurius represented both the transformer and also that which needed to be liberated or transformed. He symbolised both the *prima materia* (the lead or feces that was to be changed into gold), as well as symbolis-ing the goal of the work. *Mercurius duplex, utriusque capax* is the

Latin phrase used to describe Mercurius, and it translates into
"Mercurius, double and capable of either." The mind can trap us or
it can shape a new world for us. Jung equated Mercurius with the
transcendent function, a tricky concept to grasp, but about which he
had this to say:

> The secret of alchemy was in fact the transcendent function,
> the transformation of the personality through the blending
> and fusion of the noble with the base components, of the
> differentiated with the inferior functions, of the conscious
> with the unconscious.[6]

I believe that Mercury is the planet most closely aligned to the
transcendent function. As we have seen, it is Hermes-Mercury
who can rise to the heights of Olympus, to the transpersonal and
superconscious realms; it is Hermes-Mercury who is able to
descend into the depths of the Underworld and explore what is
buried in the unconscious; and it is Hermes-Mercury who can
bring back into everyday consciousness or into our conscious personalities what he has seen or learned when up in the heights or
down in the depths.

Mercury willing, we are going to attempt a little alchemy on
ourselves. At the beginning of today's talk, I asked you to think of
a problem you wanted to work on. Have you chosen one? Good,
now ask yourself these questions: "What is this problem forcing
me to learn? What would I have to develop, resolve or master in
myself to be able to deal better with my problem?" Take a few
minutes to think deeply about this. You may want to make a few
notes on whatever you believe the problem is asking that you learn
or develop, those things that would help solve or alleviate what is
bothering you. Now look at your notes and ask yourself, "Are
these good things that the problem is asking me to learn? Are these
good qualities or resources that the problem is asking I develop
and master?" Your answer, in most cases, is likely to be, "Yes,
these are good things." And if these are positive qualities or
resources, then how can you call your problem a problem? Who
but your best friend would want such good things for you? There-

6C. G. Jung, cited in Jolande Jacobi, *The Psychology of C. G. Jung* (New Haven, CT:
Yale University Press, 1973; and London: Routledge & Kegan Paul, 1968), 142.

fore, your problem is your best friend. For instance, if my problem were excessive, irrational jealousy, then I would need to develop greater objectivity, more detachment and distance, or I would need psychotherapy to sort myself out and hopefully I would learn a great deal about myself in the process. So is my jealousy a problem, or is it really a "friend" helping me along the way? It's a little tacky, I know, but I like this exercise. It's alchemical in the sense that you are taking something you don't like or find base (the *prima materia*, lead or feces) and turning it into gold by viewing it differently, by seeing that the problem could be a stepping stone or catalyst for your developing positive qualities which you might not develop if you didn't have the problem.

You also can see how the dichotomy between good and bad can become blurred or even transcended, because if the problem leads to something good, then it isn't an entirely bad thing. Congratulations to those of you who have just transcended an opposite — it's not something that happens everyday. If you feel "stuck," unfulfilled or unhappy in the house Mercury occupies or rules in your chart, then you are not doing something right. It is here that you can learn the wisdom of changing your beliefs, perceptions and expectations in order to alter your experience in that domain. Again, I must remind you to first clear any unconscious blockages (negative or self-defeating life statements of which you are unconscious or unaware) which are obstructing what you consciously would like to achieve. I remember working this way with a woman who had Mercury in the 2nd in difficult aspect to Pluto in the 11th but sextile Jupiter in the 4th. She wanted to be successful in her work and earn loads of money, but when I asked her to visualise herself as wealthy and successful, she couldn't do so. It turned out that unconsciously she was afraid that other people wouldn't like her if she was that way — she feared their envy and all which that entails. In order for her to realise her aims, she will have to clear that fear.

Hermes has just popped something else into my mind which I was meaning to talk about. I mentioned that he was the god of the threshold, or the god of crossroads. You meet Hermes when you have come to a crossroads in your life or you are on the threshold of a new phase in your life. Think about what it means to be standing on a threshold — you are neither inside the door nor outside the door. In actual fact you are in transition and Hermes is sometimes referred to as the god of transitions. I find this an interesting aspect, for whenever you're in transition, whenever you're moving from one major phase of life to another, the archetype of Hermes is activated. Adolescence is one such phase, and Hermes (always depicted in art as a youth) is the god associated with adolescence, when you are no longer a child but not yet an adult. Midlife is another major passage, and Hermes will be around at that time to help you find new meaning or purpose for the second half of life. In fact, any time you are in between identities or shedding your existing persona for a new one, Hermes will not be far away.

For instance, let's say you have just ended a ten-year marriage, and you are not in a new relationship as yet. You are at a crossroads, you have left your old life behind, but you don't know what will happen next. You can no longer identify yourself as somebody's wife or husband, and you may have a rather long period in limbo, grieving for the "old you," no longer standing on solid ground, no longer sure of who you are. Liminality (which is derived from the Latin limen, meaning doorway or threshold) is a word used to describe a phase when the old isn't working but the new has not yet come to replace it. In Jim Lewis' unpublished manuscript entitled Peter Pan in Midlife, Murray Stein is quoted on this subject: "Liminality is entered through the . . . internal experience of loss and burial of a former sense of self. . . . There is a break in psychological continuity, and the experience of the self and others takes on a different feeling, as though what had formerly been solid now is unreal."[7] Lewis goes on to add that during liminality, "One must be blown about the seas of possibility like Odysseus on his raft . . . accidents, dreams, meetings with remarkable strangers, and encounters at crossroads (literal or figurative) can result in totally new and undreamed of potentials being recognized and assimilated."[8] You may have to wait a while, but sooner or later, liminality invokes Hermes; through one of his tricks or an unexpected event or encounter he arranges, you are presented with an opportunity to usher in the next phase of your life. Hermes gives

[7]Murray Stein, cited in Jim Lewis, Peter Pan in Midlife, unpublished manuscript.
[8]Jim Lewis, Peter Pan in Midlife.

you the power to cross over the threshold, but you need to be open and receptive to him, and willing to take some risks. Erin Sullivan writes that "whenever things seem fixed, rigid or stuck, Hermes introduces fluidity, motion and new beginnings."[9] Do you have any questions so far?

Audience: Did Hermes get married or have children?

Howard: As might be expected of him, Hermes never settled down in one relationship—he was a bachelor god. Of course, that didn't stop him from having children. In mythology, a god's offspring can be seen as further representations of the god's nature. One of his children was called Autolycus, who unfortunately inherited some of the worst of Hermes' traits: Autolycus was renowned as an arch-thief and the biggest liar around. Another son, the ruthless Myrtilus, was a sociopath who plotted the death of his charioteer master. In some versions of the myth, Hermes is reputed to be the father of Pan, a goat from the waist down, depicted with goat horns and a beard. He was the god of forests and of pastures, very frisky, short-tempered and lustful. Pan inherited something of Hermes' mischievous nature: he particularly enjoyed hiding behind a bush and scaring travellers who ventured into the forest. The word *panic* is derived from his name. (There was a side to Hermes that was slightly wicked—a practical joker. I've observed this endearing trait in a few Mercury types, who enjoy trying things on for the fun of it: I think I'll tell my best friend that her husband is going around with someone else, and see what happens!)

Hermaphroditus, a curious figure indeed, was another one of Hermes' progeny. The by-product of a fling between Hermes and Aphrodite, he not only had both his parents' names, but he was endowed with both of their sexual characteristics as well. We get the word *hermaphrodite* from him. On one level, he represents the androgynous blending of male and female that exists in all of us. Some people with Mercury or Mercury-ruled signs strongly emphasised in their charts are psychological bisexuals. They may or may not act it out physically, but they sometimes are confused about their sexual identity because of their capacity to feel love and

---

[9]Erin Sullivan "Mercury," in *Planets*, p. 85.

attraction for both men and women. Hermes, after all, was curious about most things, and he did like to play around and experiment with different ways of being in life. Liz has spoken about the Ascendant as a means of fusing solar and lunar principles. I also believe that Mercury can serve this function as well. We've already touched upon Jung's concept of the transcendent function, which transforms the personality through the blending of opposites. As I have said, Mercury can be associated with reflective self-consciousness; it is the mind that allows us to stand back and look objectively at what is going on around us, and this helps us to decide how to act in any circumstance. There may be times when you feel it is necessary to be *yang*, that is, tough and assertive – traits traditionally associated with the masculine principle, but which exist in everyone. There are other times when you may decide that it is best to be *yin*, accepting, patient and allowing – traits that might be considered more feminine. It is Mercury in us that enables us to check out the situation and decide whether to come from a yang place or yin place, and in that way our minds can almost choose whether to act in a "masculine" or "feminine" fashion as the situation demands. It is also possible to marry the two.

Let's say you are a woman living with a man who is going through a hard time at work, and as a result he is miserable and irritable around the house. After a while, it begins to get on your nerves. It is possible for you to tell him that you really do understand why he is such a misery-guts and that you have sympathy for what he is going through, but you can still insist that you are not prepared to put up with it for much longer. In this case, you are being both loving and empathetic (the "feminine" principle), but also asserting yourself in an animus-type way. Sometimes you may be confused about which way to be. If I am in a circumstance where I can't decide whether to be tough or understanding, I try asking God, the cosmos, my higher Self or my inner wiseperson (whatever you wish to call the creative or higher intelligence which guides life) to give me an indication of how I should act. The answer may not come immediately – it may take a few days to seep through, it may come in a dream, or hit me later when I'm washing the dishes. It's like sending Hermes-Mercury up to Zeus-Jupiter for some advice, but you may have to wait a while for him to get back to you. Isabel Hickey used to comment that some people ring up the higher Self, and then put down the phone before receiving an answer. I guess what I'm doing is appealing to my intuition or "higher" mind to provide me with guidance. I sometimes even ask my higher Self to guide me to where I left my car keys. I'm surprised at how often this works.

Audience: Do all these archetypes exist within all of us, and then they are activated at different times?

Howard: Yes, I believe so. However, there will be specific archetypes which form your core Self, which are integral to your true, innate identity, and others that are secondary or less important. We all have a Zeus in us, we all have an Aphrodite in us, but I may be more Zeus than you, and you may be more Aphrodite than me. Problems arise when people twist themselves out of shape, either because of family or sociocultural conditioning, or because of the ambivalences and archetypically-based subpersonality conflicts within one's own nature. Let's say there is a little boy whose core identity is basically Dionysian: he is feeling and emotional, creative and perhaps a little scattered. If he has a father who doesn't approve of these "unmanly" traits, the boy might be coerced into behaving more like Zeus. He may even succeed in doing a pretty good Zeus imitation, but he'll never be happy or fulfilled if he has shut out or denied Dionysus in himself. If he's smart, he'll rebel in midlife.

As for the second part of your question, I would agree that different archetypes are activated or are necessary at different times in our lives, and this will probably show up through transits and progressions to the chart. Nevertheless, the core Self is still coloured by one or two particular archetypes, and always will be.

Audience: Mercury rules Gemini, the sign of the twins. Can you say more about Mercury in terms of duality?

Howard: I can illustrate it by drawing a circle on the board. What duality have I just created?

Audience: An inside and an outside.

Howard: Yes, and these two things didn't exist until I drew the circle. Before that circle appeared on the empty board, there was no duality, there was neither an inside nor an outside. You're right in thinking that Mercury lends itself to duality. Mercury (helped along by Saturn) is that part of us which draws boundaries, which distinguishes one thing from another through measuring, comparing or counting. In other words, our minds create boundaries by making distinctions between things. But don't forget that it is Mercury which also makes it possible for us to transcend duality, to transcend opposites and go beyond the realm of boundaries. Ken Wilber, the American transpersonal psychologist, is very good on the subject of duality, and I would refer you to his book *No Boundary*.[10] Wilber believes that every decision we make and every action we take revolves around the construction of boundaries. Whenever we make a decision, we are drawing a boundary between what to choose and what not to choose. We live in a world of opposites because we are always drawing boundaries. Take buying and selling, for instance. If you buy a toaster, it means that someone has sold you that toaster. Buying and selling can't exist independently from one another, so these two seemingly opposite actions are really two ends of one event. Wilber concludes that most of the problems we encounter in life are problems to do with boundaries. The more I hold onto or seek pleasure, the more I fear pain. The more I pursue goodness, the more I am obsessed with evil. The more I crave success, the more I dread failure. We live in an advanced technological world which is obsessed with progress and improving the quality of life, and yet look at the state of the planet – we are coming pretty close to destroying it and ourselves, which is the opposite of what we are aiming for.

Words (Mercury) foster boundary-making. We give one word to one side of a boundary, and another word is assigned to the opposite side. So we have light as opposed to dark, up compared with down, and good versus evil. Take the case of good and evil as an example. Most of us believe that good is achieved by getting rid of evil; if only we could succeed in eradicating or erasing evil from ourselves or from the world, we would be left just with what's good. Wilber believes that our concept of heaven is slightly

---

[10]Ken Wilber, *No Boundary* (Boston: Shambhala Publications, 1981), ch. 2.

askew — we think heaven is where all the good halves of opposites reside, while hell is the home of the bad halves. But is this true? I agree with Wilber when he says that heaven is the place where opposites are transcended, where the dilemma posed by opposites just doesn't exist — reminiscent of the gold sought by the alchemists via the transcendent function. All mystical traditions view the enlightened person as someone who has seen beyond the illusion of opposites. Rather than separating opposites and going only for the good halves, we ought to be seeking that inner psychological space which transcends and encompasses all duality.

INTERPRETING MERCURY

MERCURY IN THE HOROSCOPE

BY HOWARD SASPORTAS

Now we'll be looking more closely at Mercury in the horoscope. We'll begin by considering Mercury's sign placement, and you can refer to the guidelines I've given you (see Table 1, pages 32–33). Point one says that Mercury's sign placement indicates something about the way our minds work, how we think, learn, perceive, and digest experience. We'll start with Mercury in Aries. If this placement is not too inhibited or tempered by other parts of the chart, how would a typical Mercury in Aries learn?

Audience: It would probably learn quickly, because Aries is a cardinal fire sign.

Howard: Yes, it learns quickly and thinks fast, unless of course it is conjunct or in difficult angle to Saturn, or square Neptune or something else which would alter its expression. Fire is associated with the intuition, so people with Mercury in Aries are likely to be intuitive thinkers — that is, they grasp things whole, often in a "whoosh," and usually have no trouble thinking symbolically.

Point two states that Mercury's sign describes how we communicate and exchange ideas and information. Apply this to people with Mercury in Aries.

Audience: Ideas might come faster than they can express. Or they may blurt things out and not have too much self-control over what they say.

Howard: Yes, signs represent different styles of being. Each sign has its own style, its own way of being. A planet functions like a verb, and shows the kind of activity being done. The Moon needs

Table 1. Guidelines for Interpreting Mercury.

MERCURY BY SIGN
1) Mercury's placement by sign indicates something about the way our mind works—how we think, learn, perceive and digest experience. For example, are you an intuitive thinker (Mercury in fire) or do you have a mind which is more cool, detached and objective (Mercury in air)? Is your mind quick to grasp things (Mercury in cardinal signs), or is it too rigid and set (an afflicted Mercury in fixed signs)?
2) Mercury's sign also describes something about how we communicate and exchange ideas and information. Do you blurt things out (Mercury in Aries, for example) or are you more cautious, guarded or secretive with your words (such as Mercury in Scorpio)?
3) Mercury's sign indicates the kinds of concerns that occupy the mind, and also shows what you tend to notice and pick up on in the environment. For instance, Mercury in Libra may quickly notice possibilities for relationship, while Mercury in Capricorn will tend to notice those things which serve one's aims and ambitions.
MERCURY BY HOUSE
1) Mercury's house shows an area of life where we are likely to be restless, curious, inventive, inquisitive, adaptable, fluctuating, cunning, possibly deceitful and good at making bargains (depending on its sign and aspects). Ideally it is a domain where we stay fresh and open to experience rather than boxing ourselves in by thinking too narrowly or rigidly. Remember, we often can change something by changing our attitude and way of thinking about it.
2) Mercury's house can show the kinds of things that concern and occupy our mind. (For example, Mercury in the 6th might think a lot about health; Mercury in the 9th about philosophy, travel and meaning in life.)

Table 1. Guidelines for Interpreting Mercury (cont.)

3) Mercury's house is where we might run into issues concerning relatives, neighbours and co-workers. For instance, an afflicted Mercury in the 8th could be conflicts with siblings over inheritance; Mercury in the 10th could mean we work with a relative or sibling. Mercury in the 8th can give powerful undercurrents with relatives, coworkers or neighbours.

MERCURY BY ASPECT

1) Mercury is highly influenced and coloured by the nature of any planet aspecting it (especially the planet in closest aspect). Mars in aspect to Mercury will quicken the mind and speech; Neptune in aspect to Mercury can make the mind quite intuitive and creative, but can also produce vague and confused thinking. Our experience of learning and the educational system will also be affected by the kinds of aspects to Mercury.

2) Planets aspecting Mercury will also influence how we communicate and exchange information. Mercury-Venus will often try to say things that please or produce harmony; Mercury-Uranus is more likely to say exactly what it feels regardless of its effect on others.

3) What naturally should concern and interest us will be shown by planets aspecting Mercury. Mercury-Neptune may have an interest in Neptunian things such as the arts, healing or psychic phenomena. Mercury-Pluto is meant to probe the deeper and hidden workings of the mind and consciousness.

4) Aspects to Mercury describe something about the kinds of relationships we form with relatives, siblings, neighbours and coworkers.

5) Aspects to Mercury can give an indication of the kinds of experiences we encounter while travelling (usually taken to mean short journeys or those within one's own country).

and responds, Mercury thinks or communicates, Venus relates, Mars acts, etc. Signs are like adverbs, describing the way in which something is done. A planet will express itself according to the style of the sign it is in. So the Moon in Aries will respond in an Arien way: the Moon in Taurus in a Taurean way. Mercury in Aries will think or communicate in accordance with the style of Aries; Mercury in Taurus will do so in line with Taurus's usual style or manner. I know this is basic stuff, but I've always found the idea of the planet as verb and the sign as adverb a useful concept for interpreting sign placements.

Point three suggests that Mercury's sign indicates the kinds of concerns that occupy the mind, and also what you tend to notice and pick up on in the environment. This is rather general, but how might point three apply to Mercury in Aries?

Audience: Aries is a sign associated with initiation, being first at something. Perhaps they are looking for any chance to be first: to speak first, to learn first, to tell others about something first.

Howard: Yes, it can be a fighting mind or competitive spirit. They might also be looking for ways to use speech or action as a means of inspiring, arousing or leading other people. Joseph Campbell, the author of *The Hero with a Thousand Faces*, is a good example of someone with Mercury in Aries. He loved the intuitive world of myths and symbols, and inspired his students and followers with his original thinking, fertile imagination, and with the sheer, unadulterated enthusiasm he felt for his beloved field of study. I think you've got the point, unless maybe we need to allow more time for those of you with Mercury in Taurus to get it. Sorry, I must be nicer to Taurus. Do you want to go through all the sign placements of Mercury? You do. You sure you won't get bored doing it this way? All right, you win. What does Mercury in Taurus say about how the mind works?

Audience: It could steady and deepen the mind. They may be slower then Mercury in Aries to comprehend something fully, but once they do, they know it deeply and well. They may not want to say something unless they are sure about it; in other words, they are not quick off the mark to speak.

Howard: What would Mercury in Taurus be inclined to notice or register in the environment?

Audience: Things that would offer safety, comfort and security: ways of making money, a new home to buy, any purchase which would please them or beautify their lives in some way.

Howard: Yes, which also means they would be sensitive to anything in the environment which might threaten their security or safety. I'm glad you mention their interest in beauty. Taurus is a Venus-ruled sign, and has produced many fine artists and craftspeople. Mercury in Taurus can give a deep appreciation of art and beauty, or a deep love of nature. Although I've met some people with Mercury in Taurus who really do fit the description of a bull in a china shop, there are others with this placement who have been blessed with beautiful speaking or singing voices, and who move in a most graceful way. I'm thinking of Dame Margot Fonteyn, who had incredible style both as a person and a dancer; she certainly made good use of her Mercury in Taurus.

I must tell you a story about another time I ran a seminar on Mercury. It was in London and there were about fifty people attending. I gave them an exercise to do, in which they divided up into small groups according to their Mercury sign. So I had the Mercury in Aries group in one place, the Mercury in Taurus group sitting together somewhere else, etc. Their task was to make a list of the attributes of Mercury in their sign. The outcome was interesting, because it was so indicative of the Mercury sign of each group. For instance, the Mercury in Aries group finished first; it took them no time at all to come up with a list of what it meant to have Mercury there. I'll come to Mercury in Taurus in a minute. The Mercury in Gemini group was the largest of the twelve, and they compiled a list four times longer than any other group. The people with Mercury in Cancer completed their list and then gave each other a massage. There was only one Mercury in Leo, so I put him with the Mercury in Aquarius group just to see what would happen; they managed all right, although I did get the feeling there were power struggles going on. An argument broke out in the hair-splitting Mercury in Virgo group and one woman ended up in tears because the other members had torn her views to pieces. The people with Mercury in Libra were well-behaved; they took the task very seriously and debated their ideas quite a bit before coming up with a good list – neatly written down, of course. I can't remember the Mercury in Scorpio brigade – I must have repressed what they did. Those with Mercury in Sagittarius zipped through the exercise and then sidetracked into some philosophical discussion about astrology in general. The Mercury in Capricorn group were also well-behaved, although they kept calling me over just to make sure they were doing the exercise correctly. Those with Mercury in Pisces had a fair amount of difficulty with the task: they seemed to have quite contrasting ideas about the attributes of Mercury in their sign. Eventually we realised that the differing opinions stemmed from the fact that one of them had the Sun in Aquarius, two had the Sun in Pisces, and the remaining member had the Sun in Aries. It really made a difference whether or not Mercury was in the same sign as the Sun. I'll speak more on the relationship between the Sun and Mercury later when we cover aspects. As for the people with Mercury in Taurus – well, let me tell you . . . all the other groups had finished after about thirty minutes, but the Mercury in Taurus group needed more time. Honestly, this happened. So I went over to them and discovered that they didn't even have one point on their list. That's not exactly true – they had a few ideas on paper but then crossed out. I asked what was going on, and they told me they didn't want to write anything down unless they were absolutely certain it was fact. How concrete can you get? It's as if these people have to feel the truth of something in every single cell of their bodies before they'll say it or commit themselves to it. Truth is almost organic for them. Quite a contrast to the Mercury in Aries group, who were done in ten minutes, because they wrote down what they thought as soon as they had thought of it.

People with Mercury in Gemini often have a lot of thoughts and impressions going on simultaneously. If they are true to their natures, they'll be curious about life, experimental and open to new ideas and new experience. Usually their minds are quick, and you would expect them to be lively communicators. Infants around nine-months old, as they gradually progress from crawling to standing and walking, are at a *mercurial* stage. It's at this time that they generally relish exploring the immediate environment and

learning new words. By nature, Gemini is a sign that enjoys movement and discovering the world around them, and takes pleasure
in acquiring speech; naming things can be fun and gives you a kind
of power over something. If you have a well-aspected Mercury in
Gemini, and provided your mother has made you feel relatively
safe and secure, you probably would have had a positive experience of the practicing stage: "Oh, over here is a television set, and
over there is a cat, and look, a ball to play with, and there's my
brother pulling my sister's hair. He doesn't pull mine, I wonder
why?" Someone with Mercury in Gemini should feel good about
exploring and discovering the environment, making connections
and comparing and contrasting this with that. If this phase goes
well, they'll likely retain this curiosity and interest in the world
for the rest of their lives.

However, I've known a number of people with Mercury in
Gemini who are not curious, adventurous, or communicative;
instead, they have rigid beliefs, fixed ideas and interests, and are
blinkered like horses. Their Mercury in Gemini is blocked. It's
likely that they weren't allowed enough freedom and space in the
practicing stage (which is sometimes referred to as "the monkey
phase" of our development). They were imprisoned in playpens
and not given enough opportunity for movement and exploration.
So if adults with Mercury in Gemini aren't curious and mentally
open, it probably is due to early childhood conditioning inhibiting
their innate nature; this may show up in the chart as a difficult
aspect from Saturn, Chiron, Neptune or Pluto to a Gemini Mercury. I can give you an example of a man with Mercury in Gemini
conjunct Saturn in the 3rd house. Obviously, he couldn't remember what happened when he was nine months old, but he recalled
a later childhood event which aptly describes how he became congested in his thinking and views. For some reason, he hated his
second-grade teacher, but when he told his mother what he felt,
she attacked him for being rude and nasty and made him promise
never to say or think such things again. As a result he not only lost
self-esteem, but he also learned it was better to hide or even deny
what he was thinking and feeling if it were in the slightest bit
negative. In other words, with the help of his mother, he slipped
into a mental straitjacket. When thoughts and feelings are suppressed or disallowed, they cause psychic congestion and never

have a chance to shift or develop into other thoughts and feelings. By contrast, let's say you report to your mother that you don't like your teacher, and she responds by asking you why and exploring your feelings with you. She doesn't make you feel bad for thinking as you do; on the contrary, she encourages you to look into yourself to find out why you're having these reactions. This allows mental movement, and you may come to a point where you move beyond your initial thoughts and feelings into a whole new level of understanding or appreciation of your teacher or the situation in general. Movement (mental or physical) is experience, and gives the brain a chance to develop more fully. But if movement is curtailed, then your development is hindered, and your thinking can easily become congested and rigid. We should move on to Mercury in Cancer. How might the sign of Cancer affect Mercury's functioning?

Audience: Thinking would be influenced or coloured by feelings.

Howard: Yes, people with Mercury in Cancer can be very subjective: they think they are thinking and evaluating something rationally but in actual fact, as you say, their feelings and complexes are affecting their perception. For instance, difficulties in early bonding with mother may lead them to believe that the world is an unsafe place not conducive to fulfilling their needs. This deepseated emotional pattern will affect how they view life; they'll be predisposed to notice when someone is cold or stand-offish toward them, and perhaps not compute or register all the times other people show them warmth and genuine concern. So, according to their moods and complexes, they pick up on certain things going on around them and miss or ignore other facts or circumstances. Their thinking may be heavily influenced by the environment. When visiting a peaceful and loving household, they probably will have positive and happy thoughts. If around a place that is dark and negative, their thoughts may turn dark and negative. Cancer is a very sensitive sign that can easily "feel" into other people, "sussing out" their needs and weak points. For this reason, Mercury in Cancer can make a very persuasive talker or business- and salesperson, who knows just how to reach or get around somebody with the right pitch or line. They'll instinctively know what to say to make someone feel better or to hurt someone if that is what they want to do. Jung had Mercury in Cancer and made great use of his feelings and intuitions in his analytical work. Marcel Proust, the author of *Remembrance of Things Past*, used his Mercury in Cancer to recall his childhood and early life. He also suffered from strange allergies due to his supersensitivity to the environment, a very appropriate reflection of his Mercury sign. Besides things of the past and anything to do with home or family, what else might occupy or concern their minds?

Audience: Anything to do with survival needs, such as food.

Howard: Good thing we just had lunch. Let's move on to Mercury in Leo. Leo is fixed fire — concentrated spirit — so it should help to concentrate or focus the mind. In fact, I've found that many people with Mercury in Leo are powerful on the mental plane. If they're thinking very strongly about something, they almost have the power to make it happen. If they're holding you in a negative light (whether or not you know it), you'll feel uncomfortable around them — hard as you try to do the right thing, you'll probably end up blowing it or offending them. That's what I mean about Mercury in Leo having power on the mental plane. It can also give a bright mind, adding to one's mental self-confidence and oratory ability, although there is the danger of too much subjectivity, which can lead people with this placement to believe that their version of the truth is the only one. Mercury is either in the same sign as the Sun or in the sign before or after the Sun. If the Sun is in Cancer and Mercury is in Leo, Mercury's placement could help Cancer's confidence and courage. Both the Sun and Mercury in Leo could make one overly attached or too identified with one's own ideas and views on things, so there is not a lot of space left for other people's opinions should these differ. The Sun in Virgo and Mercury in Leo will contribute greater spirit and warmth to the Virgo Sun.

Audience: Doesn't Mercury in Leo tend to exaggerate somewhat?

Howard: I don't think they would be adverse to embellishing the truth slightly to turn something into a good story, so yes, there can be a dramatic flair to this placement. Mercury in Sagittarius will do this as well, add little bits to tales they have to tell, or turn what might seem like a minor incident into a matter of great significance.

I've already mentioned the exercise where the group with Mercury in Virgo made one woman cry because of the way they critically attacked her views on this placement. I still think this is a good position for Mercury in terms of discriminatory powers, attention to detail and the careful scrutiny of any person or situation. They don't miss a trick. I'll let you in on a little secret if you promise not to tell anyone I told you. Someone teaching this course with me has Mercury in Virgo. It shouldn't come as a surprise considering the depth of her understanding, the precision with which she explains concepts and theories, and the pinpoint accuracy of her interpretations, not unlike an Exocet missile hitting its mark.

Audience: What Sun sign is Liz?

Howard: I've revealed enough already, but what the heck. She has a Pisces Sun in a tight T-square with Mercury in Virgo and Venus in Sagittarius. And I'm sure you've guessed that she has the Moon retrograde. Okay, you really want to know, I'll tell you—her sign is, "Please do not disturb." Get it?

Mercury in Virgo needs time to fully digest and assimilate information. Like Mercury in any earth sign, people with this placement want to make sure of the correctness of what they think or say. Assimilating experience has parallels with the assimilation of food. When we take in food, we first should chew it properly, and the same advice applies to taking in things that happen to us or to what we read or are told by others; rather than swallowing something whole, it's better to chew over information we receive and mull over the meaning of events we encounter in everyday life. Chewing is an aid to the catabolic process of breaking down food so that we can retain what is nourishing and eliminate what is waste. People with Mercury in Virgo have the ability to see the good points as well as the bad points of anything they scrutinise or analyse. If well acted upon, their Mercury will enable them to hold onto what is positive and constructive from experience, and not dwell overly much on the negative things they notice. If you dwell too much on the fact that a rose has sharp thorns, you may miss the full beauty of its petals or the sweetness of its smell. You need to acknowledge the thorns, but not become obsessed by them. Also, Mercury in Virgo is a practical thinker. An abstract theory or concept is only worthwhile if it can be put to practical and concrete use. What concerns might occupy the minds of those with this placement?

Audience: Health and work issues.

Howard: Some people I know with Mercury in this sign see the tiniest, microscopic spot on their arm, and they're off to the doctors in a shot. They are also the ones who first spy the very beginnings of a crack in the ceiling, and they may have a lot of do-it-yourself books around the house on subjects like home decorating, gardening, or just fixing things in general. I'm getting silly again, so let's move on to Mercury in Libra.

Mercury in Libra often gives an interest in human relations and in the workings of other people's minds. Anyone with Mercury in this sign should strive to achieve a balanced mind, and by that I mean a good balance between thinking and feeling, between practical realism and thinking of an abstract or theoretical nature. The thing about any placement in Libra is that if it is not in balance, then it is out of balance. Those with Mercury in Libra can be incredibly accurate and spot-on in their perception of others or in the way they interpret events, but when their feelings get in the way of their rational minds, their perspective can be quite off. Sometimes they can be unstintingly objective and fair, and at other times their powers of observation go haywire—usually when an emotional complex is triggered or if someone doesn't live up to their ideals and expectations. I've seen this happen when Cancer squares Mercury in Libra; for instance, with a Cancer Moon square a Libran Mercury, or with natal or transiting Jupiter in Cancer squaring Mercury in Libra, or natal or transiting Pluto in Cancer squaring Mercury in Libra. In any case, people with Mercury in Libra are good at showing you the other side of any person or situation. So I might approach a Mercury-in-Libra person and say, "Look at this, isn't it nice?," and they might reply, "Yes it is nice, but have you noticed this flaw or this problem with it?" Or I might say how horrible something is, which sparks them into pointing out the good bits. They like a lively debate or argument, and will analyse all the different sides of a situation before coming to a conclusion, which is how they have earned their fence-sitting reputation. Ultimately, however, they most often aim to be fair and just, and they usually are not afraid to fight for what they believe in, to stand up for their ideals of truth, beauty or justice. Brigitte Bardot, the sex kitten of the 1950s turned animal rights campaigner, was born with Mercury in Libra exactly conjunct Jupiter in the 10th house. Some people with this placement are capable of expressing themselves in a typically creative Libran style: Agatha Christie, the crime writer famous for her intricately woven plots, was born with Mercury in Libra dispositing her Virgo Sun.

Speaking of crime leads us nicely on to Mercury in Scorpio. If you have this placement, it's almost like a "celestial instruction" indicating that you are meant to delve beneath the surface level of life in order to examine yourself, other people, things and ideas on the deepest possible levels. Some people call it the detective mind – always probing, always looking for motives. So if you give a present to someone with Mercury in Scorpio, the reply may be, "Thank you, how kind," but inside they may be wondering why you gave them that particular present and if there are any strings attached. As with Mercury in any water sign, there can be a secretive mind and quite a bit of caution about what they reveal to you about themselves, as if their innate instincts tell them that it is safer not to give too much away. Once something is said, how can you be sure what people will do with it? Mercury in Scorpio, like Mercury in Leo, is very powerful on the mental plane, and will defend its beliefs and opinions in a manner which would impress Joan of Arc herself.

Audience: They also know where to put the stinger.

Howard: Yes, I've found that to be true, a knack for going right for the jugular. A good example of a sharp-witted Mercury in Scorpio is the highly quotable Oscar Wilde, although its opposition to Uranus in the 9th house unfortunately landed him on the wrong side of the law of his day. Mercury in Scorpio could create a good schemer or strategist, a chess-player's mind. And it recalls Hermes

Psychopompos who could freely enter the underworld, a symbol for the unconscious depths of the psyche. What are your ideas on Mercury in Sagittarius?

Audience: This should give an interest in philosophy, religion, the laws of the universe, and travel. And since Sagittarius is a fire sign, Mercury there would describe an intuitive thinker.

Howard: Yes, as you would expect, people with Mercury here often have lively minds full of vision and inspiration. Unless this place- ment is balanced by earth signs, planets or angles in Scorpio, or a strong Saturn or Pluto in the chart, they may not think their ideas through. Sagittarius sees things whole, viewing a bigger or broader picture rather than focussing on details and pieces, and is often preoccupied with distant goals and lofty ideals. Are you familiar with the distinction between the functions of the two hem- ispheres of the brain? The left brain is concerned with rational and sequential thought; it gathers facts, analyses and compartmenta- lises, and could be related to Mercury in Gemini or Virgo. By comparison, the right brain can identify a shape which is sug- gested by only a few lines, and is associated with synthetic and holistic thinking, seeing images and patterns. This kind of thinking is more akin to Mercury in Sagittarius and Pisces. Marilyn Fergu- son, in her book *The Aquarian Conspiracy*, commented that, "the left [brain] takes snapshots, the right watches movies."[11] Mercury in Sagittarius often exhibits a natural tendency to look for meaning in events; things that happen are not just random but part of a grand design and can be viewed in the context of one's overall life plan or unfoldment.

Audience: I've known a number of people with this placement, and they all seem to talk a great deal.

Howard: Generally speaking, that is probably true, although other planetary aspects to it could inhibit the talkative side of Mercury in Sagittarius. But, yes, when excited, their minds will be flooded

---

[11]Marilyn Ferguson, *The Aquarian Conspiracy: Personal & Social Transformation in the 1980's* (Los Angeles: J. P. Tarcher, 1987; and London: Granada, 1981), p. 82.

with ideas and visions of future possibilities. Usually, they're inclined to share their enthusiasms and beliefs openly, unlike Mercury in Scorpio, which tends to keep things hidden or secret. The cardinal fire of Aries has been compared with the initial spark that starts a flame; the fixed fire of Leo is the glowing, concentrated heart of the fire; the mutable fire of Sagittarius is that part which sparkles and crackles into the air—hence the idea of Mercury in Sagittarius spreading ideas or getting others excited about a vision, plan or belief. Sometimes too much talking can be their way of staying in the head and defending against feeling. You can be in a therapy session and talk and talk and talk about what is going on in your life, and never really contact your true feelings or emotions because talking is taking up all the space.

Mercury in Capricorn brings us down to earth again. The mind has a practical bent so there can be business acumen, managerial and organising skills. Capricorn is symbolised by a goat, and I always picture this goat carefully climbing a mountain, wanting to be sure it is on solid footing each step along the way. Mercury here can give methodical thinking along with determination, persistence and staying power, and perhaps a certain eye for what will get them ahead in the world or further their goals and ambitions. In most cases, people with this placement are worriers, often imagining the worst possible outcome or that trouble is waiting around the corner. This will make them cautious and wary, not inclined to leap into something blindly even though Capricorn is a cardinal sign. Rather than get bogged down in negative scenarios of the future, I would advise them to acknowledge their fears but not dwell on them; so when they become fearful and apprehensive, they might try a little kinesthetic visualisation and picture themselves successfully accomplishing their aims and guiding a steady course through obstacles.

If you come across people with Mercury in Capricorn who seem perennially confused, disorganised or directionless, you're likely to find a Neptune aspect interfering with the natural workings of Mercury in this sign. And if you find revolutionary types or radical thinkers with Mercury in Capricorn, there is probably a Uranus aspect to Mercury. Two examples come to mind. Simone de Beauvoir, the highly original French existentialist writer who stressed that human beings have to create their own moral values in a world where there are no absolutes, was born with a close Mercury-Uranus conjunction in Capricorn. The singer Joan Baez, who is also a civil-rights campaigner, anti-war protester and committed pacifist, influenced a whole generation in the 1960s; she was born with Sun conjunct Mercury in Capricorn trine Uranus in Taurus. We also shouldn't forget Capricorn's capricious or more whimsical side: I've observed that Mercury in Capricorn (and Mercury-Saturn aspects can do this as well) frequently bestows humour and wit—usually of a dry, ironic, and self-effacing quality. The buoyant yet earthy Gracie Fields, one of Britain's most successful comediennes, had a stellium with Mars, Venus, Mercury and the Sun all in Capricorn.

Some textbooks refer to Mercury in Aquarius as an ivory-tower thinker, and, in certain instances, this interpretation does fit. Aquarius is a fixed air sign, at home in the expansive and abstract realm of the mind and intellect, and liable to dissociation from the body and feelings. To use the jargon, Mercury in Aquarius could live primarily up in the head. You might be inclined to praise the objectivity and detachment shown by some people with this placement, but you also might grow infuriated with their denial of gut emotion. They may intuit or devise divine utopian schemes and systems which are perfectly wonderful in a theoretical sense, but rather impractical or unrealistic considering the more basic, instinctive and acquisitive sides of human nature. Although it may sound as if I'm putting Mercury in Aquarius down, I'm not—we need people to inspire us with new visions, new possibilities and hope for a better future. To coin a phrase from Rodgers and Hammerstein, you've got to have a dream to have a dream come true. Mercury in Aquarius can envision a more ideal world or society toward which we can work and strive. At its very worst, however, their neatly arranged and perfectly functioning state could resemble Huxley's *Brave New World*, or the Orwellian nightmare chillingly recounted in *1984*, where one's individuality or humanity is negated and subordinated for the sake of the larger whole.

I don't want to make it sound as if everyone with Mercury in Aquarius is preoccupied only with abstract systems and utopian pipe dreams. Many are genuinely concerned with social and humanitarian problems, and are working hard to improve conditions around them. And for many of them, truth comes before social acceptability. In addition, this placement can give great clarity of mind, an ability to stand back and view situations with an awe-inspiring objectivity. When doing charts for people with Mercury in Aquarius (and this applies to Mercury sextile or trine Uranus as well), I'm often impressed by how clearly they're able to talk about themselves, by how clearly they see themselves. I sometimes get the feeling that, even if they only knew a little astrology, they could read their own charts better than I can. What comes to mind when you think of Mercury in Pisces?

Audience: A vivid imagination, but also chaotic thinking.

Audience: I have this placement and I find that I can easily pick up on other people's thoughts and feelings.

Howard: Yes, you just read my mind. I was about to say that someone with Mercury in Pisces might raise his or her hand and ask the question uppermost in the minds of others in the group. This also applies to Mercury-Neptune aspects. Pisces and Neptune both represent the blurring or dissolution of boundaries. If Mercury is connected with this planet or sign, it can be hard to distinguish your own thoughts from those of others around you. You can get the chameleonlike ones, who change their views and opinions according to whom they happen to be hanging out with at the time.

So there are a lot of contradictions about this placement: people with a Pisces Mercury often have a creative imagination and are highly intuitive and telepathic, but they also can experience a great deal of mental confusion and instability. I have a good friend with Mercury retrograde in Pisces in the 12th house (sometimes I tease him and say it's almost like not having a Mercury at all). In many respects, he's one of the clearest thinkers I know, highly sensitive, reading people and situations as accurately as a barometer reads atmospheric pressure. And yet, he is constantly misplacing his house and car keys. He visits me at my flat, throws his keys down in a different place each time, and then spends an infuriating hour trying to find them when he's ready to leave. You could say that some people with Mercury in Pisces have trouble ordering their environment. Similar to Mercury in Cancer, they tend to learn through osmosis, absorbing or intuiting information and ideas rather than learning or reasoning in a logical fashion. And as with Mercury in any of the water signs, it might be hard to fathom what they're really thinking; they can be rather secretive and often make clever strategists or good poker players. It's not always easy for them to put the mass of things they feel into words, except perhaps through poetry, music, dance, or some other plastic art form. The jazz singer Billie Holiday is a good example of Mercury in Pisces, with her incomparable voice and totally messed-up life. I've also done charts for people with this placement who suffer from extreme paranoia and a morbid imagination, which stems from projecting their deep-seated fears, anxieties and complexes onto the environment.

Before we move on to discuss Mercury aspects, are there any questions you'd like to ask?

Audience: Can you say a little more about Mercury's dual rulership of Gemini and Virgo?

Howard: I can draw some general distinctions between Mercury as ruler of Gemini and Mercury as ruler of Virgo, but you mustn't take what I have to say too literally; my interpretation just gives you a broad, almost archetypal sense of how the function of Mercury varies in the two signs. The Gemini Mercury has a tendency to move all over the place: Gemini goes here and there, exploring how one thing relates to another, making comparisons, trying to fit things into place. Virgo, however, has more to do with taking one thing and going deeply into it. Gemini will know a little something about many different subjects; Virgo will know a great deal about one or two specific topics. The Gemini Mercury likes knowledge for knowledge's sake because to know about something, to be able to name something, makes it more interesting. The Virgo Mercury likes knowledge that can be put to practical use. The Gemini Mercury receives and processes information through the mind; the Virgo Mercury picks up information through the sensations and the body, judging something by the kinds of bodily sensations it gives or by how it feels. The Gemini Mercury delights in seeing how the parts of something fit together to make a whole; the Virgo Mercury pulls things apart, dissecting and breaking down something which is whole into its component parts.

Unless Mercury is adversely aspected, Virgo is a fairly steady and reliable sign. Gemini as a sign, however, is much more changeable and prone to ups and downs. Consider the Twins, Castor and Pollux, often associated with Gemini. When one of the twins was up in heaven, it was a rule that the other one had to be down on earth. They weren't allowed to be in the same place at the same time, so they kept swapping places. Gemini (and any planet in this sign) can ascend to the heights one day, and then land right back on earth the next. Marilyn Monroe and Judy Garland were both Geminis, and the marked ups and downs of their lives and careers exemplified this yo-yo swing of Gemini. A modern example is Boy George, who reached the heights as a pop star and then hit rock bottom through drug abuse. Currently, he's trying to get back up there again. There is much more to the sign of Gemini than many Sun sign books credit it with. There is a deep side to Gemini (and Virgo as well), recalling Hermes' role as the guide of souls into and out of the underworld.

Audience: Can you say something about Mercury retrograde?

Howard: Yes, I wanted to get around to that. How many people here today were born with Mercury retrograde? Quite a few. Some texts interpret a retrograde Mercury as difficulty in communicating what you're thinking, but I haven't noticed this to always be the case in the charts I've done. I'd be curious to hear what people who have it think—if you are able to talk at all, that is.

Audience: Sometimes I have trouble with communication, and other times I don't.

Howard: Yes, the same goes for me, and I have it direct. Other people? I see you nodding your heads "no," so in your personal experience, Mercury retrograde isn't necessary linked with communication difficulties. I do believe that a retrograde Mercury inclines you to look inside yourself, perhaps to check out what you're going to say before you speak, and it also inclines you to chew over any thought or idea you have, or any information you receive before you code it or feel certain about it. Oddly enough, I've done the charts for two broadcasters who read the news on national television in Great Britain, and it just so happened that both of them were born with Mercury retrograde in Virgo. I found this odd at first, because reading the news to millions of people is a very public and outgoing use of one's Mercury. Then I thought more about it. When they read the news, they're not giving out their own opinions but supposedly just reporting the facts; and in their public lives, they often have to hide their views on things because of the high-profile nature of their job — you know the way certain newsreaders become mini-celebrities. One of them was particularly adamant I keep it absolutely quiet that she came for chart readings, just in case the newspapers caught wind of it and came out with a story sensationalising her interest in something as weird as astrology.

Audience: It's interesting that it was Mercury retrograde in the sign of Virgo, which indicates precision and skill with words and in communication.

Audience: Have you noticed anything about people who have a retrograde Mercury at birth and then it goes direct by progression?

Howard: Yes, I've looked into this. Around the time it turns direct, they do seem to come out of themselves more, opening their minds to new things and generally becoming more extraverted. Those of you born with Mercury retrograde should check out your progressions in this respect. Also, you may be born with Mercury direct, which then might turn retrograde by progression — so all of you should watch for that and see the effects it has on you. It's probably better to have Mercury direct when you are younger, because you need a free-flowing Mercury to learn as best you can and to adjust to school. It may not be so bad if it turns retrograde when you're older, because that's a time when the mind is meant to turn inward for self-reflection.

What really interests me, however, is watching transiting Mercury go retrograde and direct, something which affects us all. Erin Sullivan's chapter on Mercury in the book *Planets* contains one of the best discourses I've read on the transiting retrograde, and I'm lifting some of my material from her writing on the subject.[12] When Mercury goes retrograde, it seems to be an appropriate time for *re*doing, *re*thinking, *re*assessing, *re*evaluating – anything with the prefix *re-* in front of it. A Mercury retrograde period is a time to catch up on things, to complete unfinished projects, to write that letter you've been meaning to write or pay that long-outstanding bill, and generally to reassess the affairs of the house or area of life through which it is moving backward, and to plan your next move in this domain. It may not be the right time to take action on your plan, but it is a time to plot out future moves for when it turns direct again. You may even run into people from the past with whom something has been left hanging which needs finishing or completion. When Mercury goes retrograde, you may find that your awareness or attention naturally turns inward, affording you greater access to the contents of your unconscious mind, allowing you to explore and integrate hitherto buried or hidden feelings. By the way, Mercury goes retrograde every four months for about 22 days, and it tends to do so in cycles by element – for a couple of years it will turn retrograde in an earth sign, and then you have another few years when it goes retrograde in fire, and so on. If Mercury turns retrograde in a fire sign, you may need to reassess your direction in life or how you're using any creative talents you have, but it's probably not a good time to take risks or make sweeping changes. When retrograde in an earth sign, you may need to turn your attention to outstanding practical matters, such as a dentist or doctor appointment you've been putting off, or finally buying that washer for the leaky faucet, or getting around at last to that closet or backporch which desperately needs sorting out. When retrograde in air, it is a period to rethink or reevaluate how you relate or connect with family, friends and society in general. If Mercury goes retrograde in a water sign, your thoughts may turn to past relationships and it is probably appropriate to reexamine old habit patterns and emotional responses. I'm sure you've all noticed that Mercury retrograde often synchronises with periods when mail gets lost or delayed, telephone calls are more difficult to put through, you run into more problems with verbal miscommunication and misunderstandings, and you encounter even more

---

[12]Erin Sullivan, "Mercury," in *Planets*, pp. 94–118.

delays in travelling than usual (I'm pretty sure that British Rail must have been incorporated when Mercury was retrograde). I agree with the general consensus that says it's not a good idea to sign any contracts while Mercury is retrograde – something will go wrong or not turn out as you expected or hoped it would. I'm debating whether or not to tell you about a curious incident that happened to me when Mercury was retrograde in Capricorn earlier this year in January [1990].

Audience: Now you've got us curious.

Howard: Okay, you talked me into it. The surgeon scheduled my neck operation for January 16th, and I had to be in the hospital the day before. When I first received news of the date, I immediately got out my ephemeris and I wasn't pleased with what I saw. Mercury was retrograde and still in range of a conjunction with Neptune in Capricorn, and this transiting conjunction was square my natal Neptune and occurring in my 12th house, which you know rules places like hospitals. Also, the Moon was void of course at the exact time the operation would be happening, which, according to horary astrology, means that an event will not work out as planned. All this scared me: I was worried that there would be some sort of mix-up or confusion, they would take out the wrong thing, or the surgeon's hand would slip, or that I would be confused with someone else who was having a leg amputated or a gall bladder removed or something like that. But I decided against postponing the operation, as I was having it done on the National Health Service and it could be ten years before they rescheduled me. In any case, I didn't think the surgeon would be too impressed if I requested a change of date on the basis that my stars weren't favourable around the 16th. So I dutifully checked into the hospital on the morning of the 15th, and immediately ran into delays and problems. I had to wait three hours for the bed to be ready, and they had to give me my pre-op blood tests in the television room. Finally, I got my bed, and then had to wait for the surgeon to come to see me to discuss the details of the next day's operation. Eventually a surgeon turned up, but it wasn't the one I had been expecting would be doing the op. It turned out that my surgeon was late returning back from a skiing holiday in Aspen, so it had been decided that his registrar would do me instead. I found the registrar's explanation of the operation hard to follow—he actually described a completely different procedure from what I had previously been told. As you can imagine, I really felt terribly depressed about it all, but still didn't have the guts to call the whole thing off. Instead I took the attitude that whatever happened was my fate. Dinner came and I ate the crummy meal they served. I passed time by talking to the nurses about how I was feeling—it was okay to tell them about Mercury retrograde and the other aspects I was under. When they heard I was an astrologer, most of them were dying for me to do a mini Sun sign reading, and they kept asking if I could also read their hands or their cards. But they were kind and caring, and gave me foot massages and aromatherapy treatment to make me feel better. Around 7:30 P.M., the registrar reappeared by my bedside in an apologetic mood, "I'm sorry, Mr. Sasportas, but we have searched high and low in every department of the hospital, and it seems we have misplaced your X-rays and medical records, which means we can't do the operation tomorrow. Can you come back next Monday?" I was overjoyed, and out of there in a shot. Mercury would have turned direct by next Monday, and the Moon was much better placed on the new operation date. The whole incident left me feeling that somebody, somewhere, was looking after me. I even said a prayer of thanks to Hermes for hiding my files, which, by the way, were immediately located by the regular houseman who returned to duty two days later. This is all true, just as it happened.

We had better get going on Mercury aspects. Mercury can never be more than 28 degrees away from the Sun. If the Sun and Mercury are conjunct within 17 minutes, it is called a *cazimi*; if these two planets are less than eight degrees apart, they are considered *combust*. It's been said that the Sun burns Mercury when they are too near one another, resulting in obscured objectivity and increased subjectivity. In this sense, it is a bit like Mercury in Leo, where there can be too strong an attachment to and identification with what one thinks or believes in, leaving no room for other people's views and opinions. Impartiality is impaired and one could suffer periodically from thought overload or mental burnout. Some astrologers, however, argue that a close Sun-Mercury contact is fortunate, because it means that these two planets can work as allies in league with one another, enlivening the mind and improving the ability to communicate and express the self. As the distance between the Sun and Mercury increases, so too does one's objectivity. Mercury in the sign before or after the Sun often favours greater mental balance and a broader perspective on life simply because of the fact that two different signs are involved; however, this situation could also give rise to an identity crisis, since how you think and express yourself (Mercury) differs from the essential core of your being (the Sun). I don't have strong opinions either way, except to say that I feel more certain of a person's capacity to be objective if Mercury isn't too close to the Sun. And it's often true that an Aries with Mercury in Aries will be more adventurous, outgoing and outspoken than an Aries with Mercury in Pisces or Taurus. A Taurus with Mercury in Taurus is likely to be a lot more reticent and cautious than a Taurus with Mercury in Aries or Gemini. By the way if the Sun or Ascendant is in Gemini or Virgo (the Mercury-ruled signs), you must pay extra close attention to how Mercury is aspected. A Virgoan with Mercury conjunct Neptune will differ considerably from a Virgo with Mercury conjunct Saturn. So before you assume that all Virgos are efficient and well-organised, you had better check out the natal aspects to Mercury. The same rationale applies to someone with the Sun or Ascendant in Gemini—the aspects to Mercury will influence whether that person is a logical-thinking Gemini or a scatty one.

It's also been said that if Mercury rises before the Sun, you think first and then act; but if the Sun rises ahead of Mercury, you act first and then later seek a justification for your actions. In her book *Secondary Progressions*, Nancy Hastings shares her views on the Sun-Mercury relationship, pointing out that if you're born with Mercury in the sign behind the Sun, it will be moving direct or at least about to turn direct.[13] If this is the case, by the time you reach young adulthood, Mercury will be moving forward pretty quickly. She interprets this to mean that you will be someone who can assimilate new ideas quickly, and you would be willing to experiment with many different ways of seeing life. But if Mercury is at

---

[13]Nancy Hastings, *Secondary Progressions: Time to Remember* (York Beach, ME: Samuel Weiser, 1984), pp. 11–12.

maximum orb ahead of the Sun, it may be retrograde at birth or is likely to go retrograde by progression, which would probably turn your attention and awareness inward toward yourself.

We discussed Moon-Mercury aspects during my lecture on the Moon,[14] but I'll briefly review how they work. The trine, sextile, or a harmonious conjunction indicates a good relationship between the planet associated with emotions and feelings (the Moon) and the planet of communication (Mercury). You therefore should find it fairly easy to communicate what you are feeling. The flowing aspects also suggest a good head-heart rapport, so that there is less tension between what you think intellectually and what you feel on an emotional or instinctive level. Positive Moon-Mercury contacts also increase your sensitivity to and understanding of your environment, no matter where you find yourself. This means you're more likely to see clearly and interpret correctly what is going on around you, and you'll relate to other people in a manner which shows that you are sensitive to their feelings. With the squares and hard angles, you probably will experience conflict between the head and the heart, that is, what your head or intellect tells you to do will not be in line with how you feel about something. So your head may say get out of a relationship, but your emotions want you to stay in there. Thus, hard Moon-Mercury contacts can express themselves in self-doubt and a fair amount of uncertainty about where you stand in various situations. The Moon and Mercury are both memory planets, and when in conflict, deeply ingrained emotional complexes will colour or obscure how you interpret the environment. When you're viewing what's happening around you through the distorting lens of a complex, you may react in too touchy or oversensitive a manner to your environment. To digress slightly, Moon-Mercury contacts are interesting in synastry. You might meet someone you like a lot on first sight, but if there is an adverse Moon-Mercury interaspect, you may experience difficulty communicating verbally with one another. Conversely, if the interaspects between Moon and Mercury are good, there usually is an immediate rapport between you and the other person — you seem instinctively to know and under-

---

[14]See Part One: The Moon, in *The Luminaries*, Volume 3 of *Seminars in Psychological Astrology* (York Beach, ME: Samuel Weiser, 1992), p. 61ff.

stand their feelings, and they're receptive to how you think and what you have to say.

Mercury and Venus can never be more than 76 degrees apart, so the conjunction, the semisextile, the semisquare, the sextile, and the quintile are the most important aspects they make to one another. (Be very dubious about anyone who tells you they are born with Venus square or opposite Mercury.) The possible Mercury-Venus contacts are all fairly benign. I'd like to hear your ideas on how to interpret them.

Audience: People with the conjunction well-aspected, or the semisextile or the quintile, should communicate in a pleasing, harmonious way.

Howard: Yes, Mercury (the planet of communication) is nicely aligned with Venus (the planet of style, taste and beauty). The combination can give a pleasant speaking voice, an entertaining use of language, and an artistic mind or creative imagination. You want to use your Mercury in a way which enhances how you relate and interact with people, so you are not likely to attack or challenge them in a vicious way; you'll give others the benefit of the doubt instead. A natural appreciation of beauty is indicated, as well as an innate interest in and curiosity about anything Venusian – art, relationships, money, etc. Most Venus-Mercury aspects give affability, and often there can be grace of movement. In some cases with the conjunction or semisquare, you can be too nice or too sweet when you relate with others, acting from a superficial, unctious charm with no meat (and maybe no sincerity) to it. I keep forgetting to talk about Mercury in terms of siblings, neighbours and short journeys. With good aspects between Mercury and Venus, you'll probably like and get along fairly well with brothers, sisters and neighbours, although other aspects or placements in the chart could negate this and cause trouble. When considered separately from the rest of the birth chart, a harmonious Venus-Mercury aspect augurs well for pleasurable short journeys. If a transiting planet is bringing out your Mercury-Venus contact, you could hop on a tram on the way to work that morning and meet the love of your life, or at least someone with whom you can have a jolly good flirt. I forget, this is Switzerland – does that type of thing ever happen on the trams in Zürich? In New York, a good Mercury-Venus aspect means you are less likely to be mugged on the subway.

Audience: I know someone with Mercury conjunct Venus and he has a sideline writing love letters for other people.

Howard: What a perfect use of that aspect. It's a little eccentric, but it's authentic—he's being true to his chart.

  Mercury-Mars contacts bring together the god of the mind and communication with the god of war. The unpleasant affects of this combination can be seen most clearly in the conjunction or the hard angles of these two planets (and I include the inconjunct in this category). People with these aspects are prone to speaking impulsively and blurting out words or ideas which, whether they intend it or not, can hurt and wound others. Mercury-Mars fights with the head, and gives quick reactions. The mind is a two-edged sword which can be used to separate us from other people through critical, hostile and judgmental attitudes, but it also can unite us with others through insight and understanding. We can use words to tear down and destroy another person, or we can use words to contact, heal and move closer to somebody. Have you ever had a long period of not speaking? In the 1970s, I belonged to a meditation group which held residential "silence retreats"—a week or so among other meditators but with no verbal communication. Can you imagine me not talking for a week? To be honest, it wasn't easy, but it did make me feel more alive and vibrant inside as if I had conserved quite a lot of energy by not speaking.

  With difficult Mercury-Mars contacts, you can expect battles and power conflicts with relatives, neighbours or co-workers. If a transit is bringing a difficult Mercury-Mars contact to the fore, you are well-advised to take extra care in your interactions with others; it's a day or period of time when fights and arguments flare up suddenly or unexpectedly, when your blood boils and your short fuse is set alight by something someone says or does. With Mercury connected to Mars, you may meet Mars when travelling, so caution is advised on those days this aspect is activated. You could attract accidents when going from A to B, or burn yourself or cut yourself with a knife, particularly if you're already feeling agitated or are sitting on negative feelings. Inner discord always looks for a way out. Now, even with the hard angles, Mars has the effect of enlivening whatever planet it touches, so these aspects often give a stimulating conversationalist or someone with a lively mind who enjoys mental sparring and debate, or throwing down the gauntlet in the form of challenging, provocative ideas and statements. What would you say about the trine or sextile of Mercury to Mars?

Audience: It would add power to the mind, and force and conviction to one's words. People with this could be persuasive talkers.

Howard: Yes, I agree, although a harmonious aspect between these two planets does not in itself guarantee honesty, or that what you're being sold is bona fide. You'd be wise to think twice before buying a used car from a persuasive salesman with a Mercury-Mars trine.

Audience: What would you say about a conjunction of Mercury and Mars in Pisces?

Howard: As with any conjunction, we need to consider its placement in the context of the whole chart, but I would say that people with this aspect are born with a potent imagination, and they ought to find a creative outlet through which to express their ideas, visions or feelings. There is a strong need to communicate, and this could be achieved through dance, music, photography, painting or poetry (although words may be too limiting a medium for Mercury in Pisces).

Harmonious Mercury-Jupiter aspects are, generally speaking, very nice contacts. Because you can see the details and parts (Mercury) along with the bigger picture or larger whole (Jupiter), your mind ultimately is capable of tuning simultaneously into Channel One and Channel Two. A good Mercury-Jupiter aspect is comparable to Zeus and Hermes working together in the best possible manner: your mind is open to higher inspiration of a Jupiterian kind, but you also have Mercury's ability to apply your spiritual wisdom or understanding to everyday life. These contacts also indicate a capacity to enthuse and inspire other people with your words and ideas, although even with the flowing aspects, there could be a tendency to talk too much or periods of mental hyperactivity. Because you meet Jupiter through Mercury, a well-aspected conjunction, trine or sextile between these two planets usually suggests a fortunate or beneficent relationship with relatives; perhaps a brother or sister turns you on to meditation, or is there to help you out financially or in some other practical way. Similar benefits could come through neighbours. With Mercury in good aspect to Jupiter, travel would stimulate the mind, and you'd probably enjoy good luck on journeys, arriving in town just in time for the carnival or something along those lines.

The square or opposition (or a difficultly aspected conjunction) of these two planets can still manifest positively, but there are problems to watch out for. The conjunction or square often gives a restless, overactive mind, and perhaps a tendency to verbal diarrhoea. You might make mountains out of molehills, taking a minor event or incident and blowing it all out of proportion. Sometimes you'll suffer from bad judgment. If a problematic Mercury-Jupiter contact is hit off by a transit or progression, you may not be seeing people or situations clearly or correctly, so you should be cautious about speculative enterprises and take extra care before putting your faith or trust in someone. You probably are good at selling people your "trip," but you'll need to be careful not to put others off by your excessive zeal or over-the-top approach. Mercury opposite Jupiter can give the same difficulties as the square or conjunction, along with a real knack for starting arguments with other people over politics, religion or philosophy.

A well-aspected conjunction, or a sextile or trine between Mercury and Saturn will stabilise and focus the mind, improving powers of concentration and enabling you to think practically and logically. Even with the flowing aspects, you may be insecure about your intellectual ability or mental prowess, and yet you are willing to work hard and in a determined fashion to learn or master a subject or skill. You'll probably be careful about what you say and to whom you say it, which may be a good thing. Saturn in hard angle to Mercury indicates self-doubt about your intellectual ability, or may manifest in difficulties or slowness in learning, writing or speech. But we mustn't forget that Saturn is the celestial schoolteacher, the thorn in our side driving us on to greater achievements. Consider the literary genius Goethe, perhaps Germany's most famous writer, a Virgo born with Saturn rising in Scorpio and a wide square between Mercury (his Sun ruler) and Saturn. It took him over sixty years to complete *Faust* — that really is persistence; and he is also the source of the very Saturnian quote: "It is in self-limitation that a master first shows himself."

Audience: Don't Mercury-Saturn people need some sort of conventional recognition, such as a degree or certificate before they feel okay about their knowledge or status?

Howard: Yes, that is often the case, because Saturn may tie Mercury to conventional ways of thinking. For instance, people with these aspects might not feel comfortable or right about practicing astrology until they had earned a diploma from the Faculty of Astrological Studies or some other comparable qualifying course. How different from Mercury-Uranus people, who would gladly jump into reading charts after learning astrology on their own, not caring if they had a piece of paper to prove their worth. Any Mercury-Saturn contact can give a depressive or contemplative temperament, inclining you to dwell on the negative or dark side of a person or situation, or to worry incessantly about what tomorrow might bring. Still, Mercury-Saturn aspects usually do add weight to and deepen the mind, steadying Mercury's tendency to flit from one thing to another. Does anyone here with Mercury in aspect to Saturn have anything to say about it?

Audience: I have the square and I do suffer from self-doubts about my mind. I learn very slowly, but when I do learn something, I learn it well.

Audience: I have Mercury conjunct Saturn and I come from a family with seven brothers and sisters. Of course, I was the one who had to be responsible for them all.

Howard: Yes, siblings can be a burden or responsibility or give you a hard time if Saturn is aspecting Mercury. In actual fact, I've also seen many instances of these aspects in the charts of only children. This may suggest some loneliness in the growing-up years, or the extra burden often put on an only child to fulfil so many of mother's or father's expectations and unlived potentials. Earlier this afternoon, I spoke about the possibility of someone with a difficultly aspected Mercury in Gemini ending up in a mental straitjacket as a child. Saturn in aspect to Mercury could mean a similar childhood experience. What about these aspects in relation to travel or short journeys?

Audience: They probably would be prone to running into delays, obstructions or difficulties. Or they may travel in order to work or study something.

Howard: I can vouch for that. There is also the possibility of making a career out of whatever planet Saturn touches. So you might even get a travel agent with a Mercury-Saturn contact or someone whose job involves transporting people or goods from one destination to another. Along these same lines, a writer, journalist or teacher might be born with Mercury in aspect to Saturn. I think it's good to use Saturn aspects in this way, to turn the planet Saturn touches into a vocation you seek to master.

Okay, soldiers, forward into Mercury-Uranus. The sky god Ouranus ruled the vast, starry expanse of heaven, and any Mercury-Uranus aspect entices Mercury into the higher mental realms where visions, insights and intuitions abound. It's fair to say that a well-aspected conjunction, sextile or trine usually yields more reliable or more easily digestible and socially acceptable ideas than the hard angles, as if the person has tuned into the pulse of the collective, intuiting and promoting new concepts and trends which society or the world at large are poised to receive. Mercury-Uranus people exhibit mental wizardry, originality and ingenuity — in some cases, even genius. They can be mental gymnasts, capable of making quick connections between one topic or idea and another, which a slower thinker is not able to perceive so readily. Often equipped with a detached clarity of mind, they're able to find answers and solutions to situations which have left other people baffled. In other words, the sharp, high-speed, laser-beam Uranian mind can pierce right through problems, or, if you'll excuse the term, cut through bullshit.

Those born with a difficultly aspected conjunction or the other hard angles between these two planets might say or think things which others find too bizarre, far out, or impossible to fathom. For instance, the Mercury-Uranus people in this group may make a contribution to which I don't immediately respond or connect; but when I have the time to go away and think more about what they have said, I often discover a great deal of sense in their comments or conclusions. I do have to admit, however, that I've done chart readings for people with the square or opposition, and they say things I have a lot of trouble accepting or understanding. One occasion comes to mind, when a man with the opposition reported that he was in daily communication with beings from another solar system who fed him advice and information. It may be true, who knows? And yet, the Capricorn side of me has a little trouble digesting these kinds of notions.

If you are born with a Mercury-Uranus aspect, you'll usually say what you think even if it means upsetting, shocking or hurting others. This is quite different from people with a Mercury-Venus or Mercury-Neptune aspect who tend to share only those things they imagine others would like to hear, or which others won't find too upsetting. For Mercury-Uranus, the "truth" is more important than social niceties. With the hard angles, there often is a strained or distant relationship with a sibling or relative. You may come from a blended family, and have a half sister or stepbrother. The aspect also can manifest in a brother or sister who is a Uranian type. Have you noticed how aspects to Mercury or placements in the 3rd house can be carried by a relative? So if you are born with a Mercury-Uranus conjunction, you may wind up with siblings who have Uranus prominent in their charts; or if you are born with Mercury square Neptune, you may have a sister who is a Pisces with Neptune rising in Libra, or a brother who is a musician or drug addict. Just for the record, both Joan Baez and Jane Fonda, two talented performers also known for their anti-war and civil-rights campaigning, were born with Mercury trine Uranus. Compared with the ill-fated Oscar Wilde who had Mercury and Uranus in opposition, Baez and Fonda have been better able to get away with their "radical" beliefs.

Much of what was said about Mercury in Pisces applies to Mercury-Neptune contacts. In keeping with the boundary-blurring nature of Neptune, I find it hard to make major distinctions between its hard and soft angles to Mercury. Any Mercury-

Neptune aspect enhances the mind's sensitivity and receptivity, so it can make a person highly intuitive, even psychic – someone who often can express the self in an inspirational, poetic fashion. True, the hard angles probably contribute to mental confusion and uncertainty, but I know people with Mercury square or opposite Neptune who use these aspects as well as anyone with the trine or sextile. And there are people with the sextile or trine who are in a mess because of psychic disturbances, or alcohol- and drug-related problems. So when speaking about the meaning of Mercury-Neptune, unless otherwise stated, I'm lumping all the aspects together.

Neptune diffuses Mercury: the thinking of people with these aspects may seem vague or unclear, when in actual fact they find it hard to commit themselves to one version of the truth or to any one idea or theory because of an innate tendency to view situations and people from many different perspectives. Hence, their mental escapism or chameleonlike qualities – they may agree or go along with one set of opinions about an issue or topic, and then turn around and agree with other people who hold entirely different beliefs about the same issue. Pinning down Mercury is difficult when Neptune is aspected to it. There often is an interest in the spiritual or the occult, a mind that is receptive to God or to divine inspiration and insight, and a fairly rich appreciation of art, music or beauty in general, anything that uplifts or takes one out of oneself.

Empathy is strong, to the point of reading other people's minds and closely identifying with or taking on what others are feeling – a bit like that marvelous Woody Allen film *Zelig*, where he played a human chameleon who so wanted to be accepted by people that he literally became them when he was in their vicinity. Mercury-Neptune people are natural mediums, picking up on thoughts and feelings floating around in the atmosphere. Neptune asks that we give away whatever planet it touches, and these people are sometimes more adept at speaking up on behalf of others rather than speaking up just for themselves. A sensitivity to drugs – prescribed or otherwise – is not uncommon, and less amounts of these substances may be needed to have the desired effect. Some people with these aspects have problems with substance abuse, while others stay away from drugs or alcohol as if they instinctively know the dangers in it for them. Even with the square or opposition, you can get a good storyteller, although any Mercury-Neptune aspect can indicate someone who finds it easy to lie, deceive or distort the truth. These people remind me of Hermes when he unashamedly told Apollo he knew absolutely nothing about the whereabouts of his cattle. It is also possible that they simply get their facts wrong or draw incorrect conclusions about something. If you have a Mercury-Neptune aspect, you need to double check your facts, especially if a transit is bringing it out. For instance, if transiting Jupiter is passing over your natal Mercury and also aspecting natal Neptune in the process, you may find yourself swept away or very excited about a person, project or investment only to discover later that you were deluded or misinformed. It would be good to have a trusted friend with Mercury trine or sextile Saturn who could keep an eye on you during these times, and let you know if you were going off the wall or creating a bubble destined to burst.

Audience: I know Mercury-Neptune people who have learning problems, or who are very confused about matters of a practical nature, turning up for appointments on the wrong date, or continually getting addresses wrong.

Howard: Yes, I've seen these aspects correlate with learning difficulties, speech and hearing problems, dyslexia, and related conditions. They probably are right-brain thinkers as opposed to rational left-brain types. Mental instability in the form of paranoia or other delusional states also could be shown by Mercury-Neptune contacts. And yet, in many cases, Mercury-Neptune denotes an imaginative mind which needs a creative outlet to free itself. If you are born with Mercury in aspect to Neptune, you might have "healing hands" or emanate a vibration or presence which other people find soothing and healing. Sacrifices may have to be made when it comes to relatives or siblings, such as giving up your time to look after a younger brother or sister, or there may be a sibling who is ill or disabled in some way. And I've also seen these aspects in the charts of only children, who miss the companionship of the brother or sister they never had. Some of them may assuage this loneliness by inventing imaginary friends and playmates.

I can give you a few examples of well-known people with Mercury-Neptune aspects. Van Gogh, the intense, confused, tortured and brilliant artist, was born with Mercury in Pisces square Neptune (and Pluto) in Gemini. Although there is some uncertainty about her exact birthdate, Maria Callas, the gifted and dramatic opera singer, had a close trine between Mercury in Sagittarius and Neptune in Leo. I've already mentioned Margot Fonteyn's Mercury in Taurus square Neptune in Leo—an example of a hard angle manifesting nonetheless in exceptional presence, grace and beauty of movement. And then there is Jim Jones, the deranged manic-depressive with paranoic delusions who was the "brains" behind the 1977 Jonestown mass suicide in Guyana: he was born with an exact trine between Mercury in Taurus and Neptune in Virgo. So you see what I mean when I say that even the trines can be slightly "wonky."

Much of what we said about Mercury in Scorpio also applies to Mercury-Pluto contacts. Again, the soft angles and the conjunction can be as tricky as the hard ones, although with the trines and sextiles, it is a little easier to cooperate with, learn from and work through the traumas and difficulties associated with a typical Pluto aspect. So, as with Mercury-Neptune, I'll lump all the aspects together in this discussion. In most instances, Mercury-Pluto contacts indicate a deeply incisive and penetrating mind able to probe into the essence or heart of a matter. When Mercury aspects a planet, it will go where that planet takes it. In this case, Pluto beckons Mercury into the underworld, to look beneath the surface level of life, and to explore what is hidden in the unconscious realm. Mercury-Pluto is a mind well suited to investigative or research work, and often denotes someone who is secretive, underhanded or deceptive, saying one thing or appearing one way but actually thinking or feeling another. I believe that Mercury-Pluto people need some kind of creative outlet to express and give form to their deepest thoughts and feelings; I'm not necessarily implying they should be professional artists, but it would be therapeutic for them to find ways to communicate and release pent-up emotions. If too much frustration or negativity is allowed to fester for too long, it eventually will manifest as health problems or in the form of mental breakdown or malfunction. Mercury-Pluto contacts, especially a difficultly aspected conjunction or the hard angles, sometimes correlate with deep-seated phobias, compulsions and obsessions, and it will be necessary to ferret out the root of these disorders in order for healing to take place. Hard Mercury-Pluto aspects often give a mind which reacts to situations with great intensity, a mind that is subject to mental trauma and torture, reminiscent of Shakespeare's tragic heroes, Hamlet, Macbeth or King Lear. Something which might not faze other people too much could pose a major source of grief or discomfort for a Mercury-Pluto person.

Having a Mercury-Pluto aspect means you are powerful on the mental plane. On the plus side, you can speak or think with great conviction, what you write or say could have a transformative effect on others, and there also could be a deep love or fascination for words and language. As with Mercury in Scorpio, people born with Mercury-Pluto aspects, especially the hard angles, are often very careful about what they say and to whom they say it. They don't like to give too much away, just in case others turn on them or use that knowledge against them. Also, they do not mince words—if they want to verbally attack you, they will know just what to say to hurt you most. However, as we discussed earlier in the day, a powerful mind carries with it certain responsibilities. If you are holding someone in a negative light, that person will not feel comfortable around you, and is bound to catch your projection and act in ways which make you even more annoyed or angry.

When I first came to London in 1973, I worked at a little health food restaurant owned and run by a woman with a Mercury-Pluto square. Fortunately, she took a liking to me and I could hardly do wrong in her eyes. There were times I made mistakes or dropped plates, but she never was around when it happened. By contrast, she intensely disliked one of my co-workers. Everytime he dropped a plate, you can be sure she was in eyesight. A Mercury-Pluto mind can work magic, but there is the white kind and the black kind. Rather than cursing and freezing people with your negative attitudes, think of the good you could do if you chose to hold others in a positive light. Think of how healing and transformative you could be for them. I'm not saying that Mercury-Pluto types will find it easy to change their attitudes—it usually doesn't happen overnight. Time and honest introspection will be needed to understand why someone has hooked into your shadow and provoked a dark response in you, but it certainly is worth trying to alter your negative attitudes or perspective rather than continually creating a prison for yourself and others. What about these aspects in terms of relationships with siblings or neighbours?

Audience: I imagine there could be a lot of power games going on, jealousies and rivalries, or even sexual undercurrents.

Howard: Yes, I've found this to be the case. Also, it's possible that the death of a sibling or relative will have a profound affect on you. If your mother lost a baby before you were born, the way she relates to you and brings you up could harken back to that loss. Or a sister or brother dies when you are alive, leaving you with a sense of unconscious guilt, as if something you did caused the mishap. These feelings need to be worked through; otherwise they will haunt or torment you throughout your life.

I just have a few odds and ends to throw in here. Did you know that Machiavelli was born with Mercury in Gemini in the 5th house square Pluto in Virgo in the 8th? He was somebody who turned treachery and intrigue into a fine art. Also, André Gide, the French writer who dared to explore subjects that others of his time considered taboo, had Mercury opposite Pluto across the 2nd and 8th houses. Louis Pasteur, the French scientific researcher and investigator who worked relentlessly and against much opposition to prove the germ theory of disease, was born with a Mercury-Pluto square. The American writer Sylvia Plath also comes to mind. She contemplated death for most of her life, and finally succeeded in committing suicide one month after the publication of *The Bell Jar*, a widely read autobiographical account of a major breakdown she endured. Plath was born with Mercury in Scorpio in close trine to Pluto in Cancer, an indication that even the trine between these two planets can give an obsession with darkness and death.

Not a nice note to end on, but it's been a long day stuffed full with information and input. Get thee behind me, Mercury!

PART TWO

Venus

Love without anxiety and without fear
Is fire without flames and without warmth,
Day without sunlight, hive without honey,
Summer without flower, winter without frost.

—Chrétien de Troyes, *Cliges*

If I am not for myself, who will be?
And if I am only for myself,
What am I?

—Rabbi Hillel

THE GREAT HARLOT

THE MYTHOLOGY AND PSYCHOLOGY OF VENUS

My problem tonight is to find a way to prevent this session from sliding into soft-core porn. Perhaps I should have brought illustrative slides? In some ways a really stylish blue film might be the most direct way of communicating what is essential about the mythology of the planet Venus. But I wouldn't want to invoke the Swiss equivalent of *Miami Vice*.

We need to look first at the word "harlot," which I so carefully chose for the title of the session. There are a number of words in English which describe various faces of this central feminine archetype, but I fear these subtle differences do not translate well into German.

Audience: There is only one word for it in German.

Liz: A pity. In English we can refer to a whore, or a harlot, or a prostitute, or a hooker, or a courtesan. There are other words describing yet more aspects—hoyden, slut, and so on. There are subtle differences between these. A whore is simply for sale. A harlot may be, but the term suggests sexual license and abandon. A prostitute is more a job description, while hooker is the slang expression for the same profession. A courtesan, on the other hand, implies culture, style and skill in the erotic arts, rather like a Japanese geisha. She is for sale, but at an extremely high price, and only to those with the taste and the money.

So the harlot can be wild and abandoned, and she may not sell herself at all; or, if she does, it is not with the cold calculation of the prostitute. The etymology of the word is interesting to consider. It was once used for both sexes, to describe a rogue, and is connected with the Old French *harlot* or *herlot*, meaning a vagabond, and the

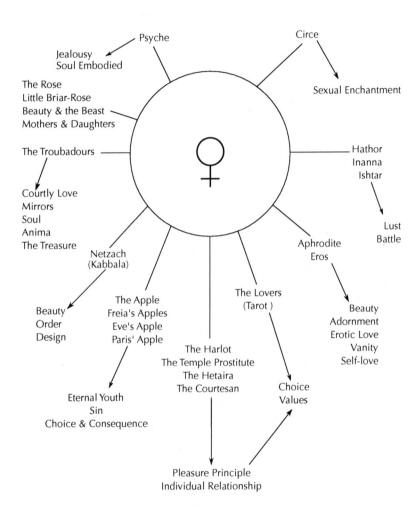

Figure 1. The mythological expressions of Venus.

Anglo-Saxon *loddere*, which means a wastrel. You can see from these linguistic origins that the feeling-tone of the word harlot is one of abandonment, rather than the trading of one's body for money. This is why I chose the word to invoke an image of Venus, for her mythic figure is very far from that of the whore.

The temple harlot was once a sacred figure in Sumeria, Babylon, Egypt and India. These women were never prostitutes in the sense we now understand the word. Some, like those who served Aphrodite's shrine at Paphos on Cyprus, were trained to be mortal "vessels" for the divine joy and ecstasy of the goddess, and they initiated men into the mysteries of Aphrodite's domain. There is a wonderful novel by Mika Waltari called *The Etruscan*, long out of print but well worth digging up in a library, in which one of the central characters is just such a woman. The beauty and erotic skills of these women were famous all over the ancient world, and it was considered a great job if you had the looks and talent to get it. Other temple harlots, like those in Babylon, were ordinary women who were expected to offer themselves once in their lives, as virgins, to the first stranger who came along to the temple precincts and made a donation to the shrine. A woman could not marry until she had performed this service to the goddess, and if no man offered for her she was humiliated and disgraced. The role of the sacred harlot was therefore to serve as a vessel for the power of the goddess. This is the archetypal equivalent of the king, who serves as a vessel for the power of the solar deity on earth. The goddess, as you will see in our diagram (see figure 1), was called Bast or Hathor in Egypt, Inanna in Sumeria, Ishtar in Babylon, and Aphrodite in Greece before she became the Roman Venus.

The temple harlot is therefore a woman who embodies and channels the essence of *eros*, which is the gift of the deity to mankind. She is sacred because of the goddess she serves and the honoured task she performs, and she symbolises the strange paradox we find in Venus, that mysterious blend of sacred and profane sexuality which defies ordinary moral interpretations. We can also look at the Babylonian ritual of the virgin being herself initiated by offering her body to initiate a stranger, and we can surmise that this symbolises the archetypal and transpersonal nature of the sexual act. There are no marriage bonds, no ties of romantic love, and no claims made afterward. This tells us something else about

Venus—she is not concerned with commitments that bind through time (Saturn), nor does she reflect the sentiment and idealisation of "romantic" love as we experience it through Neptune. All this may seem strange in view of Venus' rulership over Taurus, but the famous Taurean loyalty in relationship is based not on abstract moral promises or social codes (that is the domain of Hera), but rather on the need to render permanent any situation which provides pleasure, satisfaction and a sense of self-value.

The sacred harlot was also seen as the initiator of men, and as the inspiration for a man's virility. This is very different from the power of the lunar mother goddess, whose claim on a man depends upon her having given him life and nourished him in infancy; rather, it is the role of the goddess as the *anima* or soul image, who frees a man from the grip of the mother through the discovery of his own potency and capacity for love and joy without emotional bondage. By becoming an embodiment of the divine object of desire and source of pleasure, the temple harlot served as a kind of generator of the creative life force in men, and far from being demeaned by her role, she acquired power and importance through the value placed upon it. At the moment when a woman identifies with Venus, she becomes an individual expression of Inanna or Ishtar or Aphrodite, and finds her feminine self-value accordingly.

No doubt this is all rather uncomfortable stuff if you happen to be a stern moralist, or even an extreme feminist. But if you see this mythic (as well as historical) figure of the Venusian sacred harlot as a denigration of the feminine, you have sadly missed the point. Some of the power and sanctity of the temple harlot arises from her refusal to be bound by the laws and strictures of conventional family life; she can give herself with abandon and thereby find herself and her own capacity for pleasure without worrying about who is going to pay for the roof over her head. She is not cowed or curtailed by any husband, nor bound by any son's dependent needs. It is *her* pleasure and joy which constellate pleasure and joy in her partners, and she does not fear the giving of herself because she *is* herself.

I think you can begin to get a sense of the essence of Venus from the figure of the temple harlot. We have lost contact with this feminine archetype in modern society, for erotic love is no longer understood as sacred, and the harlot has merely become a whore. The closest modern analogy is the self-sufficient "mistress" (the equivalent of the Greek *hetaira*), who prefers to live independently yet finds her fulfillment as the friend and erotic companion of a man (or men). The so-called sexual liberation which burst upon us in the 1960s, and which is currently undergoing such a heavy moral working over because of AIDS (I hope you will reflect upon the root of the term "venereal disease"), is still horribly fraught with our Judeo-Christian ethos of sin and punishment, and usually constitutes a rebellion against Victorian morality rather than a reinstatement of Venusian values. Of all the ancient pantheon who personify the inner planets, Aphrodite-Venus is perhaps the least integrated into our present society.

We need to look more closely now at the character of Aphrodite herself. Although she is married to Hephaistos in Greek myth, it is a sort of joke marriage. She is perennially unfaithful to him, and really belongs to no one except herself. The earlier love goddesses, Inanna and Ishtar, are unmarried; they are sometimes portrayed as virgin-harlots, the word *virgo* in Latin simply meaning "unwed" or "self-possessed." I feel it is important to look at the distinctions between Venus and the Moon in this context, for these two planets are really psychological opposites, two complementary faces of the feminine. The Moon needs to belong to someone, preferably a family or group. The lunar urge to be part of a unity can include one's children, one's country, one's home town, or one's racial background, but it is essentially dominated by the longing to belong and have roots. But Venus is her own self, unconcerned with both past and future; and although in myth she mothers the occasional child such as Aeneas, she is not what we would call maternal. The iconography of Aphrodite-Venus never portrays her with a baby in her arms. She gives herself to any god or hero whom *she* desires, not any god or hero who needs and wants her. In other words, she does not barter herself for another's love. Aphrodite in myth is periodically seized with erotic longing, and plunges into a frenzy of desire for a particular lover, whom she then enchants and seduces. She certainly suffers no insecurities, but expresses an absolute power of attraction not because of what she has to offer (nurturing, care, dependability) but because of who she is. She *does* nothing in order to *be* loved, because she is the essence of the beloved.

This is another distinction between Venus and the Moon. The Moon is naturally empathetic, and responds readily to another person's feelings; the mythic Venus, on the other hand, is not known for her compassion. In fact she can be incredibly callous and unleash destruction on mortals through visiting them with unsuitable and ungovernable passions. But the Moon may also use that natural gift of empathy in order to create a sense of obligation in others. This is the let-me-iron-your-shirts-make-you-tea-and-comfort-you-and-then-you-will-owe-me syndrome, which may combine genuine caring and sensitivity with a kind of barter for emotional security. So Venus really symbolises a quality of absolute self-love and self-value, which can give joyfully to others but which does not depend upon others for a sense of worth. Aphrodite does not go out to "catch" a man at the local wine bar. She is what she is, and the man comes, in every sense of the word. Well, sorry, but I did warn you.

Now what can all this mean if we define Venus as the urge for love and relationship, as is usually done in textbooks? To begin with, I have never been happy with that definition. I think Howard is right to associate the Moon with relationship and with "first love."[1] But for Venus, relationships—interchange with others— serve as a vehicle for the gradual formation of individual values, which in turn supports the development of the central core of the personality as reflected by the Sun. When I talk a little later on about the myth of Paris, you will see that our "choices" in love are really our unconscious statements about what we value most, which we first perceive outside us and desire accordingly. Plato defined love as passion aroused by beauty, and it is in what we find most beautiful that we most clearly define our values. Where the Moon seeks relationship for emotional security and well-being, Venus seeks it as a kind of mirror, so that one may discover in the eyes of the lover the reflection of oneself.

One of Aphrodite's dominant characteristics is her extreme vanity. Now we are brought up to believe that vanity is a terrible

---

[1]See "First Love," in Part One: The Moon, in *The Luminaries*, Volume 3 of *Seminars in Psychological Astrology* (York Beach, ME: Samuel Weiser, 1992).

thing; one is not supposed to look in mirrors too often, or to spend an excessive amount of money on self-beautification. This is all "narcissistic" and "selfish" and "self-indulgent," when one should really be thinking of the welfare of others. In the fairy tale *Snow White*, it is the wicked Queen who is forever peering into the mirror, muttering, "Who is the fairest of them all?" Aphrodite's vanity makes her highly competitive and jealous of other goddesses, and even of mortal women who might challenge her beauty. This latter scenario occurs in the myth of Eros and Psyche. Psyche is a mortal whose beauty is so great that people begin to compare her with Aphrodite, and the goddess, true to character, decides to arrange a very bad end for the poor girl. This is the "catty" side of the feminine which many men, and indeed women, find so disturbing and threatening, because it seems so utterly self-centred, amoral and unethical.

But Aphrodite could never be ethical in the Saturnian, social sense, nor even in the Jupiterian, religious sense. Her ethics are those of beauty, which possesses its own innate logic. How do we decide whether a person, or a building, or a piece of music, is beautiful? It is a great mystery, but there seem to be absolute aesthetic laws which define beauty and harmony, and not merely for a given historical period according to a particular fashion. The Parthenon, for example, has always been and always will be beautiful, regardless of each epoch's trends in architecture. Some of you may know William Blake's poem:

Tyger! Tyger! burning bright
In the forests of the night,
What immortal hand or eye
Could frame thy fearful symmetry?

The tiger in Blake's imagery is beautiful, though it is deadly and "amoral." Near the end of the poem, Blake finally asks:

Did he who made the Lamb make thee?

Thus the vanity of Aphrodite is an inevitable aspect of her nature, as much as her magic girdle which renders her irresistibly attractive. She ornaments herself with gold, and is herself "golden"—an attribute which tells us about her important relationship to the Sun and solar qualities. Her husband Hephaistos, the lame and ugly smith-god, is forever making beautiful golden objects with which to adorn her. Her skin is golden, her hair is golden – in fact she shines like the Sun. She also seduces men in daylight; when she is struck with desire for the Trojan Anchises, the father of Aeneas, she makes love with him in the middle of the morning, in full view on a hillside. There is no groping about beneath the shroud of lunar darkness. This unashamed solar brightness is the creative face of Aphrodite's vanity and "narcissism."

The mythic theme of Aphrodite's goldenness leads me to her most ubiquitous symbol, the golden apple. This apple appears in many different cultures in connection with the goddess of erotic love. In Teutonic myth, it is the love goddess Freia who possesses the golden apples which give the other gods eternal youth. Wagner used this theme to great effect in the *Ring* cycle, and the barter of Freia to the giants in exchange for the building of Valhalla (the sacrifice of love for the acquisition of power) is the starting point for those inevitably accruing disasters which end in the *Götterdämmerung*, the Twilight of the Gods. The apple also appears in the Biblical myth of Adam and Eve, where it becomes the emblem of carnal knowledge; by eating the apple, Adam and Eve become conscious of their sexuality, and are expelled from Eden. In other words, the awakening of erotic feeling is a profound psychological as well as physical separation from fusion with the parent, for through it one becomes not only mortal, but free.

The golden apple also appears in the story of Paris. Paris is a young and handsome Trojan prince who has had his share of success with women, and this wealth of erotic experience earns him the unfortunate honour of being asked by Zeus to judge a beauty contest between three goddesses – Hera, Athene and Aphrodite. The prize for this contest is a golden apple. Because Paris is intelligent as well as comely, he knows that whomever he chooses, the other two will inevitably extract some kind of revenge; so he tries in characteristic adolescent fashion to evade the problem of choice, first by refusing to participate, and then by suggesting a three-way division of the apple. These typical human evasions are of course rejected. The three goddesses then parade themselves before him, the first two promising him a reward according to their attributes and sphere of dominion. Hera, queen of the gods, offers him the boon of wealth, position and worldly power; Athene, the virgin battle goddess, offers him the gifts of strategy and prowess in the arts of war. Aphrodite promises him nothing, but merely loosens her girdle. The result of the contest is thus a foregone conclusion.

As a reward for his bestowing of the golden apple upon her, Aphrodite then offers Paris the most beautiful woman in the world—Helen of Sparta, who is, inconveniently, married to someone else. This is of course no deterrent to the goddess. Helen and Paris elope together; and thus begins the cataclysm of the Trojan War. Those of you familiar with the Tarot will know that the story of the "Judgement of Paris" is portrayed in the imagery of the Major Arcana card of the Lovers. This tale is not really about love; it is about choice, and the declaration of individual values. It is a Venusian myth, not only because Aphrodite wins the beauty contest, but because Paris, in common with all mortals, is faced with the necessity of choice and its consequences. Because he is a young and amorous man, it is erotic love upon which he places the highest value. Had he been older, a seasoned warrior or ruler who had suffered a few marital disillusionments, he might have withstood the power of the love goddess, and chosen Hera or Athena instead. Thus, in relation to Venus, we must ask ourselves: What do I value most? None of us can love everybody, or value everything, despite what some Aquarians might think; and we all seek partners and friends with whom we are "compatible." This really means people with whom we can share at least some of our most cherished values.

It is the planet Venus which symbolises our capacity to form and identify what we value—the basis for authenticity in our personal choices. The story of Paris also highlights another important psychological issue, which is that ultimately we cannot evade the issue of choice and the expression of individual values. It is the gods who decide that Paris must fulfil his part in the tale; and perhaps it is the gods within us who, at some critical juncture in life, present us with a dilemma where we must choose one thing or person over another, and stand by the consequences of that choice. This to me is the shared meaning between Taurus and Libra, the two Venus-ruled signs, for Libra is deeply concerned with the process of learning how to choose, and Taurus with developing the inner strength and resources that can give one's values permanence regardless of consequences.

Many of us try to make choices based upon intellectual formulae, or upon what other people think we should do. Or we do not choose at all, but are driven into a course of action by our unconscious hungers and fears. This is compulsion rather than choice. I have encountered many people who really have no idea at all of what they truly desire and value, although they may not realise the implications of their own impoverishment. It is possible to be so disconnected from Venus' function that one is not aware of wanting anything at all. There is a kind of emptiness instead, an apathy which results in mere survival rather than any sense of deep pleasure in life. If a person exists in this state, of course he or she does not possess any individual values. There may be a veneer of so-called values, which are at bottom mere copies of what is acceptable to one's family or social circle; or there may even be an idealogy or philosophy which justifies the lack of individual desire. But in such cases there is always a huge chunk missing from the essential identity, and consequently no inner feeling of being a solid person.

Thus Aphrodite's "frenzy of desire"—the pursuit of the beloved person or object—feeds back on itself, so that what ultimately grows from it is a deepening and strengthening of one's own sense of values. There is no longing to merge and lose the boundaries of one's identity, which we find with Neptune, nor any need to embed oneself in a collective unit for emotional security, which we find with the Moon. We discover ourselves through reflecting upon what we love and find beautiful, because the object of desire is a hook for the projection of what is of greatest beauty and highest value within oneself. I think you can see why Venus is not really concerned with relationships per se, but rather with self-definition *through* relationships. There is a very beautiful passage in Plato's *Phaedro*, where he speaks of seeing mirrored in the face of one's beloved a glimpse of the god to whom one's soul belongs. This is the most profound meaning of Venus—the beloved, be it person, object or intellectual ideal, as the mirror of one's own soul.

Now if we are going to show loyalty to this dimension of the psyche which astrology calls Venus, obviously we are sooner or later going to fall foul of collective values and morals, because while one's own values may comfortably accord with those of the collective most of the time, there will usually come a day when they do not. This usually happens when a strong transit or progressed planet hits the natal Venus, announcing that the time has come to become more conscious of what we value most. The collision tends to occur most often in the arena of marriage and family, because this is the immediate collective for most of us.

Perhaps because of this basic human dynamic, Aphrodite in myth is always provoking adulterous mischief amongst mortals. Somebody is usually being cheated on, or is being struck with a highly unsuitable passion. One of the more horrific examples of both is the story of poor King Minos of Crete, whose wife Pasiphae, struck by Aphrodite's "frenzy of desire," falls desperately in love with a bull, and ends up giving birth to the Minotaur. You may well laugh, but on a more human level, desire for an excessively "unsuitable" object (whether this unsuitability is due to class, race, age, financial circumstances or any other collision with the family and social edifice) usually reflects the person's lack of recognition of some value absolutely essential to his or her development, which is in turn projected outside with portentous results.

Aphrodite's constant companion in her mischievous forays amongst mortals is her son Eros, who shoots his arrows from behind into her chosen victims. The image of the arrow is a very apt one, for we are truly "struck" with deep desire, and this is most clearly demonstrated by the kinds of feelings often experienced during important transits and progressions involving Venus. This state of desire is very different from what sociologists call "mature love," which we are in theory supposed to settle for when we are properly grown-up. Aphrodite's victims generally break their vows to somebody, not out of cold calculation or even ordinary garden-variety "bit-on-the-side" greed, but because they cannot help it — this is the "grand passion" of poetry and drama, and one feels alive as never before. Yet this grand passion is, strangely, not an end in itself, for it is a vehicle, as those who wake up afterward know all too well — an instrument by which the individual discovers a deeper and more authentic set of values, whether the relationship becomes permanent or passes away with the transit or progression.

As you can see, Aphrodite is deeply threatening to the collective, as she is in myth to the goddess Hera, her archetypal enemy. Aphrodite is an amoral goddess by conventional standards, and people suffer through her passions—families are torn asunder, wives and husbands are abandoned, children are exposed to scandal, and so on. Wherever you find Aphrodite active and amusing herself, you will usually find somebody in a dreadful emotional mess. Yet if we view her with less dogmatic eyes, we can see that she is the great affirmer of the individual, by challenging the collective interpretation of "right" relationship with the emotive issue of individual values. Whenever I have given a seminar on this dimension of the planet Venus, someone in the group inevitably gets angry, because of the hurt caused by "unsuitable" passions and love triangles. And indeed people always do suffer in these situations. Yet it is really a question of which brand of suffering we take on, for the denial of Venus results in equal if not worse misery. Triangles are a characteristic Venusian theme, and no one emerges unscathed, yet nothing constellates our growth quite so powerfully.

When we are disconnected from Venus, there are certain characteristic repercussions. One is a loss of self-worth on a very basic level, and no amount of compensation with either others' approval or a self-negating ideology can really help. If Venus in the natal chart is blocked by difficult aspects, or has vanished into the 12th house, or there are parental patterns which suggest that this dimension of life will be suppressed, then there is often a loss of the sense of spontaneous joy and pleasure and simple self-confidence which the goddess personifies.

Many people work terribly hard to compensate for this loss of self-value by overdeveloping the intellect, or rabidly pursuing worldly success at the cost of everything else, or flying up into the spirit and negating the body, or becoming someone who is most likely to be liked by absolutely everybody because they are so appallingly "nice." But the self-worth of Venus, which is more personal and body-centred than the self-expression of the Sun, cannot be replaced by any other planet's gifts. The Sun can offer a sense of meaning to life. But what use is meaning if we cannot feel happy and contented? This is the bedrock of Taurus and the 2nd house, and it begins with the love of one's own body as a source of pleasure, beauty and satisfaction. It is not only sexual pleasure, but the simple satisfactions of material life which belong to this domain—the food we eat, and the bed we sleep in, and the shampoo we use, and whether we bother to decorate the flat we live in to our own taste. I am of course really talking about whether we feel worthwhile enough to give ourselves pleasure and enjoyment on the most ordinary of levels. This can be a very painful issue if Venus is in trouble in the birth chart, for then there is often a sense of being ugly, valueless, unlovable and undeserving of happiness. And this very negative personal image of oneself usually has its roots in one or both parents, who may have had precisely the same problem with Venus. I have found that difficult Venus aspects, such as Venus-Saturn or Venus-Chiron or Venus-Uranus, recur constantly in family charts. And where we cannot value ourselves, we cannot give value to others, not even our own children.

The Venusian themes of vanity and jealousy often arise in childhood when there are problematic aspects to Venus. To some extent, jealousy between child and parent of the same sex is inevitable and natural, and part of the process of separation and the formation of individual identity. If we are to find the freedom to value and love, we must learn to cope with rivalry, for otherwise we will be perpetually backed into the position of taking what we can get, rather than seeking what we want. But sometimes this characteristic Venusian dilemma goes over the top, as it were, and the pattern repeats itself in one's adult relationships.

Powerful mother-daughter rivalry is often a feature when Venus and the Moon are in conflict in the birth chart, especially if one or the other is in Aries or Libra (the two signs which are most prone to rivalrous triangles). Often a woman, once she has borne a child, loses contact with Aphrodite and all that the mythic image symbolises within her. This may be in part because of the pattern set by her own mother, although there is also a certain amount of collective pressure on mothers to be "motherly," lest they be seen as "selfish" and "vain." I remember reading an article once in a women's magazine, where someone was loudly complaining about the fact that her mother wore the same size clothes as her, and looked like her older sister, and where were the comfortable overweight greying mothers of the past who would bake you cookies and not flirt with your boyfriends?

However, if a mother identifies completely with the maternal dimension of the feminine, and her child is a girl, Aphrodite lurks in the unconscious, and when that girl-child reaches puberty (if not before), all hell breaks loose. The mother's natural feelings of jealousy are rigourously suppressed, and may surface covertly in a subtle undermining of the daughter's feminine confidence, or a concerted attempt to prevent any loving relationship developing between the daughter and the father. Such a daughter, denied access to her father and forced into a competition she cannot hope to win, may grow up into the same kind of mother herself, and do the same thing to *her* daughter in turn. Thus we must not be surprised when we see aspects such as Venus square the Moon repeating amongst the women in the family.

Family complexes travel through generations.[2] The family complex may appear reflected by a particular configuration involving Venus, especially if it is a mother-daughter issue. Because the Moon and Venus form a polarity, it is important to be able to express both, and not to lose touch with either, even if, at a particular juncture in life, one is more appropriate to live than the other. We accept the Venusian side in a young unmarried woman, but there is, as I have said, a strong collective Hera-like pressure against it in a married woman who is a mother, and also in an older woman. Although the rigidity of these expectations has begun to break down somewhat in Europe and America, it is still difficult for many people to accept a liaison between an older woman and a younger man, although no one thinks twice about one between an older man and a younger woman. But why should an older woman not enjoy the Aphrodite side of her nature? Aphrodite is ageless, a quality of soul, and she is not limited to youthful figures and lineless complexions. Our deep-rooted prejudice against this is archetypal—we want our mothers to stay mothers, and not compete with us. And we fear rivalry with our daughters just as we feared it with our mothers. Yet nothing ages and depresses a woman faster than abandoning her relationship with this archetype. Remember that in Teutonic myth, it is Freia who possesses the golden apples of eternal youth.

---

[2]For this discussion, see Part Three: The Coniunctio, in *The Luminaries*, Volume 3 of *Seminars in Psychological Astrology* (York Beach, ME: Samuel Weiser, 1992).

You can see the nature of the dilemma which confronts everyone around the Venus-Moon polarity. How does a woman find a way to balance her maternal and erotic needs? The Moon, so wise about the inevitable cycles of time, can make the sacrifice and bow gracefully to ageing, and step aside to become the older generation while one's daughter takes her place as the younger one. But Aphrodite sacrifices nothing; it is not her nature. She will have her cake and eat it too. The same dilemma confronts a man with a Moon-Venus conflict. His need for being mothered may collide with his need for the *anima*, the soul companion, and this is classic fodder for the eternal triangle of wife and mistress. Also, the Moon and Venus represent two sides of his own feminine nature, the "family man" and the lover. The tension between the Moon and Venus is not limited to women alone.

Rivalry between father and son can also be Venus-based. When we looked at the group of horoscopes in Howard's case history,[3] the competition between Bill and Paul was rooted in solar issues — reflected by the cross-aspects of the Sun and Saturn, and by the preponderance of Leo in the family and composite charts. This is really a rivalry based on self-expression, potency and phallic power. But sometimes one can find a father who is deeply jealous of a son who is growing up healthy and fit and good-looking and attractive to women, while the father may be struggling with his paunch and his thinning hair. Men, as you have no doubt worked out by now, can also be vain. So the dynamic of Snow White and the Wicked Queen may not be a strictly feminine affair, but may be operating at an unconscious level between father and son.

Parent-child rivalry is therefore a rite of passage, and it awaits all of us to a greater or lesser degree as we develop the Venusian side of our natures. We will meet it throughout life, because where there is desire and attraction there will also be rivalry; and our capacity to handle this life dilemma with wit and integrity and confidence depends initially upon what we have learned in our childhoods, until we can bring our own self-understanding to bear on the situation. The Oedipal triangle in childhood requires us to lose as well as win, and out of encountering both experiences we

---

[3]This is discussed in Part Three: The Coniunctio, in *The Luminaries*, Volume 3 of *Seminars in Psychological Astrology*.

develop a much stronger sense of personal identity. If a child is not permitted to express rivalry, then difficulties in expressing Venus will inevitably surface later in life. Little girls are invariably drawn to dressing up in their mother's clothes, not only to crystallise a female role model, but also to surpass Mummy in feminine charms. A little girl will also try to elbow her way between her parents at the dinner table, and will try to distract her father's attention in an innocently erotic fashion, and will come knocking at her parents' bedroom door late at night because she has a "stomach ache." The parents need to be able to demonstrate a strong and healthy bond between them, while allowing the child to "win" enough to develop some self-confidence. Yet so often the mother cannot cope with her daughter's first attempts at erotic conquest, because the parental marriage is bad at core, or because the mother is lacking in confidence herself.

Perhaps we can look more closely at some of the other Venusian symbols, to extend our understanding of the planet. I have spoken about the apple, and related to this is the pomegranate, which was from Sumerian and Babylonian times onward considered a symbol of sexual ripeness and fecundity because of its myriad seeds and its red juice. The goddess is also associated with flowers, and in particular the rose—partly because the flower itself is highly suggestive, with its velvety petals closed in upon a secret core. Throughout ancient and medieval times the rose was the primary floral symbol of womanhood, and in medieval poems such as *The Romance of the Rose*, double entendres abound throughout. Lilies are also associated with the love goddess, and there is once again a suggestiveness about the shape of the flower with its long funnel and sweet scent. The scent of the rose and the lily are part of Aphrodite's essence, and her ripeness is reflected by the apple and the pomegranate.

Whenever we look at mythic images such as these, we need to remember that they are a poetic expression of human feelings and sensuous experiences. The third flower which is associated with the love goddess underlines this most clearly, for it is the poppy, whose juice puts us into a profound erotic stupour. The emotional and physical states reflected by the heady scents and textures of the rose, the lily and the poppy are part of Venus' domain, and are

a powerful dimension of sexual pleasure. If we cannot let go sufficiently to experience such states, what has happened to Venus?

Among the birds and animals, Aphrodite and her Middle Eastern predecessors are always given the dove. It is most interesting
to see that the latest goddess to inherit this bird is Mary in Christian myth, for the dove in Christianity is the symbol of the Holy
Ghost which fertilises her. I will leave you to work out that one on
your own, as I do not wish to engage in a theological discussion.
But the dove, as an expression of a particular quality of the love
goddess, is an extremely peaceable and benign bird. It is not a
predator, and when confronted with enemies will always choose
flight rather than battle. The subtle, delicious noises which doves
make are also highly suggestive, for there is no more sensuous bird
call than that of the dove. Think about the noises which chickens or
geese make, for example, or even whistling birds, which can be
musical but are not sensuous. Doves are also highly pleasurable to
touch, for they are soft and pliable, and a tamed one will nestle into
your hands. You can see that all these images—the fruit, the
scented flowers and the dove—are descriptive of the highly sensuous nature of the goddess, and of the erotic dimension of human
nature.

Aphrodite, despite her charms, is no bimbo. She is the most
cunning of deities, and can be utterly treacherous. There is a striking combination of beauty and high intelligence in this deity, and
she is not averse to strategy (the Libran aspect of her). This is a
unique combination in the divine pantheon. She is also a culture
bringer. The quality of intelligence, strategy and aesthetic feeling
differentiates her from the more instinctual attributes of the Moon
goddesses, for Aphrodite teaches the *art* of love, rather than por-
traying desire as the prelude for pregnancy and child-bearing. The
moment we refer to art, we are combining instinctual expression
with a quality of imagination and fantasy and the discipline of
craftsmanship. Aphrodite's eroticism transforms the raw libido of
physical sexuality into something completely different, which can
equally be expressed through media such as dance and poetry.

The *hetairas*, of whom Aphrodite was the patron goddess,
formed an important social class in ancient Greece. They provided
the alternative to marriage, polarising with the strictly lunar role of
the Greek wife. The hetaira was expected to be extremely well

educated and versed in politics and philosophy and the arts, as well as being beautiful and skilled in erotic pursuits. She was also highly trained in social skills, and all the subtleties of courtship and the offering of intellectual and aesthetic companionship were part of her arsenal of gifts. The world of the hetaira was a highly specialised and stylised one, and embodied the culture-bringing dimension of Aphrodite. The goddess also presided over the use of fragrances, cosmetics, oils and love potions. The word "aphrodisiac" is obvious in its derivation.

So part of the domain of Venus is the intelligent use of charm and what are called "feminine wiles." This is ironically a realm which often comes under criticism by the women's movement, although once again, if you understand the nature of the goddess, these arts are not designed to placate men, but rather, to please the deity herself, as an expression of her love of ornament and beauty. I have sometimes heard both men and women refer to this kind of self-ornamenting as "unnatural"—as though it were somehow against nature to use makeup or perfume, or choose beautiful clothes. Yet Aphrodite is as natural as any other archetypal image. It is as natural as anything else to wish to enhance and ornament and beautify. The urge to refine, to bring harmony to that which is rough and crude, to translate fantasy into beautiful forms, is an innate human impulse. We have only to look at the cave paintings in Lascaux to see how ancient and profound is our need to create beauty. This is a reflection of Taurus as well as Libra, but perhaps more the latter—and it is perhaps appropriate to remember that the Balance is the only inanimate symbol in the zodiacal iconography, suggesting a harmony designed and created by the human mind and imagination. Aphrodite's sexual skills also reflect her quality of art, for erotic accomplishment involves not only the giving of physical pleasure, but the creation and exploration of fantasy.

Audience: Is there a difference between the ways a man and a woman experience Venus?

Liz: Well, apart from the obvious, no. Not on the deeper level. But there is a great difference in how individuals experience Venus, depending on its placement in the birth chart and the degree of relationship the individual has with the planet. It is probably safe to assume that, at least in the past, Venusian qualities were largely projected by men upon women, and this is still the case to a great extent, although it is changing. There are all kinds of collective issues around being "effeminate" which have made it difficult for a man to express too much Venus. Even using a deodorant is too ambiguous for some men, never mind cologne or skin moisturiser or hair conditioner. But whether conscious or unconscious, one can still see Venus at work within the person, and it symbolises the same dimension in all human beings. And the most profound meaning of Venus, which is concerned with self-love and self-value, is the same for either sex.

The mundane expressions of Venus in both men and women are concerned with the worth of the body and the sense of being loved and contented, even in small ways which are far more important than they might seem. But as with any planet, too much Venus can be as great a problem as too little. If one identifies excessively with Aphrodite, one loses one's will and initiative. Aphrodite has no goal save to be loved and contented, and one cannot survive in life, let alone achieve anything independent, if that is the only object. There is a famous painting which portrays Venus and Mars after lovemaking, and the god of war is lying in a total stupour, blissfully contented and completely knackered. Of course that is lovely, and we can see how beauty and grace and pleasure tame the wild aggression of the battle god. But we can also look at it another way, and see Mars as having become a nice house pet, rather like a tomcat which has been neutered. He may never get up to fight again. This is perhaps too much of a good thing, and the consequences of too much Venus for a man may be ultimately more problematic than for a woman because his sense of sexual identity begins with Mars.

Men and women can both project Venus to such an extent that they have no connection at all with it inside themselves. When a person does this, he or she tends to feel worthless unless someone else loves them. There may also be a curious sense of deadness without the love of others, because Aphrodite is the bringer of joy. The extreme of this is rather like the character in John Fowles' novel, *The Collector*. One must possess a beautiful object in order to feel alive, even if this ultimately destroys the object. There are people who *must* have a beautiful lover or spouse who is desirable

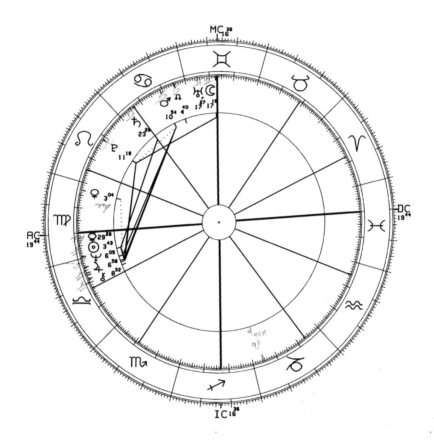

Chart 1. Lucy. The birth data has been withheld for confidentiality. Chart calculated by Astrodienst, using the Placidus house system.

to others, because without this vicarious beauty they see only their own ugliness. It is the fairy tale of Beauty and the Beast, but it often has an unhappy ending, because of the crushing possessiveness involved. This scenario may apply to a woman as well as a man, and I have met many women who project their own Venusian attributes on a male or female lover or partner, and feel perpetually insecure because the partner seems to them so beautiful and so attractive to the competition.

Another characteristic pattern can ensue if we "give away" Venus. One can become terribly dependent on the people and objects upon whom it is projected, as I have said, because this gives a vicarious sense of self-worth; and if this projection fixes itself on money or possessions, then one becomes a hoarder, obsessed with accumulating money and possessions. This is the dark troll-like side of Taurus, which springs not from real pleasure in beautiful things, but from an identification of those things with one's sense of self-value. This is of course extremely dangerous, because if one loses one's possessions, one loses oneself. I am thinking about the ways in which people reacted to the 1929 stock market crash in America. No one was very happy about it, yet the majority of people simply dug their heels in and worked terribly hard to survive and eventually recoup what they had lost. But others killed themselves, which seems to me such a pointless thing to do simply because one has lost one's wealth. It is no fun to be thrown from the top down to the bottom, but if you have your wits and your health, life surely offers many chances to recreate or reclaim at least some of what one needs. Yet these people, many of them men in their prime, thought their loss of wealth was worth dying for. This seems to me a rather horrific example of what happens when Venus is projected outside so completely that one can find no value in oneself.

I would like you to look at the example chart which you have been given this evening (see Chart 1, page 88). I chose this example because of the trapped quality of Venus, which you can see is placed in Virgo, the sign of its fall, makes no major aspects to any other planets, and is hidden away in the 12th house. Lucy is an excellent example of a person who has suffered considerably from a low sense of self-worth. She has tended to wind up the victim in most situations, particularly in her romantic life. She was married when she was quite young, to an extremely successful film producer; she was, she told me, "flattered" that he was interested in her, an ordinary woman with a middle-class background and a very prosaic secretarial job, no claim to great beauty or talent, and no real experience of men. This tells us something immediately about the patterns surrounding a blocked Venus; Lucy was so in need of *being* loved that she never really stopped to look at the man she was marrying, nor to consider whether he was truly good for *her*.

The marriage lasted for twelve years, but was effectively a nonmarriage, since Lucy's husband lost sexual interest in her very rapidly and moved on to other women. It seems that, while he was courting her, he was passionately in love; but as soon as he "got" her, the challenge was gone, and so was the desire. He did not leave Lucy, however, but maintained the outer structure of a family, fathering three children on her (all girls) and then absorbing himself in his numerous affairs and his work, which kept him constantly travelling. Lucy lived the twelve years of her marriage in a state of chronic loneliness, depression and self-abnegation, desperately trying to please her husband on the occasions when he was at home, and working constantly to understand where she had let him down.

Predictably, and perhaps fortunately, Lucy eventually went into a depressive breakdown, accompanied by terrifying fantasies of destroying her children and then herself. Her accumulating rage imploded rather than exploded, and she wound up in a psychiatric hospital and an extended course of psychotherapy. The outcome of this was a decision to leave her marriage. Something had happened to her during the breakdown; she decided that no one, to use her words, was worth "being a heap of shit for." Since then Lucy's life has improved considerably; having spent some time on her own, she has now remarried, much more happily, and many new opportunities have entered her life, creatively and personally. But it seems that she had to enter a very painful experience of self-degradation before her sense of her own worth was finally triggered.

Lucy's story is not an uncommon one, and although there are many more florid examples of the self-denigration she exhibited, probably the most characteristic manifestation of an unconscious

Venus in a woman is this kind of quiet despair within the trappings of family life. The world is full of women like Lucy, and it is primarily to their plight that the efforts of the women's movement have been addressed. Yet militant feminism does not help a woman to make a relationship with Venus; it only strengthens Mars and Uranus. The roots of Lucy's problem are not political, and the solution lies ultimately within herself.

Lucy's mother was a very beautiful and vain woman – a kind of empty Aphrodite whom many men were in love with, although it seems she remained faithful to her rather shadowy husband. This mother had spent her life obsessed with her looks and social position, and true to the darker side of Aphrodite, was not prepared to allow another female to have any share of the limelight, not even her daughter. Although there is no Moon-Venus square in Lucy's birth chart, the placement of Venus in the 12th suggests to me that there is a "Venus problem" within the family psyche. Lucy's mother is so excessive with her Venusian identification that we may assume she suffers from the same lack of self-worth that Lucy does – only she shows it in a different way, by madly overcompensating.

Lucy's conscious image of her mother was not, however, the Wicked Queen in *Snow White*. She thought her mother was lovely, helpless, pathetic, and needed looking after. Lucy was quite oblivious to the element of jealousy in their relationship, until she began to reflect upon the constant small criticisms of her appearance and behaviour throughout her teenage years, and the strange penchant her mother displayed for submerging Lucy in dowdy, unattractive clothes while she herself was always impeccably dressed. There is a nasty Catch-22 in this kind of scenario – having had her self-worth so persistently undermined, Lucy could not recognise her mother's jealousy because she could not imagine she had anything worth being jealous of.

This gives you some idea of the background to Lucy's problem. It is immediately recognisable as a "Venus wound," complete with jealous Aphrodite looming behind the personal mother. The real difficulty was never her errant husband; it was her own lack of self-value, which made her choose someone who treated her exactly as she inwardly treated herself. Now what I would like you to think about is the placement of Venus in Virgo. As Lucy begins to get in better contact with this dimension of herself, what will she find? What kind of Venus is it? This is Lucy's essential feminine self, apart from her role as wife and mother.

Audience: Has it something to do with the body?

Liz: I think so, in part. But we always need to get to the core of a sign when we interpret a planet placed there. It might be useful to imagine that Venus' sign in the birth chart is rather like Aphrodite's magic girdle, the symbol of her erotic power. Try to remember some of the myths connected with Virgo.

Audience: They are concerned with virginity and purity.

Liz: Yes, but what kind of purity? Certainly not sexual—the ancient virgin goddesses were harlots. "Virgo," as I have mentioned, simply means "unmarried" or "self-possessed," and it is this kind of purity with which the sign Virgo is concerned—the quality of inner integrity, of not being for sale. Lucy never experienced this quality during her marriage; she was indeed "bought" by promises of love, and betrayed her inner integrity by enduring great unhappiness for the sake of security. This to me is the deepest problem she has suffered because of her disconnection from her Venus. With the Sun conjuncting Neptune in Libra, there is a difficulty in defining her boundaries and expressing herself as an independent entity. We can also look at the planets in the 10th house, and make some educated guesses about the quality of mothering she experienced—particularly the exact Moon-Uranus conjunction in Gemini, which suggests that her early life was anything but emotionally safe. These are only two of the additional factors which might have contributed to her inability to live her Venus in Virgo.

Yet Lucy's essential feminine self embodies that "virgin" goddess who can give herself freely yet cannot be bought. The more value she gives to this self-contained and incorruptible dimension of herself, the more confident and lovable she feels as a woman. The time in which she lived alone was enormously valuable to her, since it is usually in solitude that Virgo's most positive attributes come to flower; and once developed, they remain permanent even if later on the person enters into another relationship or marriage.

Since Lucy is no longer afraid of establishing clear boundaries around her own needs, she now has a base from which to handle the trickier dimensions of the Sun-Neptune and the Moon-Uranus, and is less inclined to play the role of victim.

Now how do you think this Venus in Virgo might express if you saw it in a man's chart?

Audience: He would be attracted to self-contained women.

Liz: Well, that is the traditional interpretation, and it implies that Venus is being projected outside. But what does it say about the man himself, and his own values?

Audience: The same thing as it says about Lucy. His personal values involve preserving his inner integrity and not selling out to anyone, for love or money.

Liz: Yes, precisely. You see that there is no difference in interpretation on the deeper level. The more unconscious a man is of his Venus, the more likely it is that he will do the textbook thing and find a Virgo-type woman who embodies these values for him. She then becomes the object of desire, the beloved soul image. But it is really *his* soul that he needs to find within, even if he has found the right companion in outer life.

When we talk about those people and objects we find beautiful and valuable, we are also describing the complicated and subtle issue of personal taste. This is another dimension of Venus, and you can see that taste is by no means frivolous and unimportant. If it is developed—and in some people, it is not—it reflects, once again, what we value most. Now what kind of taste do you think is suggested by Venus in Virgo?

Audience: It's hard to imagine Venus in Virgo clanking around with lots of costume jewelry.

Liz: Probably not, unless the costume jewelry were handcrafted and highly individual. But usually Virgo's taste is subtle, and inclines toward things that have quality and are made to last. Since "fads" are really a kind of selling out—a bid to be just like everybody else so that one "fits in"—Virgo is not predisposed to follow-ing such trends. So even if the jewelry is huge and clanking, it will be chosen not because it is fashionable, but because Virgo feels "right" in it.

The issue of developing one's individual taste is an aspect of the change which has happened in Lucy since her breakdown and the end of her marriage. Previously, she paid little attention to how she looked, except to make the effort to please her husband. Now she is beginning to enjoy the exercise of expressing her own indi-viduality through a careful choice of clothes, jewelry, home fur-nishings and so on, all of which reflect who she is, rather than what someone else expects of her.

I would like to spend a little more time looking at the place-ment of Venus in the 12th house in Lucy's chart. I mentioned earlier that it reflects a Venus dilemma in the family psyche.

Audience: It's an inherited problem.

Liz: Yes, it is an archetypal dilemma which has been around for several generations. I think this can be said of any planet placed in the 12th; it is a powerful component in the family psyche but somehow it has not been properly dealt with. From being the "hidden enemy" it can transform into the "hidden resource" for the individual who has it in the 12th in the birth chart, if he or she can bring it into consciousness and learn to work with it. But by implication this means working on psychological issues which pre-cede one's own birth.

As we have seen, Lucy's 12th house Venus points straight toward her beautiful and narcissistic mother, as the embodiment of a Venusian family problem which has no doubt been around for many generations. Lucy's issues with her mother are also reflected by the full 10th house, which contains Mars, Saturn and the Moon-Uranus conjunction. This is a very powerful mother, and one whom Lucy experienced as controlling, rejecting and emotionally erratic. Lucy was aware of her mother's helpless unpredictability, but not of the unconscious ruthlessness in the woman, nor of the envy which she directed toward her daughter. But I will repeat again that this kind of extreme behaviour in the mother reflects a deep lack of self-value, disguised by overcompensation. Lucy and her mother have both shared the same Venus wound, but have reacted differently according to their different natures. And it is likely that the same problem existed in Lucy's grandmother, and so on.

Audience: What about the father's side of the family? Or is it just limited to the mother?

Liz: No doubt this issue has caused problems on both sides of the family. After all, what kind of man chooses a woman like Lucy's mother, if he does not have similar problems himself?

Perhaps we might look at one or two additional signs for Venus, so that you can get a feeling of interpreting the planet from a more mythic perspective. What about a fiery Venus, say, Venus in Leo?

Audience: Leo is concerned with becoming an individual.

Liz: Yes, the highest value for Leo is the expression of a unique self.

Audience: Leo needs to shine.

Liz: The Leonine need to shine is not really about impressing an audience. It is about being unique, special, a true divine child. The Sun must radiate, for that is its nature; this is why Leo loves to give, and also why it differs from the watery signs in that the giving comes not from a response to the needs of others, but from a need to give out one's own light. Leo's generosity is not sacrificial, because it springs from one's own inner necessity, not from someone else's requirements. How do you think Venus in Leo might be reflected in personal taste?

Audience: Leos love luxury.

Liz: I think this is generally true, but we need once again to look at the core of the sign to understand the "luxury-loving" side of Leo. If one's highest value is the expression of one's innermost self, then one's tastes are going to be highly individualistic and therefore usually expensive, since it is unlikely that one will find what one wants in the High Street chain shops. I think the issue is not so much luxury as optimum self-expression, which does not come cheap and which abhors the little economies which earth signs take for granted must be practised.

The same applies to the adjective "glamourous," which is also often used in relation to Leo. Once again, the real object is not to impress, since for Leo, the outer world does not really exist except as an extension of oneself. But all the fiery signs want life to be larger than life, because it is the mythic and symbolic world which is the real one for them, not the Saturnian material edifice which keeps getting in the way of imagination. The mysterious quality of glamour is deeply connected with myth, and the person who trails clouds of *mythos* behind them is usually seen as glamourous. Venus in Leo tries as closely as possible to emulate the mythic world, in style and taste as well as in ideals in love. So Venus in Leo is sometimes predisposed toward flamboyant taste, not in order to shock, but in order to bring the glory of the mythic world into the greyness of the mundane one.

You can see why I keep circling around the issue of taste in relation to Venus. How many of you feel you really have developed individual tastes, and can express them? Well, good, some of you at least have put your hands up. But this is something each person can work on. The ordinary level of this is the simple ability to walk into a shop and know that something – a garment, a piece of furniture, an ornament or whatever – is absolutely right for you, regardless of whether your friend or the salesperson tries to deflect you toward what *they* think is appropriate. Learning to develop and express one's tastes takes time, especially if this Venus faculty has been undermined in childhood, as Lucy's was. But Aphrodite is necessarily vain, so if you wish to befriend her you must be prepared to take three hours trying things on over and over again until you begin to get familiar with that mysterious feeling of what makes you attractive in your own eyes.

Audience: Could you say something about Venus in Aries? I know it's a fire sign like Leo, but it's more aggressive.

Liz: Try working it out yourself. What is Aries' highest value?

Audience: Potency.

Liz: Exactly. In common with the other two fiery signs, Aries is not concerned with what others think, but with an inner experience – in this case, potency, phallic power, the feeling of being alive and capable of making things happen. This includes the level of generating new ideas, which is also a form of potency and phallic power. You can easily understand Aries' attraction to physical activity such as sport even though it is not an earthy sign. It is not the body itself which concerns Aries, but the experience of inner fire and power which goes with competition and conquest. So Venus in Aries focusses on this sense of inner potency as the core of its lovability – the quality which makes one feel beautiful and of value.

Audience: In a woman's chart, does this mean that the only way she can feel potent is to conquer men?

Liz: That is one option. But as with Leo's love of show, it is the outer manifestation of an inner value which has many possible levels of expression. Venus in Aries certainly has a Don Juan reputation in both sexes, and it is a natural enough way of feeling sexually powerful. And there is nothing the matter with needing to periodically flex one's Venusian muscles in this fashion, unless the person with Venus in Aries happens to be your partner and you happen to be someone with Venus in Scorpio conjuncting Saturn and square Pluto. But total dependency on others, even if this takes the form of needing to conquer them, is usually a very questionable way of living Venus, because one's sense of worth is still based outside, and is therefore completely in others' hands.

Audience: What about the issue of taste with Venus in Aries? Could we say it's sporty?

Liz: That is one typical expression, although not the only one. But Venusian taste makes a statement about the person. If Venus in Aries wishes to make a statement about potency, then looking "sporty" is a very good way of doing it. We communicate all kinds of messages to each other with our clothes, rather like an elaborate code. If you are wearing a pair of joggers which have "Nike" written over them in big letters, or a ski jacket which proclaims, "Nevica," that is saying that you take your jogging or your skiing seriously, which means you are fit and health-conscious and can manage nicely on your own, thank you very much. On the deeper level, it is a statement about the power to shape your body as you wish, and it is a statement of phallic power and effectiveness, in a man or a woman. With Venus in Aries, that feeling of potency is the core of one's sense of self-worth.

We have come to the end of this session now, but I think that gives you a reasonable introduction to Venus. You will be getting a lot more of it from us both tomorrow – unless of course I'm busy in the Bahnhofstrasse exercising my personal taste in the clothing shops, and don't manage to make it back.

THE LAW OF DESIRE

AN IN-DEPTH LOOK AT VENUS

BY HOWARD SASPORTAS

For many years, I talked about Venus mainly in terms of the Eros principle, the urge for union and relationship which exists in all of us. We will be discussing Venus in terms of relationship issues in due course, but for starters, I first want to examine Venus as a significator of our value system, of what we find beautiful and desirable. Venus is an indicator of what we value or desire, of those things which we feel will give us pleasure or make us more complete and more whole. The point I'm stressing is that Venus is not just the planet of love and relationship—it also is about clarifying our identity by defining what we value, hold dear, and find pleasurable. In this sense, Venus serves the Sun, it serves the solar urge to grow and develop into an individual in one's own right: by defining your values, desires and affinities, you give greater form and definition to your unique and individual identity.

In his chapter on Venus in the book *Planets*, Robert Glasscock points out that the glyph of Venus resembles a hand mirror, and he goes on to say that what you value is a reflection of who you are, that "what we love is a reflection of ourselves."[4] And yet, it is a fact of life that many people have great difficulty defining their values; they have trouble admitting to, asking for or going after what they want. They either aren't sure what their values are, or they're reluctant or uncomfortable about acknowledging and standing up for what it is they truly desire. Because Judeo-Christian teachings seem to espouse sacrifice, suffering and self-abnegation, some people may believe that pleasure or self-gratification is a sin. The existential psychologist and writer Erich Fromm takes the view that

---

[4]Robert Glasscock, "Venus," in *Planets*, edited by Joan McEvers (St. Paul, MN: Llewellyn Publications, 1989), p. 129.

many of us are afraid or reluctant to make choices for fear of making the wrong choice. He believes that some people would prefer to live in a totalitarian state where decisions and rules are made for them, rather than face the anxieties and responsibilities concomitant with freedom of choice.[5] However, I believe that it is psychologically dangerous *not* to define our individual value system, or to lie to ourselves about what we desire or find beautiful.

The plain truth is that without a sense of what we value, we are lost, we don't know who we are. What's more, if we are not true to our values, we can never achieve a healthy self-esteem or satisfaction in our lives. If we disavow or do not act in accord with our Venus, we lose self-respect, we dirty ourselves in some way. In order to gain self-esteem, we first have to define our values and what gives us pleasure; and provided that living out our desires does not endanger or harm other people, we then need to act in ways which support our beliefs and longings. Otherwise, we are not accepting who we are, which is another way of saying that we are not showing ourselves love. And, like it or not, if we are deficient in self-love, we will be deficient in many other areas in our lives, especially in the sphere of relationship. If we don't love and respect ourselves, we will never truly believe that someone else can love and respect us. If we are not good enough, nobody else will ever be good enough.

Right now I'd like to clarify how the placement of Venus in the chart is a major clue or indication to what we value and hold dear, and to what we need to create in our lives in order to feel we are worth something, in order to gain a healthy self-esteem and self-respect. (See Table 2 on pages 102–103.) Listen carefully, because this applies to all of us. The premise I'm working from is that, by sign, house and aspect, Venus suggests those things and qualities we need to bring into our lives in order to achieve greater individuation, self-definition and personal fulfilment. For example, take Venus in the 4th house—what would you like to have or gain which would bring you more happiness and self-respect?

Audience: A beautiful home.

---

[5]Erich Fromm, *Escape from Freedom* (New York: Henry Holt, 1941).

Howard: Yes, on a very mundane or concrete level, Venus in the 4th indicates a deep appreciation and desire for harmonious and beautiful surroundings, for a home which makes you feel proud and gives you pleasure. Now, I believe that if you do what is necessary to achieve these desires, if you can create or get that beautiful home, you are realising what you value and hold dear, and therefore you will not only feel more fulfilled, but you'll actually like yourself better as well. You hear me, it's true – it can be as simple as that. Don't underestimate the importance of liking yourself. Liking yourself better means you have greater self-esteem, and if you feel good about yourself and have greater self-esteem, it follows that the relationships in your life are going to improve. And I'm pretty sure most of us would like to see improvement in the relationship sphere. Do you hear what I am saying? – the most important love is self-love. This may sound selfish, but it isn't; if you don't value and respect yourself, you will not be able to give or receive love without a host of awkward or nasty complications. Okay, what if you have Venus in the 10th house?

Audience: That means you place value on work and career, on worldly status, or serving society in some way.

Howard: Yes, and if you can satisfy those desires, you will be doing what you need to feel more beautiful and complete, which then enhances your self-esteem and self-respect, which in turn will help you in relationship.

In English, we use the word *inter*personal to describe what happens or passes between you and another person, and thus we have interpersonal love and interpersonal relationships. What I'm emphasising right now, however, is not interpersonal love but what is called *intra*personal love. Intrapersonal love is about loving yourself; it's about loving, accepting and forming a relationship with what is inside you; it's about loving and accepting *all* of yourself – even the dirty, nasty, primitive, unwashed yucky bits. I believe that intrapersonal love is the basis for achieving healthy and happy interpersonal love. Can you honestly say you love all of yourself? I've said it before and I'll repeat it again: you can't transform anything you are condemning or denying. If you are denying your nasty bits, how can you possibly do anything to work with or

Table 2. Guidelines for Interpreting Venus.

VENUS BY SIGN

1) Venus' sign is an indication of the kinds of qualities you value, find attractive or hold dear (whether these are found in a person or, more abstractly, in a work of art, a landscape, or a theory or philosophy). Developing and bringing the qualities of Venus' sign into your life should make you feel more individuated, whole and complete. You may possess talents in connection to the sign Venus is in.

2) Venus' sign says something about the image of the beloved and what turns you on. Also it influences what kinds of experiences you tend to meet in relationship — your attitude to love and other social interactions. Venus' sign can describe something about how you give and receive affection — the way you go about harmonising and sharing with others, or how you adorn yourself to make yourself attractive.

3) The sign Venus is in will colour your anima image, the image of the feminine a person carries within. Both men and women need to be in touch with and live out their Venus sign in order to feel worthy, complete and attractive as an individual.

VENUS BY HOUSE

1) Venus' house shows an area of life you are drawn to in pursuit of greater fulfillment, beauty and pleasure. By engaging in activities associated with that house and working through difficulties and issues you encounter in that domain, you will feel more complete as an individual. You may exhibit talents related to the sphere of experience associated with Venus' house.

2) There is an increased capacity to appreciate and value the sphere of life associated with Venus' house placement. In general, what we value and appreciate is what we attract to ourselves, but other placements in the chart may conflict with Venus' values.

Table 2. Guidelines for Interpreting Venus (cont.)

3) Venus' house is where we seek peace and harmony, but it is also an area of life in which we may be seductive—where we put on Aphrodite's "magic girdle" to enchant and enslave others.

4) Venus' house can be a domain where we may feel competitive or envious of people who have what we would like to have. We can also be disillusioned and critical when people don't live up to our ideals and expectations in that sphere of life.

5) Since Venus is associated with worth and value, Venus' house can be linked to issues to do with money, finance and possessions.

VENUS BY ASPECT

1) The nature of any planet which aspects Venus will influence what qualities we value, find attractive or hold dear—what gives us pleasure—whether in a person, a work of art, a landscape, etc. Compare, for instance, Venus in aspect to Saturn with Venus in aspect to Neptune. Planets aspecting Venus will colour your anima image and the image of the beloved. Aspects to Venus will also say something about how we adorn ourselves or try to make ourselves attractive.

2) The nature of any planet aspecting Venus will influence the kinds of experiences we tend to meet or attract in love and relationship. For instance, do we meet Saturn or Jupiter? Aspects to Venus will show the kinds of conflicts, tensions and lessons we encounter in close partnerships.

3) The nature of a planet aspecting Venus may show a particular talent or gift you have. Planets aspecting Venus can also influence how we fare with issues to do with money and possessions.

change these parts of yourself? Of course, you might venture so far as to recognise and accept that you have unpleasant or undesirable traits, but if you are condemning these components of your nature, you're actually making it more difficult to deal with them. Acceptance allows the healing magic to work: if we can accept that by virtue of being human, we all are born with a certain amount of greed, lust, envy, torpor, destructiveness or whatever, we can then own and form a relationship with these parts of ourselves, and this is the first step toward working constructively with them. In his best-selling book *The Road Less Traveled*, the American psychiatrist M. Scott Peck stresses the importance of self-love:

> The definition of love . . . includes self-love with love for the other. Since I am human and you are human, to love humans means to love myself as well as you. To be dedicated to human spiritual development is to be dedicated to the race of which we are a part, and this therefore means dedication to our own development as well as "theirs." . . . [W]e are incapable of loving another unless we love ourselves. . . . We cannot be a source of strength unless we nurture our own strength. . . . [N]ot only do self-love and love of others go hand in hand but ultimately [they] are indistinguishable.[6]

What we experience in infancy and childhood largely determines whether we grow up loving ourselves or not. Learning to love all of the self is dependent on the quality of our caretaker's love for us. Too often we are loved only when we display those aspects of our nature which mother finds acceptable. By the age of 1, we have a pretty good idea of what parts of ourselves win her approval, and which parts we should hide or deny. As infants, we need others to love us in order to ensure our survival; we therefore learn at a young age to suppress what is unacceptable, and to present a false self or safe face to the world. Alice Miller, a well-known Swiss psychoanalyst, draws these conclusions from her clinical work:

[6]M. Scott Peck, *The Road Less Traveled* (New York: Simon & Schuster, 1988; and London: Rider, 1986), pp. 82–83.

Accommodation to parental needs often (but not always) leads to the "as-if personality" (Winnicott has described it as the "false self"). This person develops in such a way that he reveals only what is expected of him, and fuses so completely with what he reveals that—until he comes to analysis—one could scarcely have guessed how much more there is to him, behind this "masked view of himself." . . . He cannot develop and differentiate his "true self," because he is unable to live it. It remains in a "state of noncommunication." . . . Understandably, these patients complain of a sense of emptiness, futility, or homelessness. . . . A process of emptying, impoverishment and partial killing of his potential actually took place when all that was alive and spontaneous in him was cut off. In childhood these people have often had dreams in which they experienced themselves as partly dead.[7]

And if you're still in any doubt about all this, here's one more quote for you from Nancy Friday's book *My Mother, My Self*:

We get our courage, our sense of self, the ability to believe we have value even when alone, to do our work, to love others, and to feel ourselves lovable from the "strength" of mother's love for us when we were infants—just as every single dyne of energy on earth originally came from the sun. . . . Freud, Horney, Bowlby, Erikson, Sullivan, Winnicott, Mahler—the great interpreters of human behavior—may disagree profoundly in some ways but are as one about beginnings: you cannot leave home, cannot grow up whole, separate, and self-reliant, unless someone loved you enough to give you a self first, and then let you go. It begins with our mother's touch, our mother's smile and eye: there is someone out there whom she likes to touch, there is someone out there she likes to see. That's me. And I'm OK![8]

I'm labouring this point to illustrate the fact that unless we love and place value on ourselves—all of ourselves—we hinder the full

---

[7]Alice Miller, *The Drama of the Gifted Child* (New York: Basic Books, 1983; and London: Faber & Faber, 1983), p. 27.
[8]Nancy Friday, *My Mother, My Self* (New York: Dell, 1977), pp. 55–56.

development of our true identity. In other words, the self-love and self-esteem which comes from accepting and loving all of ourselves is necessary to grow fully into our Sun sign, our individuality. You can't develop your Sun sign if you place no value on your self, if you place no value on what you want for yourself. This is what Liz and I mean when we say that Venus serves the Sun.

So what can you start doing now in your life if you suffer from a lack of self-esteem or feel that you don't love yourself enough? As we've already discussed, you can begin by looking at Venus in your chart and doing what you can to develop that area. If you have Venus in Gemini or the 3rd house, let's say, you'll feel better about yourself if you can find ways to be true to your innate love of knowledge, words and communication; if Venus is in Sagittarius or the 9th house, you should be pursuing your love of philosophy, religion or travelling. Also, if you're lacking in self-love, I would try repeating this phrase to yourself as often as possible: "I deserve love just by virtue of being." The more Saturnian among us may not agree with this statement; you may think you only deserve love if you're built or shaped a certain way, or if you do things which are worthy and laudable. Think what you like, but I prefer to believe that love is something we all deserve just by virtue of existing. I see it as a basic birthright. And I believe that you can help to heal yourself by using this phrase as a kind of mantra. In some ways, the unconscious is like a mirror: if we tell it something enough, it begins to reflect that message back to us. I admit that using this affirmation is a shortcut. You may think it's a cheat—that if you dislike yourself because of how mother or father treated you, then you can only resolve or free yourself from your complexes by having psychoanalysis five days a week for 20 years. Psychotherapy or analysis will help, but I also know from experience that telling yourself, "I deserve love just by virtue of being" will also help, especially if you remember to do so at those moments when you feel the most unattractive, the most unlovable, the most ugly, stupid, shameful or whatever. Repeating this mantra may not completely substitute or replace the need for working through childhood difficulties in a therapeutic situation, but shortcuts sometimes work . . . and this one is considerably less expensive than x number of years of analysis. Go ahead, it's worth a try.

In *Planets*, Glasscock eloquently equates the law of gravity with the workings of Venus:

> Gravity is another name for attraction. And attraction is another name for love. Quite literally, the planetary orbits of our solar system are maintained by a form of love we're pleased to call gravity. And love—in all its profundity, comedy, tragedy and ecstasy—is symbolized by Venus. So let's not shortchange her in our work with clients.[9]

Gravity keeps the planets in place, gravity holds everything together. Venus represents a similar kind of attracting force or power. Glasscock also refers to Venus as "the glue of life," the glue of the universe. And for these reasons, I agree with the importance he extends to her. The goddess Aphrodite certainly would be pleased to be looked upon in this way. As Liz would say, Aphrodite did not appreciate not being appreciated, and you had better watch out if you're not giving her due regard. Aphrodite was reputed to be the mother of Eros or Cupid, whom we know best as a little cherub shooting his arrows at his hapless victims. In earlier Greek myths, however, Eros was considered the prime creative force of the universe. Eros was there before the Titans, he was there before the world was created.[10] He was an important deity, a fully grown man instrumental in the creation myths, not that baby in nappies we so often see on the front of Valentine's Day cards. So we have the idea that love was there in the beginning, that love is a force which helped to create the universe. Love is not just an emotion, it is an energy which comes through or to you, an energy which can act as a transforming agent for yourself and for others. The power of love is alchemical—it can be very healing when someone shines the golden light of love on you. And the act of giving love can help to heal both your beloved and yourself. I believe that Aphrodite isn't only a symbol of what gives you pleasure; she is an alchemical goddess as well. I'm not just referring to sexual love here, I'm also talking about a good friendship, or the love shared

---

[9]Robert Glasscock, "Venus," in *Planets*, p. 122.
[10]Jean Shinoda Bolen, *Goddesses in Everywoman* (San Francisco: HarperCollins, 1985), p. 235.

by a teacher and student, or the love exchanged between a therapist and client. Any kind of union based on love can be healing.

Before we talk more about love, I want to say something about Venus and creativity. Wherever Venus is in your chart is where you have potential creative talent. In English, the word *talent* is an old word for money or coins. Because most people value money, and given Venus' Taurean and 2nd house connotations, she has come to be associated with money. But Venus symbolises more than money; she represents talent and creativity—skills, resources and potentials which are innate or inborn. Venus in Gemini or the 3rd can bestow a gift with words; Venus in Cancer or the 4th may mean a flair for homemaking, cooking or interior decorating; Venus in Libra or the 7th might contribute to an innate diplomacy; Venus in Sagittarius or the 9th house can indicate a talent for inspiring others with your belief system or worldview; Venus in Pisces or the 12th suggests innate healing gifts, the ability to comfort and to soothe those in distress.

There is a quote by Plato (not Pluto) which says that "All love is the pursuit of the Whole," a big statement which merits philosophical and psychological exploration. To explain it, we have to go back to my favourite place—the womb. Of course, some wombs are five-star, some are two-star, and some are shark-infested; but even if our existence in the womb wasn't ideal, it still was a place where we were in physical (and probably psychological) symbiosis with the mother, fused and at one with her body. She was the whole world to us, and therefore we felt as if we were the whole world, as if our identity encompassed the entire universe. By two months after conception, an embryo develops a rudimentary brain, and one of the first things our tiny brain registers is this sense of oceanic totality, this feeling that we are everything. Up to six months after birth, we still believe that we and mother are one. Gradually we form an ego or personal "I" and come to realise ourselves as a distinct being separate from mother and the rest of the universe; and yet we retain a dim memory of a time when we were fused with and engulfed by a caring, loving other. No matter how mature or sophisticated we become in later life, something in us will always yearn for that lost unity we felt with the universe and with that special other person, our mother or caretaker. It is this Edenic vision which is rekindled when we fall madly, passionately in love, a Moon-like or Neptunian urge to merge once again with an all-loving, all-caring other.

The kind of love represented by the Moon or Neptune implies the loss of ego boundaries, and the complete merging of the self with someone else. The love Venus seeks is different. While Venus symbolises the urge for relationship which exists in all of us, she is not that interested in losing the self or surrendering it to another in the name of love (unless Venus in the chart is in Pisces or linked up with Neptune or the 12th house in some way). On the contrary, Venusian love is that of an individual ego seeking to unite or come together with another individual ego in order to feel more complete or more fulfilled. She doesn't necessarily want to lose herself or surrender altogether her ego boundaries in love, but she does want to embellish, enhance and augment her ego identity through teaming up with someone she finds attractive and desirable. More broadly, Venus represents what we desire, what we find beautiful and what we hope to gain.

The placement of Venus in the chart describes qualities which we find attractive or beautiful, and therefore pleasurable and desirable, whether they are found in a person, a work of art, a piece of writing, or in a type of landscape. For instance, Venus in Scorpio is an indication that you will be turned on by Scorpionic qualities, whether these are found in a man, a woman, a book, a piece of music or a painting. So you may be attracted to someone deep, mysterious and complex, someone who doesn't immediately give a lot away. Likewise, you may be drawn to paintings or music which evoke mystery, intensity and passion, or adore landscapes which are dark, dramatic, full of caves, caverns and ravines. By contrast, if your Venus is in Sagittarius, you'll probably go for someone who is outgoing, expressive, even flamboyant, someone lively and spirited who inspires you with his or her vision and ideals. You may prefer wide-open landscapes, vast vistas which reflect the "don't fence me in" side of Jupiter-ruled Sagittarius. In this way, Venus' sign, and also the house it is in and any planet it aspects, gives insight into what a person is turned on by. Life is not always this simple however. Some people are afraid to be turned on, because it puts them in an open and vulnerable position. So if you're fearful of desiring something because of the exposure or vulnerability that comes with admitting to your longings, you actually may be repelled or put off by the very qualities which Venus suggests may turn you on. If you're frightened of being rejected, spurned or hurt, or if you generally feel guilty about pleasure, you may defend yourself against what you find attractive or beautiful by making an about-face and deeming it repellant or undesirable.

Venus shows what we appreciate, desire, and find beautiful. According to metaphysicians, there is a cosmic law called the Law of Desire or the Law of Attraction. This law supposes that we draw to ourselves anything we desire or appreciate—in other words, if you truly value and appreciate something, you are emitting an energy which then draws it to you. So if you were born with Venus in the 4th, and you dearly desire a beautiful living environment, according to the law of desire, this is what you should get. If only life were that simple! The trouble comes when there are other planetary aspects to Venus (or other parts of your own psychic makeup) which obstruct, conflict with or negate what Venus is so intent upon having. This can be illustrated astrologically by a very straightforward example. Let's say you are born with Venus in Libra in the 7th house, a loud and clear statement that you would appreciate and desire a loving, harmonious relationship in your life. By itself, this placement clearly cries out for love, union and partnership. This is what you value, this is what you hope to gain. But what if you also were born with Saturn in Cancer in the 4th square to that 7th house Libran Venus? Now you have a problem, because there is something else in your chart and in your psyche which is squaring or at odds with the desires of your Venus. Venus in Libra in the 7th says "I want love and relationship," but Saturn in Cancer in the 4th may indicate a part of you which is frightened of love, a part of you that is afraid of the hurt and vulnerability you may be exposed to when you open up to another person. Why might Saturn in Cancer in the 4th be afraid of closeness?

Audience: Perhaps when you were a child, you felt rejected or let down by a parent you loved.

Howard: Precisely. Most children start out in life open to feeling love for mother and/or father. But if we are spurned or pushed away, or if the object of our affection disappears or dies, we come to associate love and closeness with hurt and pain, or we decide that since we have been abandoned and rejected, we must not be worthy of love. To defend ourselves against suffering such pain and humiliation again, we close up shop, deciding it's safer to deny or hide our feelings in the name of self-protection. So although your Venus in Libra in the 7th wants a good relationship and according to the law of attraction, should draw one to you, the Saturn in Cancer in the 4th will obstruct or negate the power and force of your 7th house Venus.

Audience: How would you advise someone who came to a chart reading with this kind of conflict?

Howard: First, I would point out that they have an inner dilemma going on—one part of them craves love, but another part is afraid of it and is therefore sending out messages that keep love at bay. Then there will be the need to dig into the unconscious and the past to discover how they came to associate love with hurt and pain. In other words, there is work to be done on the hurt child of the past, and the need to redress the rejection felt by their inner child which they're still carrying around inside them. Saturn in Cancer in the 4th suggests there is a huge amount of psychological housecleaning to be done before they can feel safe and comfortable in love, before they can truly satisfy the needs and desires of Venus in Libra in the 7th. Working through the square will involve getting in touch with and expressing the early hurt, anger or pain, and then doing some reparenting—that is, giving now (in the present) the kind of love and caring that hurt child needed but didn't receive in the past.

Even though Venus shows what we value and appreciate, and therefore what we should be attracting to ourselves in line with the workings of the Law of Desire, Venus may not succeed because of our inner conflicts. We may say or think we want something, but if another part (consciously or unconsciously) fears that thing or does not believe we really deserve it, Venus' desires are likely to be overruled. We touched on something similar in the Mercury seminar, when I told you the story about how, on one level, I wanted to get better and out of hospital, but because I associated going back home with having to start work again, the healing process was delayed in spite of all the kinesthetic visualisation I was practicing.

If we are not attracting what we desire in life, we probably need to look into the unconscious and into our psychological complexes or hidden agendas for the reasons why.

Let's change gears slightly, and presume you have Venus in Libra in the 7th house opposite Uranus in Aries in the 1st. Venus in the 7th wants love and union, but what does Uranus in the 1st want?

Audience: Independence.

Howard: Yes, Uranus demands space, independence, autonomy, room to move, and the freedom to do what it likes when it likes, none of which are very conducive to the kinds of adjustments you need to make to have a harmonious relationship. In this case, it is not a fear of vulnerability or low self-esteem that hinders involvement, but rather the fear of losing your freedom and individuality, the fear of being swallowed up by another person. So here we have Uranian urges conflicting with the law of desire as laid down by Venus.

Audience: I have Venus in aspect to both Saturn and Uranus.

Howard: Yes, some people have Venus in aspect to both. For instance, if you were born in 1942 you could have a Saturn-Uranus conjunction in Taurus or Gemini, and it's possible that Venus might be linked to that conjunction in some way. Those born around 1952 could have Venus in aspect to the Saturn-Uranus square that was happening then. Saturn opposed Uranus around 1965, and then squared it in 1977, and more recently there has been another conjunction in Capricorn. Venus could easily play into these aspects. Any planet aspecting Venus suggests the kinds of issues that come up for us in relationship. If Saturn is on one arm of Venus and Uranus is on the other, a great deal of tension is produced: we want a relationship (Venus), but we fear it for Saturn reasons (the fear of vulnerability or the feeling we are inadequate or unworthy) as well as for Uranian reasons (the fear of losing autonomy). It will take quite a lot of psychological work on the self to sort this mess out, but provided that we get to the root of our fears and make peace with them, we should be able to find ways of

accommodating Venus in our lives. We are not pinned like butter-
flies to the board of fate. We do have some free will, and we can
use it to become more conscious of our inner conflicts and to do
what is necessary to resolve the tensions they create.

Audience: What if Venus is sextile Saturn, or sextile Uranus?

Howard: Venus sextile Saturn or Uranus will bring out some of the
same problems as the hard angles between these planets. The
sextile aspect (and the trine for that matter) usually does indicate
that the ego can be clever at finding ways of resolving the dilemmas posed by either Saturn or Uranus. Sextiles, in particular, offer
the promise of resolution provided that we're willing to make some
effort in that direction. I'm glad you mention sextiles: they're
important aspects which are sometimes overlooked or simply rele-
gated to the status of a weak trine. I believe they merit more attention than that. Any planets brought together by sextile have the
potential to be blended very creatively and to one's evolutionary
and psychological advantage. Sextiles are potential talents or gifts
which need some attention or working on to be developed to the
full. Venus sextile Saturn suggests that we can be loving as well as
loyal, steadfast and down-to-earth in relationship. Venus sextile
Uranus suggests we can find a way to balance intimacy with autonomy. I would encourage all of you to take time to examine, assess
and make better use of any sextiles that show up in your chart. For
instance, if you have a sextile to a planet in the 11th house, I would
urge you to become involved in a group, club or organisation of
some kind, because by putting yourself in an 11th-house situation,
you are creating more possibilities for the sextile to come to the
fore. Go for it, get involved with the principles represented by the
signs, planets and houses brought together by a sextile aspect.
Trines come more naturally to us, they land in our lap; but you
need to make a little effort to activate a sextile and get the most
from it. Before you ask, I allow a six-degree orb if the Sun or Moon
is involved, and a four- or five-degree orb for the other planets.

Audience: I have Venus conjunct Uranus and I can relate to what
you said about these two planets in square.

Howard: Yes, as Liz has often said, any aspect is like a table with two legs (is there such a thing as a two-legged table?): pull one leg, and the other leg is dragged along. So whether Venus is conjunct, sextile, square, inconjunct, sesquiquadrate or opposite Uranus, similar kinds of issues will arise. In this case, Uranus is pulled along with Venus. This can manifest in many different ways: it may indicate falling in love with Uranian types, or, more to the point, it usually means that when you fall in love, you also have to include your Uranian needs for space and autonomy and not allow yourself or your identity to become completely immersed in the other person. How well we negotiate a conjunction depends on its relation to other placements in the chart. Obviously, the ego will find Venus conjunct Uranus trine Jupiter easier to handle than Venus conjunct Uranus square Pluto. An Aquarian may have a smoother time living with a Venus-Uranus conjunction than a Taurean or someone with a strong Saturn or lots of earth.

All this talk about Venus and Uranus leads me into something I've been wanting to discuss with you in greater detail—the *freedom-closeness dilemma*. We've already touched on this conflict in my lecture on the Moon,[11] when we examined the inner ambivalence of the infant who wants to be close to mother for the love and safety she provides, and yet also is pulled by an urge to be free to explore the world beyond her knee. I'd like to carry on with this discussion from where we left off, and then we can see how the tensions inherent in the freedom-closeness dilemma are not just childhood concerns, but continue to test us in our adult relationships. In fact, the freedom-closeness dilemma is the most basic and common challenge people face in partnership: how to be close to somebody and still not lose touch with one's individual identity, how to relate, compromise and share with a mate or friend and still be true to the self.

We begin life in a state of symbiosis with the mother, but usually by five to eight months after birth we embark on what is known as a "psychological birth," that is, the process of differentiating our identity from mother. We gradually come to recognise that we are a separate person in our own right. As stated earlier, to

---

[11]See "First Love" in Part One: The Moon, in *The Luminaries*, Volume 3 of *Seminars in Psyhological Astrology*, pp. 65–66.

be separate and to stand on one's own is scary, and throughout the various phases of individuation we will repeatedly run back to mother for reassurance, safety, comfort and support. We want to grow, become more self-sufficient and explore the environment, but we also want to know that she is still around when we need her. We want mother to be there for us, but we also would like to be independent from her as well. Sound familiar? It should, because these same issues crop up again in later close relationships. The differentiation stage begins in earnest around four, five or six months old, and by nine months we grow into what is termed "the practicing stage," a time when we test and exercise our autonomy by venturing away from mother to see what else is out there in life.

As Judith Viorst points out in her book *Necessary Losses*, there is a headiness about the practicing stage: crawling leads to walking, and standing upright is a major achievement or triumph. We are excited by what we have achieved, and we start to have a love affair not just with mother, but with the world around us. In Viorst's words, we "grow drunk on omnipotence and grandeur" and turn into unabashed narcissists, "the masters of all we survey." Provided that we do not encounter too many restraints or restrictions during this period, we will grow up with a fascination and wonder for life. Built into us from this period is "that solo pilot, that African explorer, that navigator of unchartered seas," that "dauntless adventurer."[12] You can almost gauge how your practicing stage went by considering how you react when you're in a strange town on your own. Are you the kind of person who can go alone to a new place and feel excitement about what you might find there? If so, you probably fared well in the practicing phase of development. Or are you the kind of person who won't leave your hotel room in a foreign city, terrified of the unknown, afraid of what might be lurking out there? If so, your natural curiousity and adventurousness were somehow impaired or obstructed in the developmental process. Perhaps mother made you feel guilty for moving away from her, or she expressed excessive worry and concern every time you ventured away. The practicing stage teaches us to stand bravely on our own; if it doesn't go well, the joy of

---

[12]Judith Viorst, *Necessary Losses* (New York: Fawcett, 1986), p. 37.

exploration is stifled, and the prospect of discovering the world is felt as daunting.

By 18 months, however, our minds begin to grasp the full implications of our separateness. Before that, we may have reveled in our newfound powers and capabilities, but then it hits us—in actual fact we are really just a small, helpless child. Viorst compares this realisation to walking merrily on a tightrope, showing off with a trick or two, and then suddenly looking down to discover no net underneath. Margaret Mahler labelled this sobering-up period the "rapprochement" stage.[13] Aware of the dangers of autonomy, we run back to mother; but unable to forego completely the joys of standing alone in the world, we move away from her again. Then we return to her once more, but when her closeness and presence start to feel suffocating, off we go on our own. This phase is our first conscious attempt to reconcile separateness and autonomy with closeness and safety, and there is a great deal to negotiate. "How long can I stay away from mother and still be sure she'll be there when I get back?" "How much of my freedom and independence must I give up for love and shelter?" "Should I venture out on my own or should I stay with her, and if I do go away, will she accept me back again?" The key to resolving the rapproachement dilemma lies in finding the optimal distance and time you can be away from your mother/caretaker and still feel safe and secure. We have to separate ourselves and learn to stand psychologically alone to satisfy our yearning for autonomy and independence, and yet we still need to be close and loving to fulfil our longing for intimacy and security. Correct me if I'm wrong, but I'm pretty sure these issues are familiar to you in terms of your adult relationships. How many times have you felt caught in the "can't live with him but can't live without him" bind? How did you feel about leaving your partner for a week to come to this conference? If we failed to resolve the ambivalences and tensions associated with the rapproachement stage, we will be haunted by them our whole lives. The freedom-closeness dilemma, first played out with mother, is re-enacted again and again with friends, lovers and even one's own children.

---

[13]See Margaret Mahler, et al., *The Psychological Birth of the Human Infant* (New York: Basic Books, 1975).

It's not difficult to find astrological significators which correlate with the freedom-closeness dilemma. In their own way and to varying degrees, the Moon, Venus and Neptune symbolise our urge for union, intimacy, closeness, merging, and the desire to lose oneself in another person; whereas the Sun, Mars and Uranus are the most obvious indications of our need for autonomy, space, freedom, separateness and individuality. (You also could argue that, in some respects, Jupiter—the planet that likes room to move—and Saturn, the planet that enables us to draw boundaries around the self, should also be included on the autonomy and separateness list.) If you have the Moon, Venus or Neptune aspected to the Sun, Mars or Uranus, the conflict between closeness and freedom is likely to be highlighted in your life. For instance, aspects of Venus to Uranus certainly create this tension. You can get it also with Venus in hard angle to Mars, or with the Moon in conflict with the Sun, Mars, Jupiter, Saturn or Uranus.

Sign combinations can bring out this dilemma. Certain ones immediately come to mind: planets in Aries opposite planets in Libra; the Aries-Cancer square can give freedom-closeness conflicts; the Taurus-Aquarius square may manifest as the need for routine and security versus the need for space and freedom; planets in Cancer inconjunct planets in Sagittarius or Aquarius might do it; the Taurus-Sagittarius inconjunct could produce this problem, or Gemini's need for change and variety might conflict with Scorpio's need for intimacy or with Capricorn's need for security; placements in Aries versus placements in Taurus, and placements in Gemini versus placements in Taurus or Cancer also can intensify the freedom-closeness dilemma. Emphasis by house might highlight these issues: planets in the 1st opposing planets in the 7th could bring out a conflict between what you want as an individual and what a relationship asks of you; 2nd or 4th house planets inconjunct 9th house placements sometimes indicate the kinds of tensions we've been discussing. In actual fact, the freedom-closeness dilemma is virtually universal, and will show up in many different ways in the chart, even in ways I've not mentioned so far. We all have a touch of it, although some charts will boldly reveal it as a major issue needing resolution in this lifetime.

Before suggesting a formula for resolving the freedom-closeness dilemma, I'd like to look more closely at how different individuals or different couples might experience this conflict.[14] For some people, this dilemma is felt to such an extreme that it's almost pathological. I want to describe a severe case first, but remember it is an extreme and you probably don't suffer the problem to the same degree. The example I'm thinking of is when a person simply can't satisfy either of these needs: he or she finds it unbearable to be alone or separate, but being close to someone is also experienced as extremely threatening. If closeness is scary, and autonomy is scary, where is there to go? I have seen this situation in the charts of people whose Sun and Moon form a T-square with Saturn, Uranus or Pluto—aspects which indicate pretty serious difficulties or blockages with both the Sun and Moon principles. Take a Sun-Moon-Pluto T-square, for instance. If you have the Moon square Pluto, intimacy can bring up a great many fears and deep complexes, making closeness to another person a threatening prospect. Intimate relationship generates intense anxiety, as if you fear the other person will annihilate or destroy you, so you drive the other person away or run from the relationship (the Moon-Pluto aspect). But don't forget, you have the Sun square Pluto as well, which means you probably met Pluto in the process of ego formation, and this could leave you with the feeling that it is dangerous to exist as an individual in your own right.

So when you are on your own, you feel just as awful as you did in relationship, because you associate separateness with emptiness, abandonment, death and destruction (the Sun-Pluto aspect). You see the problem—being close makes you feel as if you are going to die, and being on your own makes you feel as if you are going to die. Where do you go? You may head back into the relationship, only to experience the same anxieties as before. You therefore end it and are on your own again, which feels horrible, so you try getting close again, and so on. Some of you may recognise a touch of this yo-yo style of relating in yourselves, although probably not as marked as this case. In the example I'm using, both ends of the freedom-closeness polarity are seen as totally exclusive to one another, and neither need can be gratified. To suffer not only from severe symbiosis anxiety (the fear of being close), but

---

[14]Maggie Scarf, *Intimate Partners: Patterns in Love and Marriage* (New York: Random House, 1987; and London: Century, 1987), ch. 19.

also from acute separation anxiety (the fear of standing on one's own) leaves one in a very lonely, scary place.

It's more common for couples to split and project the freedom-closeness dilemma, where one partner acts out the separateness and freedom needs, and the other is responsible for maintaining closeness and intimacy. To understand this situation more fully, we need to review the mechanics of splitting and projection. First of all, you must remember that we all have, to some degree, the freedom-closeness conflict inside us. It is an inner dilemma, an internal dispute between the urge for autonomy and the desire for intimacy. Since the ego doesn't like ambivalence, we may side consciously with one end of the polarity and deny the other. Let's say you have Venus square Uranus, and you identify mostly with Venus, thereby disavowing the Uranian side of your nature. By favouring Venus over Uranus, you are admitting to your need for union while suppressing an equally strong drive to be independent and have an identity separate from the relationship. Some people play it the other way around: they insist they're happier and freer on their own, and deny their intimacy needs. The same dilemma, and the same kind of splitting and projection, can be shown by Moon square Uranus as well. Here is what Jung said about denying or repressing a psychic component:

> The psychological rule says that when an inner situation is not made conscious, it happens outside as fate. That is to say, when the individual . . . does not become conscious of his inner contradictions, the world must perforce act out the conflict and be torn into opposite halves.[15]

According to this psychological law, if you side with Venus and disown Uranus, you are destined to attract people who are more inclined to act out the Uranian side of their natures. The situation then arises where you seem to be doing everything to foster warmth, closeness and union, while your partner carries Uranus for you—he or she is the one pushing for space, distance and more time away from the relationship. On the surface, at least, it appears

---

[15]C. G. Jung, *Aion: Researches into the Phenomenology of the Self*, Vol. 9, Part 2, *The Collected Works of C. G. Jung*, trans. R. F. Hull (Princeton, NJ: Princeton University Press, 1959; and London: Routledge & Kegan Paul, 1959), 71.

that what you are is what your mate is not. This kind of emotional division of labour creates a great deal of tension and conflict between partners: if you're the one carrying the Moon or Venus, you'll easily feel hurt and rejected and end up moaning about your partner's coldness, at the same time as your partner is complaining about feeling smothered and suffocated by you. By the way, we can split all types of emotional issues. For instance, if you are someone who habitually denies or suppresses anger, you'll most likely team up with a mate who readily expresses anger, or you'll find subtle ways to get your partner to act out your own anger for you. Or you may identify yourself as a happy-go-lucky, free and easy person, and wind up with a mate who is prone to depression and morbidity, in which case he or she is carrying your sadness and despair while you're living out your partner's unexpressed lighter side. In *Intimate Partners: Patterns in Love and Marriage* author Maggie Scarf succinctly sums up the process of emotional division of labour, which is, at root, a confusion or mix-up of personal boundaries:

> The collusive exchange of internal territories is a bargain that is struck between two interested parties. In marriage, despite all overt evidence to the contrary, there really are no victims and villains; there is a deal that's made. What is nearer to the truth, in conflictual relationships, is that an underground exchange of denied parts of the partners' selves has taken place. Then each one sees, in the partner, what cannot be perceived in the self — and struggles, ceaselessly, to change it.[16]

Scarf also speaks specifically about the freedom-closeness dilemma:

> What is fought out between the mates . . . is the problem that neither one of them has been able to address internally — the problem of how to be a distinct and separate individual while remaining emotionally attached to another human being. The core issue for these couples is each mate's inability to

---

[16]Maggie Scarf, *Intimate Partners*, p. 63.

contain, internally, both sides of the autonomy/intimacy polarity.[17]

Now, I'd like to offer you some advice (always a dangerous thing to do) on how to resolve the freedom-closeness issue. Remember that old proverb: "I looked and looked and this I came to see, that what I thought was you and you was really me and me." We are on the way to resolving the dilemma between autonomy and intimacy when we realise that it is an internal conflict. Although our tendency is to split the polarity and blame the other person for acting out what we have denied in ourselves, the truth is that we all have both needs battling it out inside us. Next, we should realise that both needs are okay to have. It's not wrong to want to be intimate and close, nor is it wrong to want space and autonomy. If we can accept that both these inner urges are legitimate, it will be easier for us to accept that other people also are conflicted in the same way, and as a result, in theory at least, we need not become unduly upset when a partner expresses either the desire for closeness or the desire to have some space away from us. What we don't like in ourselves, we have great difficulty accepting in others. So if we are terrified of our need for closeness, we won't like it when another person tries to move closer to us. Conversely, if we can't admit to the fact that we need more space and freedom away from a partnership, we are not going to be pleased when our mate demands more autonomy and independence. Owning the polarity as something contained within ourselves, and acknowledging both sides as legitimate, makes it easier for us to accept that it also exists in other people.

The next step in resolving the freedom-closeness dilemma is easier said than done: *we need to recognise clearly and consciously that a partner or loved one is not our mother.* If you unconsciously are projecting mother issues onto partners, you will feel more threatened if they express a desire for greater autonomy or separateness, because it reawakens the infantile fear of being abandoned by your caretaker, which your "inner child of the past" equates with starvation and death. Likewise, you may be terrified if they move too close, as this could rekindle the infantile fear of being engulfed or

---

[17]Maggie Scarf, *Intimate Partners*, p. 365.

suffocated by a smothering mother. By the way, women can project "mother" onto a male partner, just as easily as a man projects mother onto his wife or girlfriends. To make it as clear as possible, I'll repeat briefly the steps involved in resolving the freedom-closeness polarity: (1) Recognise the conflict as an internal one; (2) acknowledge that both the urge for autonomy and intimacy are legitimate, and it's okay for you and other people to feel them; and (3) remember that your partner is not your mother.

On one level, closeness and freedom appear to be mutually exclusive. However, with a fair amount of psychological work and effort, it is possible for you to integrate both ends of the polarity, and even to arrive at a place in which they support and enhance one another. It's a little tricky explaining how this can come about, but I'll have a go. If you're in a relationship and feel that you're still loved even when you express needs for space and freedom or for greater autonomy within the partnership, you then will feel more comfortable being close to your partner. In other words, if your partner allows you to be separate when you require, your capacity to love the other person is increased, and in this way, allowing room for separateness in a relationship actually fosters closeness. Also, if a partner can accept your differentness rather than expecting you to be a mirror image of him or her, you are freer to develop and integrate more of what is inside you, which ultimately means you will have more to offer to a mate. You no longer have to hide or deny those parts of yourself which you fear are unacceptable or unlovable. Knowing that someone will love you for all of what you are encourages further self-development on your part. Martin Buber was on to this when he wrote, "Man becomes an I through a You." For these reasons, I believe the answer to resolving the freedom-closeness dilemma is found in unconditional love, a love which accepts other people for what they are, warts and all, needs and all. Unconditional love can help heal earlier wounds to our self-esteem, when a parent or caretaker judged us as "bad" or unacceptable for not living up to their expectations and fantasies of how we should be. Unconditional love allows partners to feel okay about living out their true individuality and their need for separateness, which in turn makes it easier for them to be intimate and loving with you. In such an atmosphere, autonomy and intimacy are no longer mutually exclusive, but mutually supportive and self-enhancing. Perhaps I'm being a little naive, but I do see this as a kind of ideal toward which we can aspire in relationship, however challenging it is to make it real.

Now that we've figured out how to solve all your relationship problems, let's change gears and do an imaging exercise on Venus. It's best to close your eyes, but if things become uncomfortable for you for any reason, just open your eyes and write down what you're feeling. Take a few deep breaths, relax your mind and body, and turn your attention inward. Visualise the glyph for Venus, and then see if you can come up with any images or pictures which represent what this planet means to you. You may see a man, a woman, an animal, an inanimate object, or anything. Spend a few minutes exploring your image of Venus. Find out how it feels, what it needs and wants, see if there is anything you can do to make it more fulfilled or happy. Take three or four minutes for this. After that, say thank you and goodbye to Venus, open your eyes, and jot down a few notes about what you experienced. Then, if you wish, find a partner with whom to share what happened. Talking with someone about the exercise will bring it to life, and you may realise that more took place during it than you thought.

You can try this kind of guided imaging with any planet. Remember, if you do it on your own and it starts to become uncomfortable, just open your eyes and write about what you're feeling. I'm curious to hear what images or pictures of Venus you had.

Audience: I saw Botticelli's Venus, radiant and loving. When she came over to embrace me, I told her that I was a victim.

Howard: Yes, Botticelli's Venus—what do they call it?—Venus on the half-shell. The images that people get are highly personal, and I usually don't make a practice of interpreting them for others. It's better for you to hold the image in your mind for a number of days, and then see if its message hits home or becomes clearer. I would, however, advise you to reflect on the circumstances in your life in which you play the victim, and why. It appears that Venus would like to help you out of these situations.

Audience: I had four pictures. The first was a sensuous black cat; the second was a bird; the third was a tall, thin woman dressed in silver; and the fourth, an elfin type lady dressed in diaphanous material.

Howard: Why do you think you had so many different images? Where's your natal Venus?

Audience: It's in the 12th house in Aquarius.

Howard: Yes, I see, a very universal Venus.

Audience: I had a picture of a wizard, which turned into a mirror, and then I walked into the mirror.

Howard: We've already mentioned that the glyph of Venus is like a hand mirror, and that what we love and value is a reflection of something inside us. Funny, I wouldn't normally associate Venus with a wizard, but it's true that the energy of love can be very transformative and work magic. Maybe you have a touch of the alchemical Venus in you. You have a lot of Libran planets, don't you?

Audience: Yes, and Venus in the 9th house.

Howard: One more?

Audience: I saw a landscape with lots of green trees in full blossom—it was very calming.

Howard: Nice, so when you're feeling ill or uneasy, try recalling that image and it may help to restore your peace and equilibrium. If any of you didn't manage to get an image or picture, I wouldn't commit suicide over it. You might try this exercise at some other time. Some people don't see images easily, but even if you only had thoughts and feelings about Venus during the imaging session, you can work just as well with these.

I have the charts of a married couple, Laura and John, for us to look at in the time that's left (see Charts 2 and 3 on pages 126–127). From late 1986 to early 1988, they went through a major crisis in their relationship. The transits and progressions involving Laura's

Venus give an apt description of the nature of the crisis, so let's start first by examining her chart. Can you see immediately why Venus is an important planet for her?

Audience: Venus rules her Libran Ascendant.

Howard: Yes, you should always pay special attention to the planet ruling the Sun or Ascendant—in this case, Venus assumes importance as her Ascendant ruler. Allow me to digress slightly for a second and comment on something that could be relevant to this case study. During the Mercury lectures, we briefly discussed Alice Bailey's system of astrology, in which Mercury is considered the esoteric ruler of Aries. According to esoteric or what Alan Oken calls "soul-centred" astrology, Venus, not Mercury, is the ruler of Gemini. Now, you tell me, what do you make of the significance of Venus as the esoteric or transpersonal ruler of Gemini?

Audience: Does it imply something about finding values through relationship?

Howard: Yes, I think it does. In his book *Soul-Centered Astrology*, Oken interprets Bailey's system in a very readable and intelligent way. He theorises that Venus takes the "conflicts of duality (as indicated by Mercury, personality ruler of Gemini and planetary ruler of the Fourth Ray of Harmony through Conflict) and transforms them into a higher octave of expression . . . through the creative expression of the mind. . . ." He sees Venus as "an agent of synthesis because it is her function to blend and harmonise opposites into more creatively evolved wholes."[18] To my mind, Venus' esoteric rulership of Gemini equates love with knowledge, and I take this to mean that you can only really know something if you open your heart to it. Loving something helps you to understand it better. If you love a subject you're studying, you will learn it with greater ease and in greater depth. In effect, Venus as esoteric ruler of Gemini says that if we view all the varied facets of existence with a loving appreciation, we will learn much more about life than if we just collected facts about things. Just as there are some Ariens

---

[18]Alan Oken, *Soul-Centered Astrology* (New York: Bantam, 1990), pp. 173–174.

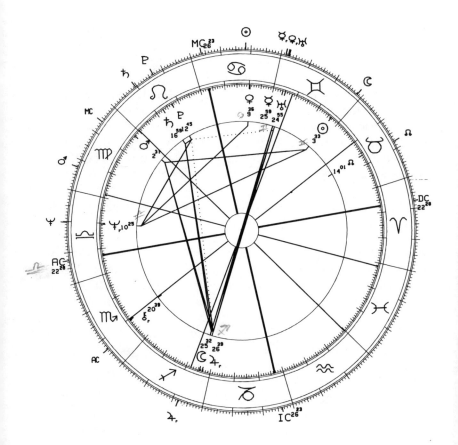

Chart 2. Laura. The birth data has been withheld for confidentiality. Chart calculated by Astrodienst, using the Placidus house system.

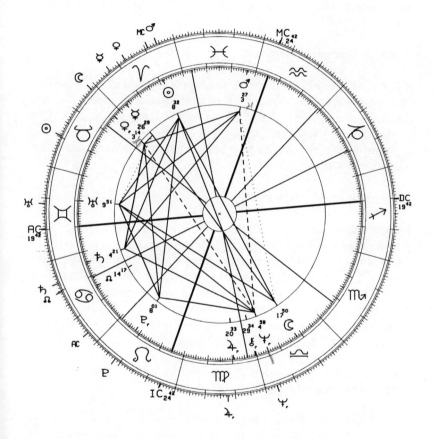

Chart 3. John. The birth data has been withheld for confidentiality. Chart calculated by Astrodienst, using the Placidus house system.

who resonate as much with Mercury as with Mars, there are some Geminis who resonate with Venus as much as with Mercury. I would venture to say that Laura is a fairly evolved and psychologically sophisticated Gemini, which means Venus is important not only by virtue of being the ruler of her Ascendant, but also as her soul-centred Sun ruler. Okay, what natal aspects can you find to Laura's Venus?

Audience: It squares Neptune.

Howard: Yes, her only major Venus aspect is a square to Neptune. This means that her Libran energy (and, esoterically speaking, her Gemini energy) is mediated via a Venus-Neptune square. She would be a very different person if her Venus was conjunct Jupiter or opposite Saturn. On the plus side, what does a Venus link with Neptune describe?

Audience: It enhances sensitivity and creativity.

Howard: Right. In fact, she works as a writer, mostly of nonfiction. Writing is an obviously appropriate form of creative expression for her, not only shown by her Libran-Venusian side, but also because she is a Gemini with Mercury in Gemini and the Moon conjunct Sagittarius in the 3rd house of language and communication. She is well respected in her field and very good at it. All right, what about Venus square Neptune in terms of love? What do you meet in love if your Venus bumps into Neptune?

Audience: Romanticism, deception, illusion, and the need to make sacrifices in relationship.

Howard: Yes, all of those things. When Venus is linked to Neptune, we probably are looking for the divine through love, seeking our lost wholeness, our lost sense of universality and oneness with all of life through merging with another person. Plato's dictum that love is the pursuit of the Whole usually applies quite well to people with Venus in aspect to Neptune, or with Venus in Pisces or the 12th house. She's changing now, but I would say that from adolescence until relatively recently, the Venus-Neptune part of Laura was looking for a lover to transport her to an ecstatic realm where she fused with something greater or other than the self, recalling the Edenic memory of fusion with an ideal mother or caretaker. This is also emphasised by the fact that Venus is in her 9th house and Neptune in the 12th, the two houses most associated with the search for something beyond the boundaries and limitations of a mundane, everyday ego-centred existence – the search for something higher. What she has had, however, is a series of lovers who have called upon her to make many sacrifices and adjustments; she has attracted relationships in which she has had to put her personal needs and wants aside because of her partners' situations or traumas. Her first important relationship began when she was about 16 and lasted until she was 21, in the course of which she had to adjust to her boyfriend's discovery that he was bisexual. She eventually married an Australian man who used drugs pretty freely, and whom she idealised even though his mental stability was questioned by many of her friends. It was a messy marriage: he was moody, jealous and prone to violence, and they soon divorced. Although there were definite periods of love and happiness in both these relationships, you can see how the more subversive side of Neptune infiltrated her Venus: the disillusionment over her first lover's admission of bisexuality, and the drugs and general craziness encountered in her first marriage.

She ultimately ended up living with and marrying John, a relationship which has lasted for over twelve years. They have two children, a boy and a girl, and own a beautiful, spacious home in northern California. In late 1986, John hired a new secretary at work, and when he started staying much later at the office, Laura grew suspicious. When confronted by Laura, John denied there was anything going on. Finally, in mid-1987 he confessed that he thought he was in love with his secretary, and told Laura that he needed time to decide between staying in the marriage or going off with his girlfriend. He boldly asked Laura whether she minded if he moved in with his secretary for a while to see if it was the real thing. Okay, here's Laura with two children and confronted by her husband in this way. How would you feel?

Audience: Angry, miserable and betrayed.

Howard: Too right. Understandably, Laura's first reaction was out-rage (she does have the Sun square Mars). But before I tell you how she handled the situation, we should look at some of the pertinent interaspects between her chart and John's, and also at the transits and progressions which were around at that time. First of all, what do you see in his chart that picks up on her Venus-Neptune square?

Audience: His Sun is 8 Aries which squares her Venus and opposes her Neptune; his Saturn is 4 Cancer conjunct her Venus and square her Neptune; his Neptune squares her Venus, and his Mars is trine to it. Also his North Node in 14 Cancer is not too far away from Laura's Venus.

Howard: Yes, well spotted. You can see that his chart is a good trigger for her Venus-Neptune square. Have you noticed how often we get involved with those people who have placements which touch off the more difficult aspects in our charts, as if we are compelled to work through our karma and complexes via close relationship? I'll be focussing mainly on the interaspects already mentioned, but there are a few other interesting connections. For instance, Laura has Sun square Mars, which means her animus image is coloured by Mars, and John fits this as an Aries with Mars in an angular house square her sun. Her Descendant is Aries, which is his Sun and Mercury sign. Also, her Venus-Neptune square dictates that she meet Neptune through love, and he has a Sun-Neptune opposition and Mars in Pisces, which makes him fairly Neptunian. In turn, she pretty well matches his inner image of the feminine: his Libra Moon lands on her Ascendant, and her Moon-Jupiter conjunction in Sagittarius is close to his 7th house. Although his Venus in Taurus doesn't link up with much in her chart, it does fall in her 7th house, widely conjunct her Taurean North Node. The Uranian connections also are worth noting, with his Uranus on her Sun, and her Uranus near his Ascendant. Their respective Marses are almost exactly opposite, which often denotes a strong sexual attraction as well as tendency to battle with one another, locking horns over various issues.

However, our main focus now is on Laura's Venus-Neptune square, which, as we will see, was activated by transit and progression during the time of the crisis in their marriage. We've already discussed some of the ramifications of a Venus-Neptune contact, but it's worth further elaboration. Venus favours equality and fairness in love, something along the lines of "I'll love you if you love me," or "I'll appreciate you if you appreciate me." Self-abnegating and sacrificial Neptune is more complex when it comes to love—in its extreme, it can manifest as "I'll love you no matter what you do or say, and I don't expect anything back in return." When these two planets are in hard angle, Venus's desire for fairness and justice in relationship is in conflict with Neptune's willingness to be extra-patient, adjusting, flexible, and understanding of partners even when they are not giving you what you need or are not being how you would like them to be. Laura found herself caught in the middle of this dilemma in 1986 and 1987 as transiting Neptune in Capricorn came to oppose her natal Venus and squared natal Neptune, and as her progressed Sun was passing over her natal Venus bringing out its square to Neptune—a double whammy hitting off the Venus-Neptune square. How should she respond? Should she kick John out for good because of his infidelity, or should she graciously allow him the time he asked for to test out the relationship with his girlfriend on a live-in basis? There is a fine line between being giving and understanding in a Neptunian way, and allowing oneself to be treated like a doormat.

In the end, I think she handled the situation very well. She sought counselling and fully acknowledged and expressed her rage and sense of betrayal; there was no way she could have, or should have, denied such human feelings and reactions. However, she couldn't help coming back to the fact that she truly loved John, and was prepared and willing to stand by him during this crisis, and to wait and see if he would return to her. John, by the way, was under challenging and disruptive transits at the time: transiting Neptune was square his Sun; transiting Pluto was inconjunct his Sun and still in orb of his natal Venus-Pluto square; and transiting Saturn and Uranus were both in the 7th, the house of marriage, accurately symbolising his conflict and indecision about staying with his wife (Saturn) or disrupting the relationship for something new (Uranus). He did go to live with his girlfriend, but eventually came back to Laura, vowing a strong new committment to her. Since then, they have made constructive changes in their relationship. Before the crisis, both of them had begun to feel like an old married couple, so after they reunited, they decided that at least once or twice a year they should leave the kids with Laura's sister and vacation on their own—a chance to be lovers rather than just mommy and daddy around the house. They instinctively were drawn to exotic and adventurous holiday destinations, which I'm sure helped to assuage John's transiting Uranus in the 7th, not to mention that transit of Uranus over Laura's Moon-Jupiter conjunction in Sagittarius. And they lived happily ever after. No, I can't promise that, but I can say that Laura's story is a good example of the kinds of issues raised by a Venus-Neptune square, and I'm pleased it worked out well for them. I remember Isabel Hickey saying that people born with this square were college students in the school of evolution, enrolled in an advanced course testing spiritual growth and development in terms of the capacity to feel and demonstrate a "higher," unconditional, selfless love rather than a love based purely on personal, ego-centred needs. In my opinion, Laura passed the test with flying colours.

THE PSYCHOLOGY OF EROTIC LOVE

A DISCUSSION OF VENUS AND SEXUALITY

BY LIZ GREENE

There has already been a fair amount of discussion of Venus and sexuality, and I would like now to focus on the aspects of Venus to other planets in relation to sexual tastes and expression. So it is likely to get more colourful as we go on.

There are one or two initial points I wanted to make. Firstly, I would like to draw a distinction between what I am calling erotic love, and what might be called the instinct to procreate. There is often an interesting overlap between these two, as may be seen in those typical situations where a couple are really hot for each other until a child is conceived, and then everything mysteriously shuts down. It might seem at times as if erotic love is one of the psyche's great tricks, arising solely to draw a couple together, and ultimately serving the procreative urge and the continuity of the species. But I do not believe this is the case. They are very different needs, and are reflected by different astrological factors.

If I were to connect the procreative instinct with planetary symbols, I would look at the Moon and Pluto in particular as belonging to this basic form of sexual expression which is part of every animal species. But we are not wholly animal, and our need for the imaginative, emotional and spiritual or symbolic dimensions of sex is as innate as the reproductive urge. The Moon is more differentiated than Pluto, and encompasses the creation and continuity of the family unit; but this too may be seen everywhere in nature in different forms.

Equally, I would not equate the Neptunian longing for fusion with what I refer to as erotic love. Sexual expression can incorporate many different needs in a single physical act, and Neptune's pull back to the waters of the womb may be one of them. But with Neptune, the sexual act is really only a vehicle, a means of transcending the anxiety of aloneness and separateness, and it is very different in feeling-tone from Venusian eroticism. There is sometimes a compulsive quality to Neptunian desire which reveals the underlying anxiety. A woman may need to be filled up, to ease her own emptiness; and a man may need to disappear into the maternal container so that he does not suffer loneliness. Sexuality can also reflect Mars, and contain elements of conquest and domination; and Plutonian sexuality may express the need to possess and overpower. Neither of these urges is really concerned with pleasure, as is the Venusian instinct.

Obviously there is no such thing as purely Venusian sexual expression, since every birth chart contains a complicated pattern of signs, house placements and aspect configurations. So I am drawing rather artificial distinctions here, but I am trying to get closer to some kind of understanding of that word "erotic." I spoke quite a lot about the "art" of love when I was discussing the mythology of Aphrodite, and emphasised the imaginative or fantasy component in Venusian expression. Venus needs to ornament, to civilise, to transform something instinctual into something symbolic and psychic—that is, of the psyche, the soul. The process of human creativity is, in part, concerned with the transformation of instinctual urges through the magical medium of the imagination. You should read Jung's *Symbols of Transformation*,[19] which is concerned with precisely this issue. Erotic love reflects the imaginative process at work on the primal instinct of procreation— as Plato called it, passion aroused by beauty.

Erotic love concerns individual relationship, because beauty is a highly individual business, and reflects individual values. So erotic love may be seen as a form of communication—the airy side of Venus—which differentiates it from the procreative urge, which could satisfy itself through any fertile member of the species. Venusian sexuality is a profound expression of individuality, a unique selection of the beloved from a million others who might serve the same biological purpose. It is a creative act, rather than a compulsion. This brings me to another distinction I wish to make,

---

[19]C. G. Jung, *Symbols of Transformation*, Vol. 5, *The Collected Works of C. G. Jung*, trans. R. F. Hull (Princeton, NJ: Princeton University Press, 1956; and London: Routledge & Kegan Paul, 1956).

between sexual taste and sexual compulsion. Taste is a matter of choice and, as I have said, of individual values. Compulsion is mutually exclusive with choice; one simply *must* perform a particular act, and often there is great shame, not only about the act itself, but about the impotence one feels when in the grip of a compulsion. If we consider the awesome range of human sexual preferences, we will rapidly discover that many of these are not really preferences at all, but are compulsions.

Now inevitably the question arises of whether there are "normal" and "abnormal" sexual preferences and tastes. This is a highly charged area of discussion, as is evidenced by the various laws made over the centuries which prohibit one or another sexual act. It is even a highly charged issue among astrologers, who persist in describing certain aspects as implying "perverted" sexual behaviour. It may be argued that sexual activity between two consenting adults is the business of those two adults alone, and we have the right to interfere as a society only when someone is unwillingly victimised, such as in a case of child abuse or rape. But then we are on broader ground, and are speaking of "criminal" or "antisocial" rather than sexually "abnormal" behaviour. You can see what a complicated business it all is.

My own feeling, as an astrologer and an analyst, is that, apart from the broader issue of injuring an unwilling victim, a particular form of sexual expression is a problem only if it becomes a problem for that individual. In other words, if someone is tormented or distressed by his or her own compulsions, then there is a problem. But if it is a preference, and does not cause the individual to suffer conflict, and the partner is consenting, then I do not feel I am in any position to pass moral judgment about what is normal or abnormal for that person. Sexual expression is a manifestation of the whole personality, and there are many permutations which can occur within the framework of what is "normal" for any particular individual. And that is as much as I can say about it. So you will find, as I talk about the aspects of other planets to Venus, that I will not be describing these issues from the perspective of normal, abnormal or perverted. If someone comes along for a chart reading, and they are suffering conflict or pain around some sexual issue, then the chart can be extremely helpful in highlighting the emotional issues which might contribute toward the conflict. If there are compulsive patterns at work in a person's sexual life, these will usually reflect parental rather than specifically sexual *ℎ* issues, since I have found that where we are compulsive, the family complexes are usually alive and kicking within us. These family patterns may or may not include a sexual level of expression, but often I have found that the same psychological dynamic is at work in two people, one of whom expresses the conflict sexually and the other in some altogether different arena of life.

So, in sum, I feel Venus tells us about what is most beautiful and pleasurable and "right" for an individual in terms of erotic fulfilment, but Venus may be distorted, blocked or mixed up with other issues because of our unconscious compulsions. Since our compulsions are usually parent-linked, they are also linked with the universal human dilemma of separation; and I would even go as far as suggesting that we cannot fully live Venus until we are separate enough from parents and family background to develop our own individual tastes and values. Ambivalence is the charac- *ℓ* teristic emotional tone of most compulsions, and reflects the profound and primal problem of wanting to leave the womb and wanting to stay in it at the same time. We unconsciously express our regressive longing through many symbolic gestures and actions, some of which are reflected in sexual compulsions.

For example, a man may be a compulsive transvestite, who slips on his wife's underclothes while she is out not because he enjoys it, but because he cannot stop himself. Such a compulsion can make a more conventionally minded man feel deeply ashamed and guilty; he may begin to lie, which compounds the guilt; and if he is caught, and his wife is equally conventional in her thinking, the results can be devastating—he may lose his home, his marriage, his children and his social standing because of his "perversion." He may know the danger, and it may well be part of the compulsive excitement of his cross-dressing; and he may even unconsciously set himself up to be caught because he feels he deserves to be punished. What then are we looking at? It is rather pointless to look at his Venus square Saturn or opposition Neptune and say that it "makes" him perverted. These aspects say nothing about cross-dressing. But if we look at his compulsion through symbolic eyes, we can see that, in becoming a woman for a time, wearing and smelling and touching a woman's undergarments, he is drawing closer to some comforting as well as erotic feminine image which he cannot experience in any other way. And what might this image be? I would be much more interested in helping him to explore his early life with his mother, and discovering what feelings he experienced that seemed so compulsively necessary to him, than in classifying his transvestite compulsion as "perverted."

Venus' erotic preferences can also be identified because they bring joy, whereas compulsions, while often providing tremendous excitement as well as release of a kind, are rarely joyful. Sadomasochistic sexual behaviour, for example, has little or no joy in it, although it is usually highly compulsive on both sides. Such patterns are rarely connected with Venus in the chart, except in terms of style and ambience. The desire to inflict pain is usually connected with the desperate need to feel powerful; it compensates for the profound terror of being helpless, victimised and tormented at the hands of a parent with whom one is erotically enmeshed. There is great rage in such behaviour, which is linked with feelings of deep impotence and compulsive parental attachment rather than sexual delight. The sexual masochist at the receiving end merely acts out the unconscious side of the sadist, and vice versa; both suffer from the same wound, which may in other people not be sexualised at all, but may be displayed in subtler, noncorporeal ways. Divorce lawyers are familiar with the term "mental cruelty," which is a nonsexual form of sadism rooted in the same kind of complex.

Sexual expression, as I have said, is a reflection of the whole person, not a thing unto itself; and many sexual compulsions are not really about erotic love at all. This is the point I am making with the examples I have given. Because the body is the first experience we have of ourselves, early wounding and trouble in the mother-baby bonding process are often reflected later in life through sexual compulsions. This relates to Howard's talk on the Moon and "first love."[20] Erotic feeling is a normal part of a baby's world, as well as of its mother's, through the experiences of nursing and touching and cuddling. If too many destructive, manipulative or humiliating

---

[20]See "First Love," in Part One: The Moon, in *The Luminaries*, Volume 3 of *Seminars in Psychological Astrology*.

elements enter into this earliest relationship which is so body-focussed, it is not surprising that these elements will surface in adult life when we are back again in a naked, intimate embrace with another person. These issues are lunar rather than Venusian, but usually they get very entangled with each other, and it may be important to disentangle them in order to understand what we need for our own fulfilment.

There is no planet aspecting Venus which I would consider "bad" or intrinsically pathological in terms of sexual expression. Even difficult contacts such as Venus-Saturn or Venus-Chiron reflect emotional conflicts which, although they may become enmeshed with sexual issues, have more to do with the person's sense of self-worth, or lack thereof. Since I don't wish to do a cookbook list—you know the sort, Venus-Sun, Venus-Moon, Venus-Mercury and so on in order—I will move around with these aspects as the spirit takes me. Someone asked me about the meaning of Chiron earlier, and I would like to begin with Venus-Chiron contacts, since this gives me a chance to deal with both issues at once. I have taken my time observing Chiron, and am now convinced, after several years of watching it, that it is extremely important and should be placed in the birth chart as well as tracked in progressions and transits. That is why you have not heard me talk about it in past seminars; I feel uncomfortable teaching theory unless I have direct practical experience to back the theory up. I have got this now with Chiron, so I am including it in this session on Venus aspects, and you will be hearing Howard and me mentioning it throughout the week.

Chiron seems to partake of both Saturn and Uranus, between whose orbits it moves, and appears to have both a personal dimension and a collective one. I have found that it reflects an area where one feels deeply wounded in some way, irrevocably damaged by factors over which one has no control. In this way it resembles Saturn, which usually describes that sphere in which we feel inadequate, inferior or unable to express ourselves freely, and where we tend to build rigid defenses which protect our great vulnerability. But Chiron's wound is different from Saturn's. Usually Saturn reflects the parental background quite faithfully; it describes qualities which were somehow lacking, thwarted or misused within the family psyche, and which were either given no encouragement or were actively undermined in one's childhood. But Chiron seems to reflect a more general source of hurt, usually a collective problem, which makes it impossible to "blame" anybody in particular. It is a sort of "rotten luck" planet, and this impersonal quality reflects its connections with Uranus and the other outer planets. Where Saturn compensates with highly personal defence mechanisms, Chiron turns us philosophical, for only a broader vision of life can help us cope with the wound.

The mythology of Chiron is very telling in this respect. The name Chiron (more correctly, *Cheiron*) means "hand"; from this word we get the term "cheiromancy," the art of reading palms. Chiron's parentage varies in myth. Sometimes he is presented as the son of Centaurus, the child of Ixion (who offended Zeus and was imprisoned forever in Tartaros, tied to a burning wheel). This Centaurus sired several half-horse, half-human progeny on Magnesian mares, most of whom were wild and drunken (like the satyrs, another half-animal, half-human mix); but Chiron was the wisest and most civilised. In another version of his birth, he is the son of Kronos (Saturn) and the nymph Philyra, who turned herself into a mare in order to avoid the old Titan's attentions. Saturn being Saturn, however, doggedly persisted in his courtship, eventually turning himself into a stallion to win his prize. The grotesque child of this union was Chiron; his mother abandoned him in disgust and he was subsequently raised by the god Apollo, who taught him the art of prophecy. Chiron is therefore a god, but he is also an animal, with a bestial as well as a divine face. He makes numerous appearances in the myths of the heroes, usually as their wise tutor, possessed of the gifts of prophecy and healing. Yet Chiron is also a savage hunter, a dark and disturbing figure whose wisdom does not cancel out his primordial nature.

The story of Chiron's wounding has several variations. According to one, the hero Herakles, engaged in a furious battle with a group of drunken centaurs, accidentally wounded his old friend Chiron in the knee with a poisoned arrow. The poison was the blood of the monstrous Hydra, the nine-headed creature which Herakles had to destroy as one of his Twelve Labours, and all his arrows were tainted with it. Although the hero drew out the arrow, and Chiron himself supplied the healing herbs for dressing the wound, they were of no avail, and he retired howling in agony to his cave. Yet he could not die, because he was immortal. In another version of the story, Chiron was accidentally wounded by a poisoned arrow that pierced his left foot while he and the young Achilles were entertaining Herakles on Mount Pelion in Thessaly. After nine days of agony, Zeus took pity and placed Chiron among the stars, as the constellation of the Centaur. It is important to note that in all the versions of this tale, the injury is accidental, and the wound cannot be healed.

I would recommend Melanie Reinhart's book, *Chiron and the Healing Journey*,[21] in which she discusses the psychological dimensions of this myth in great depth. I would like to focus on this issue of the accidental wound, because it reflects a basic unfairness in life which I feel we have a very hard time accommodating. Those of us involved in astrology (and psychology, for that matter) are particularly inclined to find "answers" for human suffering, and this is one of the themes which seems to surround the planet Chiron. In order to cope with the feelings of woundedness, we tend to seek intellectual or spiritual understanding, because the idea of a disorderly or chaotic universe, where unpleasant things happen accidentally or undeservedly, is a deep offense to our Judeo-Christian ethos. But there seems to be no answer to Chiron. One cannot blame anybody, not even oneself. Plato believed that 95 percent of the universe was under the benign governorship of Reason, but 5 percent belonged to Chaos, and could not be explained or controlled. Chiron seems to embody that five per cent, which we keep trying to justify by philosophical concepts such as karma, or psychological concepts such as family complexes. Neither of these approaches is very helpful when dealing with Chiron, natally or in transit or progression.

So Chiron requires us to accommodate a wound which will not heal, regardless of how much psychotherapy, meditation, homeopathy, acupuncture, macrobiotic dieting or astrologising we do. Learning to accommodate this wound usually involves great effort at understanding why, as far as understanding can go; and while Saturn builds protective bastions against the threat of injury, Chiron attempts to become philosophical about it all. The fruit of this is not only a deeper and broader grasp of the issues around

---

[21]Melanie Reinhart, *Chiron and the Healing Journey* (New York: Penguin, 1990).

Chiron's sign, house and aspects; it is also a more tolerant and
compassionate attitude toward people and life in general. Chiron
forces us to grow up, for it is really the child in us who cries, "But it
isn't *fair*!"

Wounding in the knee or foot may reflect something about
injury to our capacity to stand firmly, and to move out into life with
confidence. Freud thought that wounding in the foot in dreams
was an image of castration. Our feeling of potency is injured by
Chiron. The understanding or skill we develop (*cheiron*, the Greek
word for hand, suggests being skilled, handy, accomplished) compensates for our feelings of impotence and pain. If we put together
Chiron and Venus, then there is likely to be a wound to our sense
of self-worth, our belief that we are beautiful and lovable. This is
often reflected by a sense of woundedness around the body (the
Taurean side of Venus), a feeling of being ugly or flawed in an
irrevocable way. Although there may be no justification for this
feeling in adult life, there is often a kind of "unfair" justification in
childhood – one might be the only black child in the
neighbourhood, for example, or one might be overweight, or one
might not fit the prevailing collective standards of good looks.
Children can be extremely cruel with their mockery and rejection
of anyone "different" (as can adults), and this is one of the "unfair"
facts of life which Venus-Chiron often has to face.

Whom can we blame for such things? Venus-Chiron often compensates by developing great skill at beautification and ornament;
it is one of the aspects which I have come to associate with considerable talent in fields such as fashion design and beauty therapy.
Because Venus is also connected with the body's pleasure, with
sensuality and erotic fulfilment, there may also be a feeling of
woundedness or inadequacy here as well; and often the compensation is the development of erotic skills, such as the Greek *hetairas*
acquired. Venus-Chiron may become a talented lover, who is
drawn to relationships with those who are equally wounded and
need healing. The Libran side of Venus may also reflect Chiron's
wound, and a sense of isolation and inability to relate to others is
sometimes reflected by this aspect. There may be great shyness
and diffidence, and a feeling of being different and unacceptable.
The person may make great efforts to learn as much as possible
about human relationships, and may make a skilled marriage

counsellor or therapist. You can see that all these typical Venus-Chiron compensations are likely to be deeply satisfying and rewarding. But they do not make the wound go away.

Audience: Is Venus-Chiron like Chiron in the 7th?

Liz: There is a similar feeling, as there also is with Chiron in Libra. But the issues around the body, and the feeling of being unattractive or worthless, do not seem to be the focus with Chiron in Libra or the 7th. That is more a reflection of Chiron in Taurus or the 2nd house.

Audience: Can Venus-Chiron be a motivation to learn more about love?

Liz: Yes, certainly. That is what I meant when I said that the person may make a great effort to learn about human relationships, emotional and intellectual as well as sexual. The motivation to transform a wound into an art is very powerful with Venus-Chiron. That is the most creative dimension of the aspect. The darker side is of course the ongoing pain, which may lie quietly under the surface but will usually break into consciousness when the aspect is triggered by transits or by someone else's planets in a synastry contact, or even by the planets in the composite chart of a relationship. There is also a manipulative component which I have observed with these Chiron wounds, as there is with Saturn— Venus-Chiron, like Venus-Saturn, may repeatedly choose partners who are themselves wounded, because one feels "normal" in comparison. As the old saying goes, in the country of the blind, the one-eyed man is king. Chiron is readily projected, just like Saturn, especially when it is square or opposition Venus; it is much more difficult to live consciously with one's feeling of inadequacy. When the wound is projected, it is the partner who has the "incurable" problem, and one may have an unconscious investment in their *not* healing.

I have also frequently seen Venus-Chiron try to compensate by "transcending" the wound. This may involve a philosophy which prescribes overcoming the lower nature, and rising above such base things as erotic urges. It is an attempt to spiritualise sexuality in order to avoid the woundedness of the body. This usually causes considerable trouble, because Venus does not enjoy being transcended. It will be obvious that the mythic Aphrodite is hardly going to put up with this sort of attitude; and the planet, like the goddess, will usually take revenge by striking from behind. Then one falls desperately in love with a totally unsuitable person, and discovers that inner planets should not be messed about with.

Audience: I remember that when Chiron was crossing my Ascendant by transit, I had a lot of dreams about wounded men whom I had to heal.

Liz: Chiron transits are extremely interesting to watch if you want verification of these mythic themes of wounding and healing. I am not surprised by what you say, as I have encountered this dream motif before with powerful movements of Chiron.

Audience: Would you be wounded by a Chiron transit, or healed?

Liz: It seems to do both. The type of experiences which I have seen accompanying a Chiron transit seems to reconnect the person with much older hurts, and there is often a lot of pain involved. But it is usually not unproductive pain; realisations occur at the same time, and one has the chance to face issues from the past that need dealing with. This does not mean nothing "good" ever happens under a Chiron transit. There are sometimes reconciliations or resolutions of old conflicts. But I am not inclined to glamourise this planet, since I think it is a very difficult one for us to deal with. The uncivilised nature of Chiron in myth is reflected in the sometimes sudden and painful nature of Chiron experiences in actual life, and this often involves becoming uncivilised oneself, or being exposed to another person's emotional explosiveness. I mentioned earlier that there is a Uranian component in Chiron, and it seems to show itself through the suddenness of events which occur around a Chiron transit.

There is a great paradox in this business of wounding and healing. Often we carry hurts about which we know nothing; they lie in the unconscious and we do not understand the powerful effect they have on our outward behaviour. A Chiron transit, by pulling the defensive cover off these old wounds, can be healing because we become more conscious of who we are. This is a kind of cliché in psychotherapy—it is when we begin to feel our conflicts and our pain that we are on the threshold of healing, or coming to terms with things. When something is unconscious it cannot grow or change. So, like Uranus, Chiron is an awakener, even though the awakening may come through a painful experience.

Audience: What sign do you think Chiron rules?

Liz: I really don't know. I am not very happy about assigning it to any sign. I know that some people associate it with either Virgo or Sagittarius. But it does not really belong to our solar system; it is a maverick, a big asteroid which wandered in and got caught by the gravitational pull of the Sun. Eventually it will leave again, like a comet does. Because of this alien quality, I am uncomfortable about slotting it neatly into the planetary rulership system. Its behaviour in psychological terms is that of an alien who has wandered in; and I work with it as though it had no rulership of any sign. It is a kind of indigestible, wild bit of life, like Plato's 5 percent of chaos.

I would like now to look at Venus-Moon aspects. Howard has discussed these aspects quite comprehensively,[22] but there are one or two points I would like to add about the archetypal dynamic between these two planets. I mentioned already that there is an innate conflict between the maternal and erotic, symbolically reflected in the enmity between Aphrodite and Hera in myth. The hard aspects between Venus and the Moon are particularly important in terms of love and relationship, because the security needs are in conflict with personal values, and there is often a deeply uncomfortable feeling that one must choose between them. I do not believe squares and oppositions "fate" us to have to make such a choice; but this is how the hard aspects make us feel. Because any planet aspecting the Moon has relevance to the psychological inheritance from the mother, a hard Venusian aspect (or for that matter the sextile, trine and conjunction as well) implies a conflict in the mother between these two sides of her own feminine nature.

---

[22]See "First Love" in Part One: The Moon, in *The Luminaries,* Volume 3 of *Seminars in Psychological Astrology,* p. 62ff.

If we are given such a model, we will not at first see how the two opponents could be reconciled.

Jung wrote about the problem of a "split anima" in men, between the mother image and the image of the beloved. This conflict often results in a man marrying a maternal woman and, finding himself deeply dissatisfied on the erotic and soul levels, creating a second relationship with a lover or mistress. Usually in such a case the mother repressed one side of her nature (usually the erotic), which communicated itself to her son in a very powerful unconscious way. Venus-Moon conflicts in men tend to reflect a propensity for dividing women up into those who are appropriate to marry, and those who are good to take to bed; and the two seem in eternal opposition. That there might be women who combine the two seems to elude such a person. If the man leaves his wife and marries his mistress, he will soon begin to perceive her as maternal, and will once again seek his erotic fulfilment outside the marriage. The fear of the mother's unconscious sexual feelings is usually so great that it is too disturbing to allow a partner to be both sexually and intellectually exciting, and emotionally supportive and containing as well.

In women with these aspects, the issue is the same, but the split usually appears within the woman herself, rather than being projected onto a partner. If the mother represses her Venusian side in favour of the security of home and family, she will inevitably feel jealousy when her young daughter begins to develop as an attractive young woman — particularly if the relationship with the husband is fraught. Thus Venus-Moon often suggests a deep, albeit unconscious, rivalry between mother and daughter. In order to remove herself from her mother's domain, the daughter may reject all maternal identification, acting out her mother's shadow instead and becoming a true *hetaira* who relates to men through the Venusian erotic and intellectual channels the mother cannot reach. Such a daughter will usually be Daddy's favourite, unconsciously playing his anima, and finding that she winds up in triangles later in life involving married men.

Equally often, I have seen this rivalry between mother and daughter generate a great fear of the mother, which may result in the daughter suppressing her own erotic side in order to stay out of the line of fire. One can sometimes see the scenario of the attractive, sexually provocative mature woman with a plain, overweight daughter trailing downcast behind her; the daughter has been so undermined by her mother's unconscious sabotage that she has opted to stifle her own Venusian self-worth as a woman. When such a daughter grows up, she will invariably choose a man who wants her for her maternal qualities, and will usually wind up having to contend with a rival in the form of her husband's mistress, who, as I have suggested, suffers from exactly the same conflict, expressed in mirror image reverse.

I am to some extent caricaturing these Venus-Moon dynamics; but one can see them displayed to a greater or lesser degree, and sometimes just as floridly as I have portrayed them. Jealousy and rivalry between women is a characteristic of Venus-Moon, even with the soft aspects; although much depends on how the mother has handled her own issue. On the simple interpretation level, Venus-Moon reflects a challenge to combine these two facets of the feminine, because one possesses both to equal degrees, and needs to find a way to live them. The more negative face of these aspects tends to make its appearance partly because, until quite recently, motherhood really ended a woman's Venusian life. Before the advent of birth control, she could not decide when to have a child, or how many; and, equally importantly, on a collective level there was something "wrong" with a mother who enjoyed herself too much and "ignored" her child—not to mention the "abnormal" woman who opted not to have children at all. Despite many changes in the collective image of women, we are still faced with the great challenge of balancing Venus and the Moon. For a person with these planets in strong aspect in the birth chart, this challenge is one of the major themes of life.

Audience: Is this similar to Venus in Cancer, or the Moon in Libra?

Liz: Some of these elements are present, particularly with the Moon in Libra, because this also makes a statement about the mother. We might say that the Moon in Libra reflects a Venusian mother, a woman who possessed a strong aesthetic sense and a need for lightness and romance in her life. Whether she lived this or not, the chart cannot tell us, although other placements such as Saturn, Neptune or Pluto in aspect to the Moon or in the 10th might suggest she did not. Venus in Cancer does not make the same statement about the mother; it reflects a person's own individual values, which are likely to be traditional and family-based, although not devoid of romantic feeling. Sometimes in myth Aphrodite favours marriage, as long as the erotic side of the marriage has some life in it. Our modern exponent of this combination is Barbara Cartland, whose novels, although appallingly written, seem to sell in millions. These books invariably present a highly charged sexual attraction which ends in a happy marriage.

The Moon in Libra, and Venus in Cancer, both combine Venusian aestheticism and romantic feeling with a need for security and roots. But they do not in themselves suggest a split, of the kind I spoke about earlier. This kind of splitting is characteristic of the two planets combining, for a planet is a dynamic energy, and each has its own "personality" and needs. Ancient Greek society built this split into its structure, by creating two classes of women — wives who stayed at home, bore children, and looked after the household, and *hetairas*, who provided intellectual, aesthetic and erotic pleasure and stimulation. There is of course a replay of this in modern times, although it is not made explicit; and understandably many women are quite fed up with it.

Audience: I am a man with a Venus-Moon square, and I find that I can't enjoy romance without actually thinking of making it permanent.

Liz: I am not sure whether you think that is a problem; I would not say it was, unless you are trying to pattern yourself after a collective image of how men are supposed to behave in relationships. But the need for romance and stability together is what happens when the two planets combine their energies. If you don't feel a split between them, why should you want to create one?

Audience: My need for security is a little obsessive. I can't just enjoy someone's company, I am thinking of ways to bind them right from the start.

Liz: I think there may be other factors involved here, such as a deep insecurity which makes you feel you cannot relax without guarantees of permanent love. This suggests a problem with separation, which is not really a Venus issue. Because of this anxiety, there might be too much weight on the Moon, and Venus is not really being consciously lived – in other words, you do not value yourself enough, but depend instead on formal commitment to ensure that you are loved. Do you have a Venus-Saturn aspect, or a Moon-Saturn?

Audience: I have the Moon in semisquare to Saturn, which is in the 7th house.

Liz: Then I would emphasise that your "heaviness" in relationships springs more from a deep fear of rejection – probably a legacy of your childhood – and not from the combination of Venus and the Moon, which rightly needs a blend of domesticity and erotic pleasure. This is the signature of a romantic, not of a Don Juan, although many men are so frightened of their romanticism that they are compelled to play Don Juan to avoid feeling vulnerable.

Audience: What about homosexual relationships?

Liz: The dynamic is the same. If Venus and the Moon are in conflict, we can identify with one and project the other on a member of the same sex, just as easily as on one of the opposite sex. In most relationships, heterosexual or homosexual, one partner usually aligns more with the "caretaker" role and the other more with the "beloved playmate" role. Hopefully one can have some of both, and in a dynamic relationship these roles are fluid and both people will play them at different times. Where there are Venus-Moon conflicts, it can go to extremes, and the roles become fixed and almost archetypal because of the projections involved. The same propensity for triangles exists in a gay relationship with Venus-Moon conflicts, and also the same requirement to combine security needs with erotic fulfilment.

Audience: I have a friend, a woman of 64, who has Venus conjunct the Moon and square Mars. She has always had lovers younger than herself, and has never had any children. Now she keeps finding herself in competition with the mothers of her boyfriends.

Liz: The penchant for beautiful young men is a characteristic of Aphrodite, who unlike the Moon is ageless and transcends time; and it seems that your friend has identified all her life with Venus, and has acted this out in her relationships. But the lunar side of her nature has obviously been deeply suppressed, and the rival has materialised not just in the form of a "maternal" wife, but in the literal guise of her lovers' mothers. The lunar need for family seems to have surfaced in an unconscious choice of son-lovers. Probably these mothers she antagonises are very like herself, but with the split tilting the opposite way.

Audience: She doesn't believe me when I explain it this way.

Liz: Well, why should she? It is much easier to blame those horrible mothers for her troubles. If a person identifies so completely with one planetary principle, there is not a lot of room for objectivity about oneself, because archetypal energies have a way of taking over consciousness and distorting our perceptions of life.

Audience: I would like to make a comment about living both Venus and the Moon together. In the Middle Ages it was acceptable to be married yet have an adoring lover who wrote you poetry and went on knightly quests for you, but didn't have a sexual relationship with you. But that kind of romance is not acceptable now, and your partner might not like it.

Liz: You are describing the strange ethos of courtly love, which reached its height in France in the 12th century with the love songs of the troubadours. This may initially seem like a way of resolving the Venus-Moon dilemma, but I feel it is really a Neptunian path, incorporating a sacrificial element which is in fact inimical to Venus. Also, it arose out of a medieval Catholic collective, and although it was sometimes considered heretical (because of its links with the Cathar heresy), devaluing of the body and of erotic feeling was implicit in its philosophy. Courtly love required that the woman be married; and although the rules were constantly broken by imperfect mortals, its philosophy required abstinence on both parts, and considerable frustration and suffering which, in theory, transformed base love into a spiritual experience. Any psychoanalyst would read this setup as highly Oedipal, since the passion of courtly love depended on the object remaining unobtainable—the adored parent who is forbidden because of the incest taboo and the parental marriage. In the end you must sacrifice your fantasy of perfect love with your father because he is married to your mother. In psychoanalytic terms, this process of Oedipal defeat and sacrifice, if it is not too harsh or humiliating, is one of the building blocks of the mature ego. In the Middle Ages, it gave rise to a terrible sexual intensity, an erotic swoon that bordered on a religious experience. This is Neptunian stuff, not Venusian.

I have met people, particularly those with Venus-Neptune aspects, who still pursue such a sacrificial love, although they usually do not do it because of a mystical-artistic philosophy. They do it because they cannot help themselves; they are in the grip of a compulsion. They find themselves desperately longing for someone who is unobtainable in one way or another (married, a member of the priesthood, living four thousand miles away, or just emotionally uninterested or incapable of commitment), and I think the Freudians are right in connecting this kind of compulsion with an unresolved Oedipal dilemma.

Venus, as we have seen when we explored the mythology of Aphrodite, is not inclined to sacrifice anything at all, let alone the pleasure and fulfilment of the body. Nor is the Moon sacrificial by nature, although it is sympathetic. The courtly love triangle is not a way of resolving the Venus-Moon dilemma, but is an escape from it. If there is a conflict between Venus and the Moon in a chart, but there is a benign aspect from Venus to Neptune (or something similar), the individual may use the trine to escape the friction of the hard angle. We tend to do this with our trines, because they are reliably comfortable; and it is human enough to avoid the difficulties involved in confronting both ends of a hard aspect by jumping out of the hot place into the gentle harmony of another planet's trine. That is why Grand Trines are so ambivalent; they offer gifts, talent and luck, but they provide a perfect cocoon in which to hide from one's T-square or Grand Cross. Dealing with Venus-Moon in an honest way is not a very glamourous or mystical pursuit, since it confronts us with our all too human needs.

I remember reading a rather amusing article in a magazine some time ago, written by a woman whose complaint was that mothers did not look like proper mothers any more. She felt there was something deeply offensive about women who could carry off wearing their daughters' clothes, and looked as though they were still sexually alive and exciting, instead of settling into comfortable middle age with a nice padding of extra weight, a tightly permed head of grey hair, dowdy clothes, and no interest in flirting with the daughter's handsome boyfriend. I found it fascinating that someone would write such an article, because it seems to reflect a change which is taking place in the collective. Once upon a time things were so apparently simple; mother was Moon and daughter was Venus, until she married and became mother, at which point granddaughter was Venus, and so on. This is very comforting, and also very ancient and archetypal; but it does not take into account the real human problem of all that frustrated unconscious life which surrounds an unlived planet and spawns all kinds of family complexes.

Audience: What happens if Mars is linked up with a Venus-Moon square?

Liz: Perhaps we should look at Venus-Mars now. Many writers describe this aspect as contributing a considerable degree of sexual charisma and attractiveness, for they are complementary principles and in myth are portrayed as lovers. The characters of both Aphrodite and Ares are self-centred and self-gratifying, although their approaches are different; and in this sense they have a lot in common, as do the signs Aries and Libra. If you watch an Aries and a Libra operating together, you will see how deeply similar they are. Aries is usually very direct, coming straight out and saying, "Do it my way." Libra says, "What a good idea. But I would feel happier sitting down for just a few minutes and making sure we've looked at every point of view, even though of course you are right." After several hours of long, convoluted discussions, Aries finds that the plan has changed considerably from the original, but still thinks that it is his or her idea; and the Libran goes away smiling because everyone is happy. Both are cardinal signs, and reflect the wilfulness of their rulers. So you can see that combining the planetary principles will produce a very powerful drive toward pleasure and self-gratification, combining Venusian style and Martial assertion, which is difficult for an innocent bystander to resist.

Audience: If they conjunct in Aries, does that make the Martial side stronger?

Liz: In outer behaviour, yes; the assertive qualities will show more obviously through the personality. If the conjunction occurs in a Venus-ruled sign, then the Venus component will be more obvious. But the signs are really like garments; they describe the manner in which the planets express themselves. But they do not change the nature of the planets. Venus-Mars in Taurus or Libra may be very charming and peaceable, but if you think about the fact that with any Venus-Mars aspect, one's personal values combine with one's aggressive instincts, you will realise that this delightful charm masks the proverbial iron fist in the velvet glove. The Venus-Mars combination, which ultimately serves the development of the Sun, combines fighting power with the capacity to beautify and bring joy. That is a potent combination. If the two planets are in hard aspect, the essential meaning is the same; but on a conscious level the person often feels torn between needing to maintain harmony and needing to assert the self. I have seen the squares and oppositions, and the conjunctions as well, behave in a very contrary way at times, where the individual is all charm and adaptability and grace and then suddenly kicks you in the teeth. This happens when too much identification with one planet results in a backlash from the other one (which is a characteristic of hard aspects).

I am thinking of a client whom I worked with, who has the conjunction in Pisces, with a Libran Ascendant. Venus is therefore his chart ruler, and even more powerful because of its exaltation in Pisces. The Venusian side is at first glance much more obvious in his personality. He can be incredibly sweet and gracious and pleasant and polite, and then suddenly he will say something truly vicious and destructive, intentionally hurtful, whenever his Mars, like Achilles, gets fed up with being dressed in drag. There is a great backlog of rage in this man, because he has identified almost totally with Venus.

Audience: Is he homosexual?

Liz: Not in his sexual tastes. But I think I mentioned earlier that sometimes we can see the same psychological dynamic expressed in different ways through different people. The important issue is not whether he is homosexual or heterosexual, but how he relates to the masculine and feminine sides of himself. He has considerable anger toward women, as well as being very seductive with them; and he practises a covert but not uncommon form of sexual cruelty, a subtle rejection and denigration of women's bodies and sexual desires, as a means of feeling more potent. This is also a characteristic which I have seen quite often when Venus stifles Mars. We might see this as a "sexual" problem, but it is really a problem of potency, for Venus can emasculate Mars, just like in the famous painting, and then Mars sits and seethes in the basement.

If there is too great an identification with Mars, and Venus is blocked, it is the sense of self-value which has been lost, and one of the commonest manifestations is extreme jealousy and possessiveness. Mars is very proud of its autonomy; a Martial temperament truly doesn't give a damn what anyone else thinks. Like Frank Sinatra, they do it *their* way. Venus, on the other hand, feeds off the love and approval of others for its sense of value. Aphrodite could not possibly survive without her crowd of adoring youths at her feet. So you can see that if a person with Venus-Mars tries to be too assertive and macho and tough, there will be a tremendous secret dependency on the love of others for a sense of self-worth.

There is a kind of androgyny in the Venus-Mars combination, which may also be evident in the person's sexual style in a very attractive, creative way. The excitement of challenge and conquest combines with the love of pleasing and being pleased, and this can result in being comfortable with a spectrum of sexual roles, both active and passive. We might say that Venus and Mars, when they are able to blend, offer the person a capacity to understand sexuality from both the male and female points of view, which can give an extremely rich and rewarding erotic life.

Audience: Would this be possible if they are in square?

Liz: Squares and oppositions, as I mentioned earlier in connection with Venus and the Moon, do not mean that we are forced to choose. They reflect the ego's perception that the conflict is irreconcilable, and usually involve the repression, at least in part, of one of the planets involved in the aspect. But the ego's perception is not the only truth, as anyone who has worked in depth psychotherapy will know. Most of the deep transformations which occur in therapeutic work spring from the ego confronting other dimensions and perspectives of the psyche, and changing accordingly. In other words, the distinction between hard and soft aspects is really the difference in how we perceive our reality. Such ego perceptions can be altered and expanded, and nothing shifts them more powerfully than an encounter with what was previously unconscious. I believe that it is possible to get great harmony and benefit from squares and oppositions, although this usually means exploring the unknown dimensions of the personality; and the harmony may not be possible all the time, especially when a difficult transit triggers the natal aspect. In compensation for the bumpiness of the ride, the hard aspects offer a dynamic energy which is very exciting and which, for many people, may be preferable to the easy, relaxed feeling of a trine or sextile. If we can learn to stand in the middle and appreciate both ends of a hard aspect, we may find that it has more to offer than the soft aspects in terms of vital life energy. So, in short, yes, it is possible with a Venus-Mars square.

Family complexes also have a great deal to do with our perceptions, since if we have seen an apparently irreconcilable conflict in the family, we are not going to instantly know that there is a possible route through. We will grow up assuming that such conflict will always exist. Then the mechanism of repression is very understandable, because who wants to be in a state of constant turmoil, perpetually at war with oneself, when there seems no possible resolution? Jung wrote about something he called the *transcendant function*, a reconciling principle which can bring about a creative resolution if one takes a different attitude toward an inner conflict. Usually, as I have said, we disown the uncomfortable end of a hard aspect—or even the entire configuration—and then it appears in our lives outside, over and over again, in one form or another. If we have got as far as recognising our own ambivalence, rather than blaming the external world and the people in it, that is already a great leap forward in learning to handle a hard aspect. With the soft aspects, we seem to have an innate assumption that it is possible to have our cake and eat it too. Because we are open to possibilities (the sextile and trine have been equated respectively with Mercury- and Jupiter-type energies), we can usually find ways of combining the planetary principles without a lot of effort. Venus trine Mars assumes that one can please people and get one's own way at the same time. Venus square Mars worries itself half to death with the fear that one will automatically lose love if one asserts oneself; and the person's behaviour, because of the stress and anger this anxiety generates, may create the very thing they fear. It is difficult for us to see the extent to which we create our own reality and draw predictable responses from others, while thinking we are doing something quite opposite. Yet an objective observer can often see it clearly enough.

Perhaps we could look now at Venus-Uranus aspects. These have a peculiar reputation in terms of sexuality, and a number of older textbooks—and even a few newer ones—refer to perversion and homosexuality. I have already made my point about such classifications. Alternatively, the hard aspects of Venus and Uranus have a reputation for being incapable of commitment, which is also, from what I have seen, not a valid interpretation. We need first to examine Uranus, and have a sense of what this planet really represents, before we combine it with Venus to see what results might arise. In myth, Ouranos is the original sky father (the name means "starry heavens"), who exists before there is a manifest cosmos. Like our Judeo-Christian idea of an invisible, omniscient, transcendant deity, Ouranos symbolises the plan of the universe which precedes its creation. He is what in esoteric teachings is called the Mind of God. One of William Blake's marvellous paintings portrays the Divine Architect bent over his drawing board, wielding a pair of compasses; I have always thought this was the most vivid image for the planet Uranus that I have yet seen. So we are confronting something that is pure collective mind, a perfectly functioning system or design which has yet to be made manifest in the world. When it is manifested, through the Saturn function, it is "castrated" (this is the mythic enactment)—for any idea, once imprisoned in form, is no longer fluid and self-generating, but has become static and bound by time, space and the limits of individuals.

Now we come to the part of the myth where Ouranos fertilises Gaia, the Earth Mother, and she bears him the Titans and the Hundred-Handed Giants. These creatures are earthy and therefore flawed; they do not reflect the perfect idea of the progeny of heaven; so he dooms them to imprisonment in the underworld. The result is that Kronos (Saturn), one of the Titan children, armed with a sickle given to him by his mother, leads his brothers and sisters in a revolt against his father, and castrates him. Amongst other things, this story seems to describe something fundamental to Uranus: an ideal of perfection which, when challenged by a flawed reality, reacts with rejection, repudiation or dissociation – and attempts to imprison the offending reality in the underworld of the unconscious.

In one version of this myth, the drops of blood from Uranus' wound fell on the earth and produced the Erinyes or Furies (goddesses of vengeance), while the severed genitals, falling into the sea, fertilised it and engendered the goddess Aphrodite. This strange image seems to suggest that, although the collective ideal of a perfect world may be shattered, the human urge to create beauty is its offspring. So there is a harmony between Venus and Uranus on the aesthetic and intellectual levels (Libra), but a deep conflict on the "Titanic," body level (Taurus). The archaic Greek myth of Ouranos' conflict with his Titan children was absorbed into early Orphic teaching (the first centuries A.D.) and exercised profound influence on the early Christian church as well, for the earthbound Titans were equated with the sinful, corrupt human body, whose pleasures had to be sacrificed in order to release the spiritual, Uranian spark within.

From the Uranian point of view, no body, however beautiful, can be perfect, simply because it is mortal; and no society, however sound, can measure up to the vision of the perfect world. I think you can begin to see what this combination of planets might produce. On the creative side, there is often considerable artistic talent and intellectual capability, particularly in fields where the aesthetic and the mathematical combine – such as architecture and musical composition. There is also a high ideal of what ought to be possible in the realm of love, and a willingness to look beyond what *is* to what *might be*—hence the reputation for erotic experimentation with which Venus-Uranus is sometimes associated. Venus-Uranus will expand the socially defined rules of relationship in its quest for bringing together ideal and reality, and may abandon quite a few people along the way. But this is not sexual "perversion"—the person's values are constantly buffeted by a changing and ever-expanding collective ideal, and it becomes impossible to "settle" for something simply because no one else has come up with anything better. I remember reading in one of Charles Carter's books that William Blake, who had Venus trine Uranus, maintained a very stable and conventional marriage, but had the curious habit of receiving guests to tea in the nude, because he believed the human form to be divine.

There are also considerable problems inherent in the combination of Venus and Uranus, and these generally circle around denigration of the instinctual side of life. Venus-Uranus does not lack loyalty or the capacity for commitment; but it can have difficulty in sustaining emotional and physical intimacy, because the Uranian perfectionist's eye recoils from too prolonged an exposure to emotional and instinctual needs. There may be a tendency to cut off and dissociate at regular intervals, which comes across as "cold" and can be inadvertantly hurtful to a more watery temperament. And the fantasy of sexual love may always be more exciting and beautiful than the reality, because the sweating bodies get in the way. Venus-Uranus loves thinking about love, and even talking and philosophising about it; but there may be little self-love, because Uranus can devalue Venus' sensual side, and one may project onto others the hated imperfection one unconsciously feels in one's own body.

Audience: Isn't Venus-Uranus very unstable in its affections? I thought it was associated with divorce.

Liz: It was in older textbooks, when divorce was much more difficult and only the brave undertook it. Now you could associate any planetary aspect with divorce, especially in America. But no, I don't believe that Venus-Uranus indicates instability on an emotional level. I have known people with this aspect to be loyal almost to the point of stupidity, because they have a Uranian ideal

of fidelity which ignores the fact that they are miserable in a relationship. But it is very difficult for Venus-Uranus to be happy
within a Saturnian type of marriage, where the primary concerns
are security and family structure. Venus-Uranus needs intellectual
companionship above all, or, put more simply, it needs a friend
before it needs a wife or husband. The hard aspects (especially the
opposition) may reflect a person's tendency to identify with Venus
and disown Uranus, in which case it is usually the partner who
acts out Uranus and leaves. But whenever I have seen a client who
has been left, and I see Venus and Uranus in hard aspect in the
natal chart, I am inclined to wonder whether the errant spouse has
been firmly, albeit unconsciously, driven out, and whether my
client might not be feeling a secret relief in the midst of the pain
and hurt pride.

Venus-Uranus needs a certain amount of practical planning.
Because of the tendency to dissociate from the feelings, and to
measure all relationships against a perfect ideal, there is a deep
need for breathing space in a relationship, so that fantasy can
periodically drive away the oppressive vapours of too much famil-
iarity. The more things are taken for granted in a relationship, the
less room there is for the excitement of surprise and unpredictability. Venus-Uranus, if there is no conscious provision for this, can
display the unpleasant habit of creating crises and breaks in order
to generate an atmosphere of excitement. But the root of this is not
inability to sustain a commitment; it is inability to sustain too much
ordinary life. If we do not recognise such a need in ourselves, we
may clutter up our days with routines and rituals which, although
safe, choke the life out of love. Nothing does this as quickly as
marriage and family, which is why anyone with this aspect needs
to find the courage to build breathing space into the marriage,
rather than having the marriage explode like the proverbial time
bomb.

Venus-Uranus is not, after all, a difficult combination to understand, nor even to work with if certain important factors are taken
into account. If you have this aspect, and your partner has the
habit of doing all the hygienic rituals with the bathroom door open,
stop watching and go for a walk instead, and then your ideal of
beauty won't take such a battering. But the uncompromising and
reforming nature of Uranus can tend to inject an element of inflexi-

bility into one's values, so that another person's perfectly appropriate differences automatically appear as flaws which must be corrected. Also, some very painful difficulties may arise when a person is too insecure to acknowledge their need for periodic withdrawal. If one needs constant emotional reassurance, it may seem very dangerous to say, "I'm going out with my friends for the day, I'll see you this evening." One's partner might retaliate, and then one might be rejected. But if Uranus is repressed for too long, it will find a way to break apart the relationship by one means or another.

Alternatively, if the Venusian side of the aspect is repressed, then the person may go about declaring that he or she isn't interested in commitment, and is a free spirit, and so on; and this kind of behaviour can be exaggeratedly and unnecessarily hurtful, under the guise of "needing space." But sooner or later our blocked planets come to meet us, and you will recognise by now how Aphrodite typically behaves when she is ignored. The repression of instinctual needs which is characteristic of Uranus may eventually erupt as a compulsive passion; or the person may be trapped by an event such as a pregnancy—one's own or one's partner's. I have seen this more than once with Venus-Uranus people who identify too strongly with Uranus.

We can learn a good deal about the natal aspects from watching their dynamic in synastry. When one person's Venus is strongly aspected to another's Uranus—especially by hard aspect—there is often a tremendous electric charge at first meeting (the classic "love at first sight" experience). But the synastry aspect rightly has a reputation for instability, because once the relationship becomes closer and more familiar, a tension develops which pushes the people apart as often as it draws them together. Usually it is the Uranus person who abruptly withdraws, emotionally or physically, leaving the Venus person anxious and unhappy. But this may be unconscious, which is why sometimes it seems to be the other way around—it may be the Venus person who acts out the withdrawal, fed up with the instability of the relationship and giving the Uranus person a jolt which may ultimately help them to discover their own Uranian needs.

Although erotic fantasy may be extremely important for a person with Venus-Uranus in the natal chart, sexual experiences are often a vehicle through which one gets in touch with a more incorporeal level of relationship. In alchemy, there is a process called the *sublimatio,* in which the *prima materia,* the base matter, is distilled through the cooking process into an invisible vapour which is its essence. Uranus subjects us to this kind of experience; it breaks apart the concrete form of any personal planet it touches, releasing an essence or core idea which is much like Plato's concept of the Divine Idea preceding manifest reality. This emphasises the Libran dimension of Venus, while denying the Taurean. Viewed through a Uranian perspective, physical love is a symbol, a reflection of something nontangible that exists beyond time and space and the experiences of the body. Venus-Uranus often has a unique capacity to love the idea of the individual, their human essence, the meaning of their existence; but it is harder to love the flesh day in and day out, and there is often a curious detachment which allows the Venus-Uranus person to maintain the idea of the relationship's continuity even if the relationship itself has ended or is severed by circumstance. This may be reflected by the typical Venus-Uranus request: "But can't we remain friends?" Venus-Uranus can comprehend the deeper meaning of friendship, which exists whether you are with your friend or not. One may not see a friend for ten years; but nothing has changed, and the friendship remains despite time and distance. You can see that this aspect does not deny the ability to love; but it is the kind of love which may be inexplicable and even profoundly painful to many people.

I have mentioned that the darker face of the aspect can be reflected in a deep repulsion toward the body. Often this problem is projected, and one of the most common expressions of this is the abrupt "turning off" which can occur once a sexual fantasy has been actualised. The person is then compelled to pursue the quest for the perfect partner, incarnated in the perfect body; but of course the real object of one's repudiation is one's own physical reality. Sometimes this problem with the flesh is felt internally, and is reflected by a chronic discontent with one's own appearance. Somewhere inside is an image of the perfect body one "ought" to have, and no amount of dieting, exercise or cosmetic surgery will ever be able to produce it.

Audience: Is it like Venus in Aquarius?

Liz: As I have mentioned before, there will always be similarities between a planetary aspect and the planet placed in the corresponding sign or house. But we need once again to remember that signs and houses do not reflect dynamic energies; the former describes qualities and the latter a sphere of expression. So some of the same detachment, idealism, aesthetic and intellectual ability, and dissociation from the body may apply to Venus in Aquarius as well as Venus in the 11th, but it is more in the nature of a manner of behaviour rather than a dynamic motivation.

There are many ways in which Venus-Uranus can be made reasonably comfortable within a stable relationship. It is a good idea to be cautious about signing anything in too much of a hurry (although Venus-Uranus may initially be in a great hurry); and it might even be wise not to marry, but to live together instead, or to buy a house with two separate wings and an interconnecting door which can be locked. Or one might make sure that one's work involves some independent travel, and that one has an entirely separate group of friends and interests. In short, Venus-Uranus needs sometimes to feel single rather than the permanent half of a couple. Too much "we" is anathema, unless it is an ideological "we," which is acceptable. Venus-Uranus not only needs fantasy; it needs newness and experimentation, and this does not mean memorising page 75 in your copy of *How to Keep the Romance in Your Marriage*. That is Saturnian, not Uranian. Do any of you remember Woody Allen's film, *Everything You Wanted to Know About Sex But Were Afraid to Ask?* One of the scenarios involves a couple who only get turned on if they have it off in dangerous situations, such as lifts, buses, display sofas in department stores and so on. The illicit element in erotic love can be a great stimulus to Venus-Uranus.

How many of you have a strong Venus-Uranus aspect? Do you feel confident enough to tell your partner you need time off sometimes?

Audience: I am afraid of saying it, because there might be a reprisal.

Liz: There is more likely to be one if you *don't* say it, and it will come from within you. You have illustrated my point very nicely.

Perhaps we could look at Venus-Mercury contacts now. I know that Howard talked about these yesterday, but there may be some additional features which could prove interesting. In myth, when Aphrodite and Hermes become lovers, they produce a child called Hermaphroditus, who possesses both male and female sexual organs. This curious mythic image might suggest to us a quality of androgyny, a detachment from any particular role in matters of love. Like Uranus, Mercury seems to constellate the aesthetic and intellectual dimension of Venus. I have found that these aspects (and they can never be anything beyond a conjunction or sextile, or the minor semisextile or semisquare, because both planets tend to cling closely to the Sun) reflect a pronounced love of beauty, in thought, word or form; there is often a marked elegance of speech and style.

As you might expect, because of Hermes' clever and inquisitive nature in myth, Venus-Mercury can also be quite detached and devoid of inhibitions, not for the sake of unconventionality, but because of sheer playful curiosity. There is a rather pointed story about Aphrodite's love affair with Ares, which drove her husband, the lame smith-god Hephaistos, into vengeful fury. He spun a golden net so fine that it was invisible, and draped the net around the bed in which the lovers met; and when they were asleep after their lovemaking he wrapped it around them and hoisted them up in the air in full view of the other gods. All the Olympians, Hera in particular, stomped about behaving like Mary Whitehouse, complaining about Aphrodite's shamelessness and perfidy and so on — all except Hermes, who moved closer to get a good look, and merely laughed and declared that he would have liked to be in Ares' place. (Later on he was.) He is the only deity who does not censure Aphrodite, because he is utterly amoral himself. This playful face of Hermes, and the verbal dimension of erotic love, are both reflected by Venus-Mercury, which can find talking or being talked to a very exciting element in lovemaking.

Hermes is a *puer aeternus*, a permanent adolescent; he does not grow into a mature husband, but remains a charming and tricky youth. This quality is also reflected in Venus-Mercury, which may find scenes of heavy emotional intensity rather offputting. The natural medium for this aspect is the romantic letter or telephone call (or even the romantic fax, which is the preferred courtship style of someone I know who has Venus sextile Mercury in Gemini). You can no doubt work out from what I have been saying what typical problems also accompany this combination. It is not possible to have a square or opposition between Venus and Mercury unless your computer has gone berserk, and the planets are both light in nature; and there may be so much charm, aestheticism and intellectualising that one's values become postured and shallow. There is also a marked distaste for open confrontation, which means that evasiveness or even outright lying may be used to deflect nasty scenes. Those with meatier planetary aspects to Venus (such as from Saturn or Pluto) may find Venus-Mercury disturbingly cool; for although there is no lack of capacity to love, it is love with a light touch, airy rather than earthy, and more of the mind and spirit than the body or the heart.

Audience: Can you say something about a retrograde Venus?

Liz: Any retrograde planet reflects a turning inward or "backward" of its energy and drive. This may mean a certain amount of frustration in terms of its expression in the world, but it also releases the introverted function of the planet, so that it manifests more as an inner reality. When Venus is turned inward in this way, the capacity to express erotic love on the body level may be somewhat inhibited; but the inner image of love, and of the beloved, becomes extremely powerful, activating the imagination and the translation of that image into symbol and art. For example, a retrograde Venus conjuncting Mercury may find it easier, and perhaps ultimately more rewarding, to write about the experience of love, conjuring out of the inner world images which have greater depth and meaning for the person than the more conventional forms of fulfilment which we define as "happiness."

There is, as I have said, an element of frustration in all this, but if we consider the alchemical axiom that it is frustration of instinctual drives which ultimately leads to their transformation into alchemical gold, then this frustration may not be at all a bad thing. It is never total anyway, but is usually experienced more as a limitation which must be accepted. Often there is a kind of shyness or social clumsiness about a retrograde Venus, since the elegance and skill of a more extraverted Venus will operate on the inner, cerebral level rather than the outer one. There may also be considerable awkwardness in sexual matters, because the beauty of the fantasy may supercede the pleasure of physical encounter. A retrograde Venus does not thwart the capacity for sexual pleasure. But it may not be the most important aspect of relationship, and there may be inhibitions which need to be honoured because of the inner richness of feeling which results.

Perhaps we could move now from Venus-Mercury to Venus-Pluto. After all that lightness and delicacy, I think we need a little more red meat in our diet. You should have the hang of working with Venus aspects by now. Would anyone like to offer an interpretation of Venus-Pluto?

Audience: I keep thinking of Carmen.

Liz: Yes, she is a good illustration of Venus-Pluto, whether one lives her oneself or falls in love with her in a partner.

Audience: What about Penthesilia, the Queen of the Amazons? Didn't she battle with her lover King Agamemnon during the Trojan War?

Liz: Well, actually, she battled with the hero Achilles; he was her lover, not poor Agamemnon, who had a Venus-Pluto wife called Klytaemnestra who murdered him in his bath. But yes, the Queen of the Amazons, who engages in deadly combat with the man she loves, is another good image for this aspect. The "battle of the sexes" is certainly a view of love which is close to the heart of Venus-Pluto, as is control through sexual power, illustrated by Carmen. Klytaemnestra and Medea, another savage heroine of myth, are good images of the vengeful side of Venus-Pluto, which can never forgive hurt or rejection. What are the values of Venus-Pluto?

Audience: Intensity and passion.

Liz: I would agree with that; for Venus-Pluto, a relationship without passion is really rather a bore and not worth bothering with. What Venus finds of greatest beauty and value becomes mixed

with the raw Plutonian battle for survival; and this results in a taste
for theatre which brings the life-and-death struggle into the realm
of emotional and erotic satisfaction. Sexuality for Venus-Pluto is
not merely a matter of physical pleasure, any more than it is for
Venus in Scorpio. It is a gateway to experiencing the drama of the
passions, and the losing of the ordinary everyday self in the great
struggle of life. Venus-Pluto seeks an experience of deepening and
transformation, a movement from the everyday world into some
heightened archetypal realm where everything matters terribly.
Often this can be reached only through pain and conflict, which is
why the aspect has a reputation for complicated relationships and
psychological game-playing.

Because this combination may not sit well in a chart with many
cooler or more prosaic signs and aspects, I have found that there
are characteristic defence mechanisms to repress it. It is not an easy
aspect to live in the modern world, particularly for men, since the
crime de passion is no longer recognised as noble (it is merely sordid)
and the dramatic scene is no longer rich and releasing, but merely
hysterical. This kind of behaviour is acceptable only in Continental
films. So the tendency for deep, irrevocable attachment is often
covered over by a kind of callous promiscuity in the first half of life,
as if Venus-Pluto were pretending to be a particularly jaded sort of
Venus-Mercury or Venus-Uranus. The person may have a great
fear of encountering a "fated" relationship from which they cannot
extricate themselves, and this fear may in part be justified, since
once Venus-Pluto becomes deeply engaged, it does not easily
become disengaged. Often, therefore, the aspect is projected.
What do you think the result of this might be?

Audience: The person will find a partner who causes all the emotional trouble.

Liz: Yes, that is usually the scenario. The partner may be psychologically damaged, or pose some insurmountable problem (such as
an existing marriage), or be too possessive or emotionally demanding or controlling. I have known a number of men with Venus-
Pluto who are unconsciously very manipulative and controlling,
trying to protect their vulnerability and intensity of feeling while
"winding up" their partner and provoking her into acting the

aspect out through jealous scenes. But the combination of planets is in itself not inimical, as Venus-Saturn or Venus-Chiron might be. There is a certain affinity between Aphrodite and Hades in terms of unbridled passions, although Hades takes his rather more seriously. And the aesthetic dimension of Venus can combine with Pluto's sense of drama, which can reflect considerable theatrical ability. Love and life are enlarged and rendered huge and mythic. If you have a fight, it isn't a cool little exchange; it means all the crockery gets smashed, and everything is over, *final*, and you're going to go off and throw yourself under a bus. Yet the dramatic skills and sense of timing are there in the background, because Venus cannot resist making art out of life.

Audience: Can you talk about the difference between Venus-Pluto and Venus in the 8th house?

Liz: We seem to keep coming round to this question with every Venus aspect. Once again, there are many similarities. But the 8th house is a sphere of life; it is the arena in which one meets and experiences Venus. Because it reflects experiences that are beyond one's ego control, which erupt from the unconscious or invisible level, Venus is met through "fated" encounters. There are often painful but deeply transformative experiences in relationships of every kind, which can include such things as the death of a parent at an early age, or the loss of a lover or spouse. The experiences are of course not necessarily tragic, but they have the 8th house characteristic of erupting from the depths and taking over one's life, revealing an inner world which one did not know existed. With Venus-Pluto, because the planets reflect our own dynamic needs and drives, the person *actively seeks* experiences which carry the necessary intensity and depth, even if this intent is unconscious and projected upon a partner.

Venus-Pluto can be extremely unpleasant if it is disowned and acted out unconsciously. The same might be said of any planetary aspect with Pluto, because Pluto requires great emotional honesty, with self and with others, to offer up its best. Otherwise it may become a destroyer, and behave in extremely ugly ways behind the scenes. If you have Venus-Pluto in the birth chart, the need for drama and intensity needs to be included in your emotional spectrum, even if you have a nice polite Moon in Libra or a rigourously controlled Capricorn Ascendant or a reasonable, civilised Aquarian Sun. This may pose many problems, and the individual may face the thorny issue of emotional self-betrayal more than once in life — particularly if the parents were uncomfortable with their child's erotically precocious intensity and gave loud messages that it was shameful and unacceptable.

I have found that this last point is one of the primary reasons why a Venus-Pluto person may try to disown the aspect, which almost always brings out its worst manifestations. A child's eroticism is well understood and recognised as natural and healthy in analytic circles; but the average parent is often not able to accommodate or accept Oedipal dynamics, particularly if the parental marriage is dicky[23] and recognition of sexuality has been a dirty no-no for a few generations. Every family must contend with jealous, competitive feelings as well as erotic triangles; they are simply a fact of life, and part of childhood development. But as a culture we are not very well educated in these things, and prefer to pretend they are not there unless we are hit in the face by them in a more vicious form such as child abuse. If you are a Venus-Pluto child, your early erotic feelings will have probably been more intense and obvious than those of many children, and there is a great likelihood that they were not welcomed.

For example, if you were a rather aloof, shy, Saturnian sort of father who worked hard for the family but did not express emotions easily, or a more cerebral, Uranian type of father who enjoyed an intellectual rapport with his children but recoiled from too much kissing and cuddling, you would find your little Venus-Pluto daughter very disturbing when she kept trying to crawl into your lap and unconsciously aroused unwelcome sexual feelings in you because of her inexplicable sexual magnetism. Although this is a perfectly natural situation, and can be handled with grace and care if one is conscious, try to imagine yourself as the average father. You would be horror-stricken as you found yourself becoming excited, and your guilt would make you push your daughter away

---

[23]This British word may be unknown to American readers. *Dicky* is colloquial, combining several nuances and referring to something shaky and not in good condition.

in an overly brutal fashion which she would inevitably interpret as rejection and disgust. The child will then associate expression of erotic feeling with rejection and disgust, and will grow into a woman who is terrified that, if she expresses her sensuality and eroticism, she will be humiliated and abandoned. And because Venus-Pluto reflects a peculiarly intense and fixed kind of love, there is great pride involved, and the wound is never forgotten. It is then not surprising that Venus-Pluto people, when grown up, may play some rather awful power games in order to avoid ever being humiliated in this way again.

Audience: Would the same thing apply to a mother-son relationship?

Liz: Yes, certainly, although there is perhaps a little more acceptance of such feelings in women toward their children because of the erotic dimension of breastfeeding. But it takes a very psychologically aware mother to consciously acknowledge her son's sexual feelings toward her, and to respond to these feelings with care rather than with either disgust or manipulation. This latter may also be a reflection of Venus-Pluto's difficulty, since if the parent is caught in his or her own unconscious need to possess, the child's sexuality may be used in order to preserve the early parent-child bond beyond its natural life. Such manipulation not only offers a rather horrific role model to Venus-Pluto; it may also leave deep scars of rage which make the person very afraid to risk losing sexual control in adult relationships. Hence there may be a good deal of frustration with Venus-Pluto, because of the fear of becoming addicted and used through one's erotic needs.

I would not necessarily read all this into Venus-Pluto unless it combined with particular parental significators in the birth chart. But it is common enough, given the collective climate around the issue of children's sexuality. Freud did us a profound service in finding the courage to face this Plutonian realm head on, although he may have got rather dogmatic in his efforts to squeeze it all into a neat system; but most people do not know anything about this dimension of life other than that it has something to do with wanting to have sex with one's mother and all that sort of filth. I think that if you have Venus-Pluto in the birth chart, you had better read a little Freud and Klein as well as Jung, and embrace the psychological dimension of life for the sake of your own well-being. If we return to the basic premise that Venus reflects our most permanent values, then Venus-Pluto finds the depths of human nature of the highest value, and will always benefit from exploring them voluntarily rather than involuntarily because of crisis and suffering.

Audience: Does Pluto destroy relationships?

Liz: Pluto will attempt to destroy that which threatens its survival. Since it is a collective planet, survival for Pluto means survival of the most primal instinctual needs, and any refinement, containment or balancing of those needs with more individual ones constitutes a threat. This is why Pluto needs to be made conscious, and we need to become more aware of where we are tribal creatures, ready to attack anything which requires us to develop as individuals. If we remain unconscious of these primitive needs and emotions, and cannot find a way to incorporate them in our lives, then we may inadvertently try to destroy things which we may actually want and need very badly. Certainly Venus-Pluto, particularly the hard aspects, may engage in the unconscious sabotage of a much-valued relationship. But this usually occurs because there is a big dissociated chunk of primitive emotion knocking about in the basement, and therefore an unconscious fear of losing control (which constitutes a threat to survival).

Audience: I know a man with Venus in Scorpio opposite a Moon-Uranus conjunction in Taurus. This man never married, and seems to spend most of his time meditating. He is very spiritual, and rejects sexual love.

Liz: I wonder where his Venus in Scorpio is hiding.

Audience: That is what I would like to know.

Liz: The Uranian influence on both the Moon and Venus might reflect his need to pull away from the instinctual world and find freedom in Uranus' "starry heavens." But the placement of these planets on the Taurus-Scorpio axis is rather troubling, because both are deeply sensual signs; and it seems that Uranus has taken over everything, and that there is a great imbalance. I would say that this man probably suffers from a great fear of the body and of his sexuality, which may be linked with experiences with his mother in childhood. If you recall our discussion of Moon-Venus, there is usually a conflict in the mother between maternity and erotic feeling, and the child may react to the overpowering threat of the mother's unconscious sexuality by dissociating from instinctual needs in adult life. This is not to say that your friend's spiritual endeavours are "wrong," since they are a characteristic and healthy reflection of Uranus. But there is too much repression here for Venus in Scorpio and the Moon in Taurus. There is no balance; he is running away from himself.

Audience: Could we correlate Venus-Pluto and Venus in the 8th house with the Persephone myth?

Liz: Yes, this myth in many ways portrays the process of Venus-Pluto, although it can be understood on other levels as well. With the hard aspects of Venus and Pluto, the aesthetic, light side of Venus may at first shy away from the darker dimensions of love, and life will usually bring about a forcible initiation into underworld feelings and instincts. The Persephone story reflects the invasion of compulsive desire, which is portrayed as a rape because it is apparently unwilling. Yet if we look carefully at the myth, we can see that Persephone wanders off into danger alone, as though something in her seeks this experience in spite of herself; and although her mother Demeter tries to keep her virginal, Gaia, the Earth Mother who is simply another form of Demeter, colludes with Hades and opens a passageway in the earth for him to abduct his prize. This myth is full of subtleties of a Plutonian kind, and is not what it seems to be at first glance. The feeling of involuntary or forced submission to fate which often accompanies Venus-Pluto relationships usually reflects the same subtlety, and is also not what it seems at first glance.

I associate the Persephone myth with the experience of puberty, because of the sense of the body being unwillingly invaded by biological changes and compulsive feelings of a new and frightening kind. It is not surprising that many adolescents try to escape into religious or spiritual preoccupations at such a time, for this is one of our most characteristic human efforts to keep Pluto at bay. Yet the outcome of the myth is a Persephone who can inhabit both upper and lower worlds, which may also be seen as the potential of Venus-Pluto.

Audience: What happens if your Venus is in strong aspect to another person's Pluto?

Liz: The Pluto person is the one who will experience Plutonian feelings, and much depends upon how they handle it. The Venus person embodies qualities of grace or charm or beauty which activate very powerful, intense emotions in the Pluto person. Pluto's intensity in turn is very attractive to the Venus person, who values it and finds it beautiful; so there is often a powerful sexual chemistry with this synastry combination, even if the aspect is a difficult one. But if the Pluto person is disconnected from these primitive emotions and therefore threatened by them, then there may be a power battle, because as I said before, Pluto will try to destroy whatever challenges its survival.

A general rule in synastry is that we experience others through the lens of our own planets. If someone's whatnot lands on your Venus, what you will feel is Venus, which means that you become aware of this dimension of yourself in that person's presence. If it is their Sun conjuncting it, then you may feel beautiful and loved and worth something as a person. If it is their Saturn, you may also feel loved after a fashion, but you may also feel criticised or burdened in some way. If it is their Pluto, you may, once again, feel loved and attractive, but you may find their intensity disturbing or controlling. There is often a degree of emotional blackmail and manipulation at work with the hard synastry aspects, although this usually reflects fear from childhood issues which has risen up to infect the present relationship. But any strong contact to your Venus from another person's planets will make you much more aware of your own values, even if the process is stressful.

We have time to cover one more of the Venus aspects. Howard has done some things with Venus-Saturn, and hopefully we will cover Venus-Neptune and Venus-Sun later on. So perhaps we can finish this session with Venus-Jupiter, which is more fun than

Venus-Neptune, and gives us a happy note on which to end. Does anyone what to comment on this combination?

Audience: Well, I am thinking of Zeus. He is very promiscuous and is always chasing a new lover.

Liz: Yes, there is that side of Venus-Jupiter. And it does indeed sometimes get acted out in the unending pursuit of an ideal love. But Jupiter does not seek perfection as Neptune does; it seeks constant growth and the unfoldment of new potentials. If this is possible within a relationship, with a partner who can move along and keep pace, then Venus-Jupiter is not subject to the kind of disillusionment which so often afflicts Venus-Neptune, and may be perfectly capable of loyalty. It is boredom with a narrow relationship which drives this combination into constant new love affairs.

Zeus in myth is endlessly fertile and creative, and not just in terms of his fertilising women. He changes shape with each new encounter, amusing himself by becoming a swan, a bull, or a shower of gold. So we know that the component of imagination and fantasy is very important to Venus-Jupiter's values in love, and too much sameness and routine in a relationship is anathema. Zeus also falls in love a lot, which reflects an innate romanticism, a belief in the Grand Passion complete with Tchaikovsky's Violin Concerto in the background. Love needs to be a Great Adventure for Venus-Jupiter, a voyage of discovery and exploration, and the world must open up and grow larger as a result. So there is a certain element of opportunism in the combination (sometimes material and sometimes on subtler levels), since Venus-Jupiter will usually not bother with a relationship that offers no possibilities for the expansion and enriching of one's life in one way or another.

Zeus is one of the archetypal *puer aeternus* figures, which means that one is happiest when one feels things are not yet complete. The highest value for Venus-Jupiter is the sense that one has not yet exhausted the creative possibilities in a relationship, that there is more to learn and discover sexually and emotionally and intellectually. The feeling that there is no further to go, that things have reached their natural limit, that it is time to settle into a permanent state of being rather than of becoming, will usually drive Venus-Jupiter out of the relationship—whether literally or on an emotional level. Or, if the puer qualities of Jupiter are projected, one may unconsciously drive the partner out, so that one's life can once again have an open door to the future.

Zeus is a sensuous deity, and Jupiter, although it is a fiery planet and belongs to the realm of the intuition and the imagination, also has great fun playing about with the earthy world. Zeus mates with mortal women in myth, and although he is an Olympian, unlike Ouranus he does not repudiate what is made of flesh. But he must bring drama into corporeal life, which is what Venus-Jupiter wants from its romantic enterprises. This drama is not the heavy meat of Plutonian struggle, but the radiance of Camelot, where all princesses are exquisitely beautiful and all knights are brave and noble. Venus-Jupiter has little tolerance for tragedy and suffering, and can display considerable callousness when the going gets rough; life ought to be happy, not dripping with pain, and the Venus-Jupiter person can become very impatient and irritable if long-term problems arise within a relationship which require sacrifice and the patient enduring of difficulties. That is the dark side of the aspect.

There may also be great impatience with another person's slower responses – "We've known each other for three weeks, why aren't you ready for total commitment? Why isn't the potential I can feel happening *now*?" One can see this impatience with the limits of other people in Sagittarius, which often finds waiting a very difficult thing to do. One should be at the goal post immediately, or it can't be the right relationship. There is a difficulty in waiting and letting feelings develop over time. This includes the sexual side of a relationship, which, if the earth does not move on the first night, may be dismissed as a failure too quickly. Richard Idemon always used to describe Jupiter and Sagittarius in terms of the feeling of being special, because Zeus is the king of the gods. One ought to be exempt from ordinary human problems, because one is special. This feeling – "I have the *right* to be happy!" – may seem very inflated and narcissistic to those with Venus in aspect to heavier planets. But we all create life situations through our unconscious assumptions, and Venus-Jupiter, because it expects to be happy and assumes its right to personal fulfilment, often attracts very fortunate situations which arouse the envy of other people. That is the bright side of the aspect, which often receives a very high return on its belief in the ultimate goodness of love and life.

PART THREE

MARS

Aggression is not necessarily destructive at all. It springs from an innate tendency to master life which seems to be characteristic of all living matter. Only when this life force is obstructed in its development do ingredients of anger, rage or hate become connected with it.

—Clara Thomson

THE WARRIOR AND THE WOMANISER

THE MYTHOLOGY AND PSYCHOLOGY OF MARS

BY LIZ GREENE

As we are dealing with the theme of Mars today, we can be a good deal more aggressive. Howard and I were talking yesterday evening about the exercises in guided imagery for Venus which he has been giving you, and we were trying to think of something suitable which might help to crystallise the meaning of Mars. We decided that you could close your eyes, get an image for your Mars sign, and then punch the person sitting next to you.

Do you all have the diagram for the mythic images associated with Mars? (See figure 2 on page 178.) One simple definition of Mars is that it is the fighting principle for the Sun, and in a sense the fighting principle for all the inner planets which lie within its orbit. The necessity for a fighting principle is obvious, since there is a big world out there in which sooner or later one will meet conflict or challenges to one's individuality, one's values, and even one's physical and psychological survival. Inevitably, we must all fight for what we are, beginning with the struggle to emerge from the womb. Mars was considered a malefic principle in medieval astrology, a "baddie," and this connotation still clings to the planet in more "spiritual" astrological approaches. But although the whole thorny realm of aggression and war and conflict is not what we might ideally include in a perfect world, and learning to work with Mars in a conscious and constructive way is no easy task, without Mars we are impotent, and then someone else's Mars will beat us to pulp. This is a simple, pragmatic approach to the planet's value which appears to elude many astrologers.

I will be talking quite a bit about the issue of impotence on all levels, and about what happens to us when Mars is not expressed in the chart. This tough little planet gives us our initial definition in life; it is the most basic instrument of separation from the womb

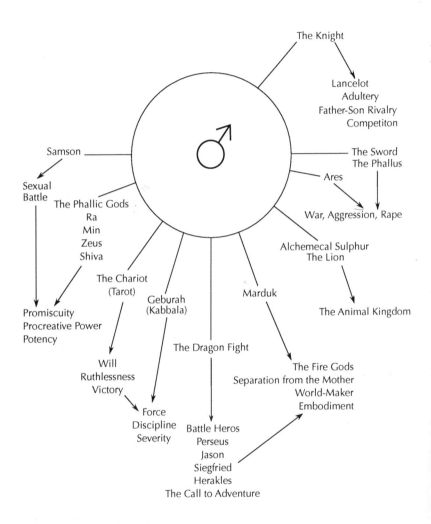

Figure 2. The mythological expressions of Mars.

and the collective, because the moment we take a stand over what we are or want or value, we define ourselves as irrevocably separate from others. Once Mars is brought out into the open, and the statement is made, it cannot be unmade, any more than we can crawl back into the womb once we have begun to breathe independently and the umbilical cord is cut. So there is an absolute and irreversible quality about Martial action, which is one of the reasons why many people have trouble owning the planet.

Mars cannot speak in conundrums and double meanings to cover its tracks; it simply says, like Martin Luther (who had Mars as one of his Sun sign rulers), "Here I stand, so help me God." Even if one apologises and makes up afterward, one can never go back to that state of perfect fusion which existed before the quarrel. In romantic relationships, the "first quarrel" is a huge watershed, and afterward nothing is ever quite the same. At the beginning of a love affair, Neptune and Venus preside, and it feels like two hearts beating as one—you must all know those three-handkerchief films like *Love Story*, where "love is never having to say you're sorry." Mars cringes at that kind of sentiment; the only time we experience the reality of two hearts beating as one is in the womb, and all that fusion ends at birth. Those wonderful feelings of perfect empathy and understanding are shattered when Mars makes its entrance and an argument ensues which defines the separate identities of the two people. It is the first crack in the encircling walls of the Paradise Garden, and even if the crack is patched up very quickly, the serpent has somehow managed to get in. So part of us fears Mars, because once we have acted on our own behalf, we cannot go back on it.

Do you all remember that phase of the hero's journey where he must fight the dragon or the dark twin? This is the emergence of Mars, which is the hero's sword and fighting spirit. At a certain point in the Sun's development, Mars must be invoked to defend the growing individuality. In my session on the mythology of the Sun,[1] I talked about the Babylonian fire god Marduk, who must do battle with his mother Tiamat, and then cuts up her body and

[1]For a discussion of this myth, see "The Hero with a Thousand Faces," in *The Luminaries*, Volume 3 of *Seminars in Psychological Astrology* (York Beach, ME: Samuel Weiser, 1992), p. 94.

creates the manifest universe. Marduk's battle epitomises the function of Mars, which not only fights against the regressive pull of fusion with mother and collective, but must also perform the ruthless task of objectively viewing and defining reality (cutting it up) in order to create an individual life. If we consider Marduk's battle on a psychological level, anger, aggression and assertion of self are the primary implements of separation from the mother and formation of individual ego ground in the early stages of life. These primitive emotions are the weapons by which we fight the dragon, which every mother, even the best, must become at a certain stage of her child's development.

Certain mythic heroes are unmistakably Martial in nature, like Marduk. The hero's journey is essentially a solar journey, but some of these journeys have a more combative element, while others, such as that of Odysseus, depend more on cleverness and guile. And there is inevitably some stage of the journey which involves battle or resistance against a foe, even if the hero is a relatively peaceable sort. Jason must slay a dragon to acquire the Golden Fleece; Perseus must slay the Medusa to win his Andromeda; Parsifal is a gentle fool, not a warrior, but even Parsifal must fight. In Wagner's opera, his battle involves resisting the wiles of Kundry, as well as battling with the castrated sorcerer Klingsor. Both are reflections of Martial strength, for refusal based on one's own values is as much a battle as the more aggressive clash of weapons. Siegfried, on the other hand, is the classic Martial hero, with a sword of power bequeathed him by his grandfather Wotan. We might even extend our mythic interpretation to suggest that the hero's symbolic phallus, the magic sword such as Excalibur in the Arthurian cycle, is itself a most vivid symbol of Mars, wielded by the solar hero.

Siegfried has another relevant Martial attribute: he is invincible except from behind. He can be destroyed by a knife in the back, which is what happens to him in the end. Siegfried is bold and fearless, but he is not especially wily, and he allows himself to become the victim of treachery because he thinks with his "sword." The invincibility of Mars can only be sustained when one is facing an honest enemy. The Martial function is not gifted at dealing with undercurrents and enemies who creep up from behind, although Mars placed in subtler signs such as Pisces, Cancer and Scorpio can develop a better capacity to cope with indirect confrontation. The Martial nature may be insensitive and crude, but it is essentially open and honest and straight. As long as one can trust the enemy's honour, one can fight fairly and even lose gracefully to fight again another time. But it is the knife in the back which defeats Mars, and there is no sharper hidden knife than emotional manipulation.

One of the most difficult childhood issues for the expression of Mars is the family background where the fighting is covert. This implies a family problem with Mars, where overt aggression and separativeness are shunned, and all efforts at getting what one wants are forced into unconscious operation. I have found that manipulative illnesses (and many apparently organic ailments have a manipulative component) are invariably bound up with a badly afflicted Mars in the horoscope, and all the anger and aggression and will are compressed into a form of covert control of others through bodily symptoms. This is usually a pattern learned from the family, and it may go back for many generations.

The hero who to me best epitomises the Martial nature is Herakles. He was terribly popular with the Romans (Hercules) as well as with the Greeks, who thought of him as the ideal hero. Yet he is not a very intelligent character, and performs a chain of real blunders in his heroic career. He is always accidentally killing someone (Hippolyta, Queen of the Amazons), or accidentally wounding friends (Chiron), and then he scratches his head and says, "Oh, sorry, I guess I was a bit too forceful." There is a slightly blundering quality about Mars, something slapstick and a little stupid, until it is in the arena of battle and shows its real gifts.

Audience: What happened to Chiron?

Liz: It is worth remembering this myth, because it has bearing on the symbolic meaning of Chiron as well as on the nature of Mars as reflected by Herakles. Herakles has just finished killing the Hydra, the nine-headed monster which lived in a slimy cave, and he has stopped to visit his friend Chiron for lunch, carrying a quiver of arrows which are smeared with the dead Hydra's poisonous blood. As the two of them are sitting having a good chat, Herakles makes a clumsy movement, and one of the arrows in his quiver accidentally nicks the centaur in the thigh. One cannot blame Herakles, but it is typical of him, and Chiron has an incurable wound as a result; the poison cannot be drawn out and there is no antidote. This results in Chiron becoming a wise healer, but no doubt in darker moments he would have settled for being an ordinary unwise centaur and not an archetype of the wounded healer. If we want to take the symbolism to its inevitable conclusion, we might say that it is often because of the Mars function – the unforgettable poisoning experience of rage and aggression – that we carry scars for life, although it is usually, as in Chiron's case, somebody else's Mars which inflicts the wound.

The pattern of Herakles' twelve labours is an interesting one, for he undertakes them in expiation of another accidental killing. Each labour is a kind of mini-myth in itself, and each one is also a facet of Mars' training ground. It is as though the cycle of the twelve labours describes the many faces of battle to which we will be subjected during a lifetime, and to which we need to learn to respond with a strong Martial function. Herakles comes out of these labours having learned rather more polish and self-containment, but he is still Herakles.

The battle with the Lernean Hydra, which I just mentioned, is a very good example of these Martial tests. The Hydra has nine poisonous snakeheads, lives in a cave in the middle of a swamp, and is killing off the population of the countryside. Herakles goes along with his club – a unique weapon in myth, and unmistakably phallic – and expects that he can easily conquer the creature, because his club has always been effective (his basic principle is, "If it moves, club it"). But the Hydra frustrates him. First it hides in the darkness of the cave, and he has to spend some time working out that he must shoot flaming arrows into the cave in order to drive the monster out into the open. Here is Mars confronting an opponent who does not play by honourable battle rules, but hides in the darkness of the unconscious; so one must learn the art of effective provocation as well as insight into the enemy's motives, both of which might be reflected by those flaming arrows.

Then, when the Hydra finally swarms out to the shadowy cave entrance, Herakles discovers that if he clubs one of its heads, it sprouts nine more. This is a deadly opponent indeed; force alone can achieve nothing except making the enemy stronger, and

Herakles comes near to being destroyed himself. Here Mars must learn that overt aggression can sometimes increase the aggression of others, achieving nothing in the end but one's own defeat. Then the hero remembers that the only thing which can destroy the Hydra is sunlight. So he gets down on his knees and lifts the creature up into the light, and that is the end of the Hydra. This symbolism is very striking, and one of its meanings might be that Mars needs to learn the necessity for apparent humility and the foregoing of pride for a time (bending the knee) in order to win. The Hydra, like many inner and outer enemies we meet in life, is defeated if enough consciousness and openness is brought into the situation. I am sure many of you will recognise those situations where anger and even long-standing hatred can be diffused by open discussion and an honest airing of the problem. And even if painful decisions must be made and the enemy remains an enemy, at least we will not be poisoned by invisible emotional under-currents—particularly our own.

The cleaning of the Augean Stables is another striking labour which Herakles must undertake. This mythic image has become part of our ordinary language, and we speak of an awful mess which we must somehow clean up as an Augean Stables. Herakles is told to clean the stables within a certain time limit, but the place is so full of cow dung that it is quite impossible. He obviously cannot use his club, since it is excrement and not an enemy which he must deal with, and even using his hands would be useless in the allotted time. Mars here has to serve as a cleansing agent, sweeping away with surgical precision what is useless and out-worn in life. This "getting rid of all the old shit" is another facet of the Martial function, and is related to our capacity to make decisions which rid us of an outgrown and smelly past.

The Hydra might be seen as an image of human hatred, unfor-giveness and emotional poison, and as with every character in a myth, it is within us as much as the hero is. Perhaps it is a Pluto-nian creature, with roots which reach back through mother to the dark complexes of the family past. We need Mars to cope with this evil in ourselves as well as in the world outside. But the Augean Stables reflect all our inherited psychic dross, the waste which has accumulated over many generations, the habitual patterns which drag us down into inertia and smother us with their stench and weight. Herakles eventually gets an inspiration: he rechannels a powerful river by moving its bed, so that the water flows through the stables in a great torrent and washes them clean.

This image might be describing a rechannelling of emotional energy (water), a release of feelings which can wash away all the dross in one enormous flood. Therapeutic work, particularly the cathartic kind, often involves this process: emotions which have been moving into other channels are redirected toward oneself and the anguish of one's own situation, and the realisations effect an outburst of feeling which can change many old, entrenched patterns of behaviour. This too is Martial, for the emotions involved are usually unexpressed anger and outrage, and a sudden realisation of what one has been putting up with for far too long. There is a stage of healing childhood hurts which generally involves being pretty furious with one's family, and outraged on one's own behalf. This is the stage of "parent bashing." Although it is not a very helpful place to get stuck in, and needs ultimately to mellow into comprehension and compassion, it is often a necessary temporary cleansing process, especially in a person who has defensively idealised a deeply abusive parent and has never dared to face the reality before.

These two labours I have described both provide many insights into the challenges which Mars must meet in life, and the appropriate ways in which to deal with them. Because Mars is an "antisocial" planet (it serves *me*, rather than society), life will sooner or later temper the aggressive instinct in us, because other people will not put up with a rampant Mars. At best, they do not like us, and at worst, they lock us up. If we can respond to these "tempering" experiences in the way that Herakles learns from his labours, we can express Mars in a much more positive, contained (rather than repressed), and creative way.

If we move on from Herakles to the Greek god Ares who becomes Mars in Roman myth, there are several interesting images to consider. First of all, Ares has no father. He is created by the goddess Hera parthenogenically. Hera is in a state of great rage because her husband Zeus has produced the goddess Athena out of his head without a mother, and this is a profound insult to the domain of marriage, family and childbirth over which Hera presides. So Ares is the product of the goddess's furious revenge, or, if we wish to be especially Freudian today, a product of her penis envy. She is determined to compete with this offending god who has created a female child of the spirit (wisdom) without her, and generates a son-phallus of her own who will fight for her. Where Athene is not mothered—she has no part in the realm of the body and instincts—Ares has no father-principle in him, which I understand to mean that he does not spring from logos, from the spiritual or intellectual dimension of the masculine realm. He is male, but he is pure instinct, without any reflective or symbolising capacity.

Thus, although Ares is unmistakably phallic and male, he does not partake of the Olympian gods' detachment. He is lunar and chthonic, and Homer describes him as a kind of big thug, three hundred feet tall, hairy, brutish, but invincible in battle. He is stupid and clumsy, but he has the light of the Berserker in his eyes, the divine inebriation of war. The Berserker is the Teutonic version of the spirit of Ares, the warrior who is drunk on the wine of combat. When a warrior is taken over by this spirit, nothing can harm him; he can go right through the enemy's battle lines without a scratch. There is a kind of folklore about this in military circles, even today, and certain soldiers—especially those such as the SAS[2] who surround themselves with the mystique of secrecy—become mythic in stature because they seem to be invincible. In Britain we have this fantasy that the men of the SAS can do anything, and the regiment itself feeds the fantasy in us and in its men for its own psychological and political reasons; films such as *Who Dares, Wins* portray this fantasy of daring and invincibility most clearly. But the strange thing is that, when an archetype such as this is invoked, it does seem to manifest in "real" life. We ordinary folk can experience this divine inebriation of Ares in a typical pub fight, or when some danger threatens and suddenly the instincts take over and we act decisively and courageously in a way we could never dream of doing when ordinarily sober and fearful. We are "taken out of ourselves" and can perform amazing feats of bravery and physical strength that would be utterly impossible with everyday consciousness.

---

[2]British Special Air Service, the crack troops who operate in greatest secrecy on particularly dangerous military and political missions.

The Norse and Teutonic image of the Berserker is an interesting one to consider in the light of history. The coasts of Britain were once subjected to repeated Viking and Saxon invasions, and one can imagine how utterly terrifying it must have been to see these blonde giants swarming off their dragon ships, wearing their horned helmets and wielding their enormous swords, quite mad with the Berserker's light in their eyes. There is a powerful sexual component to this energy, which is reflected in all the phallic symbolism of the horns and swords. I would also connect this spirit of Ares with religious and political martyrdom, which can be just as inebriating and full of sexual passion. This dimension of Mars has mostly died out in Judeo-Christian culture, but we do not have far to look to locate it alive and well in other religious and political persuasions. There is also some of this quality in the dedicated competitive athlete, and we can see certain participants in a rugby or football match or in the Olympic games who are suddenly "taken over" and perform outstanding feats which, all too often, they cannot repeat later. The Martial personality needs regular doses of this energy, whether on the mental or emotional or physical level, because it is a connection with the archetypal realm and gives the person's life a feeling of vitality and meaning.

In myth, the god Ares is irresistibly drawn to Aphrodite, who has the power to tame him through his desire for her. In this respect Ares reflects the hero Herakles, who was also tamed through sexual desire by the Queen of Lydia, called Omphale (which means navel). Omphale has such absolute erotic power over the hero that he allows her to dress him up as a woman and toy with him as though he were a large, cuddly tomcat. You might remember the painting I mentioned of Ares and Aphrodite, where he is completely passive after sex, sprawled by her side, satiated and somnolent. Ares can thus be tamed through erotic feeling, through beauty and pleasure, whereas the excitement of conquest only leaves him hungry for more conquest.

The mythic image of Ares tells us that we are dealing with a raw archetypal force, a basic instinct of survival. There are other symbolic images in our diagram which can help us to see subtler dimensions of this instinct. In alchemy, Mars is equated with the principle of sulphur, and is portrayed most often as a wolf. The wolf also turns up in Greek and Roman myth in connection with

Ares-Mars, and the god Mars in fact fathers the twins Romulus and Remus who, suckled by a she-wolf, grow up to found the city of Rome. Mars in this guise is the wolflike lone fighter, the Clint Eastwood of the planetary pantheon. Alchemical sulphur is a symbol of the aggressive instinct, the primal life force, in its bestial stage before it is subjected to those transformative processes which will result in its humanisation, the birth of the new King who is the alchemical gold. In other words, Mars is the primitive, animal form of the Sun.

Thus the solar hero, before he becomes human and develops the capacity for reflective consciousness, is the wolf, the burning alchemical sulphur. This profound symbolism is easily observed in a young child, who at a certain age—usually around two years old, which has led people to describe this stage as the "terrible twos"—begins to behave appallingly, throwing tantrums and being generally disagreeable and perverse. This early rage, which is a perfectly natural aspect of early development, is intolerable for many mothers who have a problem dealing with Mars in themselves, and this can lead to many problems later. But there is something about this primal rage which is really a statement of separateness, and it is the true beginning of the formation of individuality. The rage of a two-year-old needs containing and tempering, but if it is forcibly repressed or blocked through guilt and emotional blackmail, it cannot move beyond its animal form, and the sulphur never transforms. It just goes on fuming and giving off sulphurous smells, and it is a great shock to many people in psychotherapy to discover the "terrible twos" still steaming away inside like an active volcano.

Alchemy gives us some very striking images of the process by which the wolf is transformed into the King. His paws are cut off, and he is placed in a sealed flask or alembic and then cooked. Yet he is not killed, for he is recognised as divine—the theriomorphic form of the alchemical gold. There is a strange paradox in this barbaric image which combines recognition of the highest value with the necessity for suffering and transformation. The wolf howls and makes a dreadful fuss, but the alembic remains sealed, for otherwise no King is born, and no gold formed. We may look again at the experiences of rage in childhood and see that, symbolically, this is the process by which the young child's anger is contained yet not destroyed. The same situation often occurs in psychotherapy, where one may go through a prolonged period of anger toward the therapist which is acted out in varying ways (ranging from chronic lateness or forgetting the cheque book to overt verbal abuse) but which needs to be both acknowledged and contained at the same time.

It is interesting to think about your own childhood, and whether you can remember ever being really angry. Did you ever throw a proper tantrum? Could you express rage and be disciplined without being made to feel you were worthless? Were you slapped or beaten if you expressed rage? Or was the message of repression so absolute that you simply never experienced any emotion resembling anger? I can remember once, when travelling in America to give a seminar, watching a very sad television programme about a schizophrenic serial murderer whose mother was being interviewed. She said defensively, "My son was such a good, obedient child. He was never angry or difficult." Obviously not all well-behaved children grow up to be serial murderers, but I could not help feeling a small shudder at this complete obliteration of the Mars function, which erupted later in life in a particularly horrifying example of berserker rage.

Parents are not responsible for our essential character, and a difficult Mars in the birth chart is not "caused" by parental treatment. But the way in which Mars, the rudimentary Sun, is handled in childhood can make a great difference in terms of how we approach this side of ourselves in adulthood. In many ways a collision of the child's Mars with the parent's, resulting in a beating or an argument, is healthier than the profound castration which results from being taught that anger and aggression are in themselves bad, dirty or immoral. The guilt which arises from such a message is corrosive, and we all tend to feel a little guilty about Mars anyway because, as I have said, the god Ares is basically antisocial and three hundred feet tall, and one would not like to meet him in a dark alley.

A blocked Mars results in a feeling of impotence and victimisation, and great unconscious rage which can express itself in a variety of ways. Since Mars, as myth tells us, is most amenable to seduction, it is often the seductive rather than the aggressive parent who performs the early castration. This is the parent who says,

"If you go on like this you will hurt me so much. And I have already been so badly hurt by your father/mother. I hoped that you would champion me, and take my side. Now even you are behaving like that terrible brute/bitch, injuring me when I am already so unhappy. I am so disappointed in you, I thought you were a better, more loving person." I see that some of you are smiling; perhaps you recognise this piece of dialogue?

Mars can be naturally cruel as nature is cruel, but it is not malevolent. Animals fight to the death, and hunt each other, and live by a ruthless law of survival of the fittest, but they are not innately sadistic. I do not believe that gratuitous cruelty is an inherent attribute of Mars. Blind aggression and crude insensitivity may be, but it takes a special kind of wounding to produce the manipulative cruelty which may be the darkest expression of a thwarted, unconscious Mars. The Martial gods are not by nature vicious; Ares may be a thug, but he observes a soldier's code of honour in battle. Herakles is not sadistic either, merely stupid and blundering at times. But if Mars is castrated (like the sorcerer Klingsor in Wagner's *Parsifal*) and subjected to powerlessness over many years, then it can become very poisonous indeed. This castration may in part be parental, as we have seen, but it also may be the product of a conflict within oneself, where the basic temperament is too peaceable and idealistic to easily integrate such a primitive energy. I feel astrologers make a great mistake if they interpret Mars as innately malefic.

The rage of a blocked Mars can be directed against oneself as well as against the world outside. This is particularly the case with a gentler or more dissociated temperament, such as a dominant Pisces-Libra combination, or a lot of Aquarius. This may result in self-destructive behaviour, emotionally or physically (difficult Mars aspects are known for being accident-prone); or it may lead to a typical group of illnesses which seem to embody frustrated Martial energy. No other planet turns up so frequently as a trigger by progression or transit, or as a natal "hot spot," when emotionally linked symptoms (such as migraine headaches and colitis) erupt. Mars seems to be a major key to physical as well as psychological health, and I am not referring to exercise and diet. Obviously the Moon, being a reflection of the body itself, is important in this context. But there is no emotional state so destructive to the body as repressed rage and feelings of impotence.

Audience: Could this be related to cancer?

Liz: I assume you mean the illness and not the sign. Yes, I believe it is. I was going to talk about this, because there is a great deal of medical evidence emerging which suggests that there may be a particular psychological portrait which accompanies certain forms of cancer. This does not imply that getting cancer is one's "fault," and obviously there are other factors involved; but there may in some cases be a connection between a person's inability to deal with difficult emotions and their susceptibility to the disease.

The personality profile which many doctors seem to feel has a connection with cancer is one where a great deal of acquiescence and wish to please are dominant qualities. It is a little too simplistic to assume that if you go around saying "yes" all the time and never get angry, you will get cancer. But inability to acknowledge, let alone express, one's justifiable anger and right to assert oneself can be, very literally, deadly. Sometimes Martial symptoms are so obvious that I am amazed the person has not made the connection between the weekly migraines or bilious attacks and the Sunday dinners with one's mother-in-law. Martial symptoms are a wonderful emotional barometer if one learns how to read them, for all of us at one time or another find ourselves carrying a nice package of rage which cannot be acknowledged or expressed. There is something very straight and obvious about Mars, even when it is working underground through the body. And we need to remember that Mars is a physical-instinctual planet just as the Moon is. The myth of Aries' parthenogenic birth tells us this. The other face of the warrior is the Martial illness, which is what happens when you take the Berserker, bind and gag him, and dress him up in a city suit.

I have mentioned several times that Mars is a powerful trigger for other transiting and progressed planets. Because of its direct, physical quality, it seems to reflect a manifestation process—just as the progressed Moon does, but with considerably more force. For example, a major transit, such as Pluto over the natal Sun, or Neptune square the natal Moon, or Uranus trine natal Venus, can remain within orb for a long period of time – in Pluto's case, sometimes two to three years. The transit may be said to reflect a process at work, and the entire two-year period is occupied with that process, although it may seem quiet or inactive for long periods while things are at work on the inner level. But when transiting Mars makes a hard angle to the transiting configuration, events tend to occur, or emotions break out which generate change. The phallic, penetrating quality of Mars is very much in evidence in this trigger activity. Mars will also act as a trigger for a progressed planet which is sitting within orb of an aspect to a natal or other progressed planet. Now the cycle of Mars around the zodiac is roughly two years, although it does not spend the same amount of time in each sign – it has a retrograde cycle just as all the other planets do. But if we work with his rough orbit, there is a hard aspect of Mars to each point in the natal chart approximately every six months. Thus Mars will trigger a slow body such as transiting Pluto several times during the course of the transit, and the events which occur at those times will be connected in meaning, if not in outer form, because they are relating to the same underlying process.

If we have a friendly relationship with Mars, we know what we want and can ask for it from others. Different people have different ways of pursuing their objectives, depending upon the sign and aspects of natal Mars; and of course we all want different things at different times in life. But the capacity to "know what we want and do what we have to do to get it" (as Jung once defined masculinity) is dependent on an individual being able to express Mars in a conscious way. The personal style of Mars in Pisces, Cancer or Libra may be much gentler and more indirect than that of Mars in Aries or Leo, because the desire nature is balanced and modified by the need for others' acceptance and approval; but Mars is still Mars nonetheless. And one extremely common result of a disconnected or thwarted Mars is a chronic state of depression.

Obviously a period of depression can arise from perfectly understandable external causes such as separation or loss, and we all experience it at one time or another. But chronic depression has deeper roots, and I have found that all too often the taproot is a profound sense of impotence, frustration and rage, generated by the feeling that one has no capacity for choice, nor power over one's own life. Depression is usually not experienced as overt misery; it is more usually a state of apathy and deadness, where nothing is worth bothering with, not even anger, because it is assumed that nothing will change anyhow no matter what one does or says. Many people dissociate from this kind of deep depression, and consciously gear themselves up to keep the surface of life functioning, finding escape routes such as compulsive work, large doses of television, sex, alcohol or tranquillisers when the repressed blackness threatens to break through into conscious awareness. But break through it does nevertheless, often as illness or tiredness or inability to sleep properly. Mars here inverts and turns against the individual, so that one destroys all one's potentials. It is a kind of death wish, although thoughts of death are not often conscious.

This can be a very serious problem, and I feel it is bound up with a poor relationship with Mars. This planet is concerned with the basic instinct of survival, and while the Sun might reflect the will to live in terms of a sense of meaning, Mars reflects the will to live on the physical-instinctual level. Sometimes the escape route from this dark tangle is provided by a philosophy or ideology of nonattachment, which can find its way into politics as well as into religion. This approach labels personal desire as selfish, and thereby condemns the principle of Mars, dooming it to the underworld where it must function as covert rage and envy. I have found that those who are most angrily vocal in their condemnation of individual striving usually have a powerful but difficult Mars in the birth chart. You can see that Mars is not very good on committees and makes a very poor socialist, because it is not interested in principles; it is interested in survival and gratification of desire. The realistic and sometimes ruthless thrust of Mars wants reward for effort made, and cannot be deflected by arguments that such rewards should be sacrificed on behalf of those who could not or would not make the effort. Since Mars is present in every horoscope, this obviously poses a difficulty for a more idealistic nature, particularly if, as I have suggested, one of the unconscious issues behind such global abnegation is a sense of personal impotence arising from childhood.

One can almost smell the god Ares clanking around in the basement in such situations, furious and frustrated and beating his sword against the locked door. Fanaticism is also often the product of a blocked Mars, because the more uneasy we feel at that sound of banging and shouting coming from behind the locked door, the more blindly emotional and even violent we become in our efforts to convert others to our conscious viewpoint. I have never found an honestly expressed Mars to be fanatical; one pursues one's own goals and other people are left alone to get on with theirs. The history of religious persecution has a good deal of Mars in it, but it is a sick Mars, corroded by guilt and castrated by condemnation of the body and the instincts. It is really very dangerous to go through life repudiating Mars too strongly. Whatever our conscious reasons might be—ideological, religious, or simply the fear of loneliness or separation—the price for others as well as ourselves may be too high.

We need now to consider the issue of what we call masculinity in relation to Mars. Since both men and women have Mars in their charts, it may be assumed that both men and women have a need to express the masculine side of their natures. But as the medical symbol of "male" suggests (it is the astrological glyph for Mars), the expression of Mars may be more basic, urgent and literal for men than it is for women. Our sense of sexual identity and confidence begins with the body itself, and the physical condition of impotence is a more threatening, painful and often degrading experience for men than many women realise.

Often a "Mars problem"—a conscious or unconscious feeling of impotence or castration—will be passed down psychologically through the men in a family. Since the father is for every male child the first channel through which the masculine archetype is met, a father's weakness and inability to express Mars can mean that his son has no model for how to feel potent. Feelings of impotence in a man can express themselves in an obvious way—for example, the traditional "henpecked" husband, resentful but unable to show his anger or say no, who escapes his rage toward his mother-wife by emotionally disconnecting but who performs a kind of covert sabotage at every possible opportunity. The son of such a man may despise his father for his weakness and try to compensate by becoming a psychological bully, attempting to reverse the pattern by controlling his women through conquest, rejection or even violence. Yet inwardly he will suffer from the same feelings of impotence and weakness, hidden not only from others but from himself.

The violent or controlling man and the passive, impotent one thus suffer from the same dilemma with Mars, although ironically these two will usually despise each other if they should meet socially. The extreme of the macho man thus mirrors the extreme of the "wimp," although neither is quick to acknowledge that they are hurting from the same wound. This is the pattern from father to son in many families, although it may disguise itself as an external problem such as a hardworking father with a wastrel son, or vice versa. And there is bound to be competition and covert warfare between a father who is insecure in his masculinity and a son who is struggling to find it. If this kind of problem with Mars exists in a woman who projects it onto men, then she may find herself having to deal with two men in her life—husband and lover, husband and son, successive lovers, or whatever—who appear to represent these opposite poles, yet who are secretly identical in their difficulty with Martial masculinity. The woman with a controlling or bullying lover may consciously try to choose a passive, compliant man afterward, only to discover that she feels victimised by them both in different ways, and suffers just as much from a feeling of impotence within the relationship.

We could go on ad nauseam exploring the myriad emotional scenarios which reflect this problem of masculine potency. But all these characteristic scripts reflect a dilemma around the simple Martial principle of knowing what you want and doing what you have to do to get it. More importantly, we perhaps need to consider what this pattern might look like in the birth chart, and what we can do about it. One aspect which often suggests a problem of feeling and expressing potency is the square or opposition of Mars to the Sun. Whatever the natal relationship between these two planets, they need ultimately to be friends, for Mars must offer the Sun its fighting power and the Sun must provide meaning for Mars' battles. If the Sun repudiates Mars (in other words, if we disown our aggression because it challenges our self-image and our conscious goals), then we may have vision without any capacity to put it into action. Then it seems that "other people" (partner, parent, child, employer, government, society) reject our creative efforts, and obstruct us with their ruthless selfishness. I feel this is true for both men and women. If we try to be the Sun without Mars, we castrate ourselves, and wind up inauthentic and power-less; and our projected Mars will come back at us from the world outside.

The issue of others' violence is a thorny one, and one cannot attribute everything to one's own personal projections. Violence exists in the world and always has, and sometimes whole societies are the victims of it. It would be absurd then to speak of one single individual's projected Mars invoking a Hitler, a Stalin, or the IRA. Yet when violence enters our lives on a one-to-one basis, we must consider whether there might be something in ourselves which is being triggered at the time, manifesting "out there" in true Martial fashion. There are people who are violence-prone, and where there is a pattern of this kind, we must look inside, however pain-ful it might be, if we are to break the chain. I have sometimes upset women clients with violent husbands by suggesting that there might be something within them which unconsciously colludes with or helps to invoke the violence already existent in the other person. I find absurd and dangerous the ideological viewpoint that all violence perpetrated by men on women is due to men's basically vicious natures. Being subjected to a man's violence is a terrifying and degrading experience, and merits absolute sympathy as well as legal protection. Yet there are some very uncomfortable issues raised, not least the one of why some women stay married to husbands who knock them about.

When a negative Mars erupts within a relationship, it is usually the problem of both people. If one carries around a deep rage which is unacknowledged and unexpressed, then one may pro-voke a partner to act it out, thereby achieving a kind of release while at the same time preserving apparently clean hands. And to put it very bluntly, there are some extremely subtle ways in which a woman may castrate a man and drive him to the point of blind rage which pass under the guise of loving self-sacrifice. You should all read Eugene O'Neill's *The Iceman Cometh*, which offers a terrify-ing portrayal of this mechanism. Because as a society we condemn acts of physical violence while ignoring those acts of emotional violence which are disguised as martyrdom, we find it painful to confront these issues in ourselves and others. Yet there is a kind of sweet, passive, "nice" personality, found in both men and women, which has the most remarkable knack of repeatedly arousing anger and aggression in others.

I will give you a personal example of this—a small incident which occurred a few years ago and which has remained in my mind as a kind of vignette of typical projected Mars interaction. My doorbell rang just after midnight one weekday night. I was in the middle of an interesting conversation with my partner, and was also getting ready to go to bed; and although, as Howard implied when he said that my sign was "Do Not Disturb," I may sometimes err on the side of being too firm with my boundaries, I think even a triple Pisces with Neptune conjunct the Sun, Moon and Ascendant would have been mildly disturbed by what followed.

There on the doorstep was a chap who looked as though he had stepped out of Haight-Ashbury in 1966, complete with beads, lovelocks down his back, and a sweet, we-are-all-one smile. He said, "Hello, I'd like to have my chart done." I counted silently to ten and said with reasonable politeness, "As you obviously have my address, it would be considerably more courteous to write to me or phone for an appointment. I don't do people's charts at midnight." He replied: "Oh, but I really feel the need for it now." He went on smiling that sweet smile, not in the least bit aggressive, and all the while I could feel myself becoming angrier and angrier. It wasn't just that he had no sense of another person's privacy. There is a deep unconscious aggression in such behaviour, of which he was completely oblivious. I said, "Well, that's too bad, isn't it, because you'll just have to survive without it. This is not a booth at a fair, open 24 hours a day for your convenience. Go away and don't ring this doorbell again." At this, he said with perfect ingenuousness, "Why are you getting so angry? Do you have some kind of problem with anger?"

I think I should be given due credit for not murdering him on the spot. I merely slammed the door in his face, and he no doubt went away convinced that I should have been available to him, and must therefore have a serious problem dealing with my aggression. Yet because he did not display overt anger, he could justify his own behaviour. He saw himself as a flower child, full of peace, love and humanitarian spirit; yet he expected the world to give him absolute unconditional mothering, any hour of the day or night, and if it did not, then he would vent his rage through accusing others of being "unevolved." He was utterly lacking in boundaries and therefore blind to others' reality, and when that reality impinged upon him unpleasantly, it was invariably the other person's fault. I can imagine him wandering through life with that sweet smile, leaving behind him a trail of enraged partners, employers, friends and acquaintances, and giving from time to time a weary, poignant sigh at the evil, aggressive state into which the world has fallen because of its greed and selfishness.

There are humourous elements in this story, but it illustrates a profound and disturbing point. If this man gets assaulted or draws violence from others — and with such behaviour, he inevitably will ring the wrong doorbell sooner or later — whose responsibility is it? There are many kinds of invasion and control, and some are very subtle, and force others to do one's will through playing on their feelings of obligation and pity. I think you can see what I am getting at when I say that the eruption of violence within a relationship may be the creation of both people, not just the uncontrolled aggressiveness of one. How would you feel after months or years if you were reminded gently every day of how selfish and unloving you were if you did not give your partner precisely what he or she needed, especially after all those sacrifices (which you might not have asked for in the first place)?

This is often what happens when Mars is repudiated and forced to operate through unconscious channels. Being the victim of another's abuse, verbal, emotional or physical, is a horrific experience, but I believe we must find the courage to look at the element of collusion in it. I can see, looking back, why I might have attracted that flower child to my doorstep; at the time I was still struggling with the issue of having the right to possess boundaries (which is in part a Mars issue), and he was the personification of a guilty inner voice telling me I should put the needs of others first. But he was at far greater risk than I, for I had merely to close the door in his face; but had I been six feet tall and drunk, he might have wound up in hospital. His anger was totally unconscious, global and unforgiving rather than specific and reality-linked, and stretching back to a childhood where he was no doubt deprived of the unconditional loving every child needs.

We all have Mars in the horoscope, and the issue of psychological separation from others through openly expressing one's aggression inevitably confronts us all. Violence and victimisation are Mars issues, taken to the extreme; and if we are caught in a repeating pattern of being the passive recipients of another's rage while believing that we are devoid of any ruthless survival instinct ourselves, then it is time to ask what might be going on with Mars in the birth chart.

Audience: I wonder if, when someone is raped, there is some link between Mars in the two charts. Might this be an example of what you are saying?

Liz: This is an extremely charged issue, and I am reluctant to get into it without sufficient time to deal with the emotions it might arouse in members of the group. I do not believe any woman can be "blamed" for rape, and there is around us a very dangerous collective attitude, a relic of medieval Catholicism which believed women were the tools of the devil, and which often makes women feel so guilty and ashamed that they are often frightened of reporting a rape to the police for fear of being accused of "causing" it. This attitude is within the woman herself, as much as "out there," but it is deeply entrenched in the collective psyche. This having been said, I think there are individual cases—especially that murky area where the rapist is known to the woman, an ex-boyfriend or ex-husband or casual friend—where there may be collusion involved, and where a woman's deep suppressed rage toward men may unconsciously set up a situation where the rage is acted out. I have encountered such cases, just as I have encountered cases where a woman was truly foolish in wandering about alone in an area known to be dangerous; and it is rather pointless to argue that there "should" be no such areas in a perfect society. The reality is that there are, and only a deeply unconscious person would tempt fate (or their complex) by blundering unaccompanied into New York's Central Park or the alleys of London's Brixton late at night.

In sum, I think it depends upon the individual situation. Sometimes there are difficult Mars contacts between two people which are set off by the same transit, and I have seen this in cases of couples where rape or violence erupts between them. However, in contrast to this, a recent chart example of a rape comes to mind, that of a 16-year-old girl who was assaulted during the transit of

Pluto over her natal Moon. Her mother came to see me about it, and since the rapist was an unknown man, it was obviously impossible to obtain his chart. But the girl had been out late at a disco, and was walking home alone through a rather insalubrious area of London. I will leave it to you to consider whether some element of self-destructiveness might have been at work—or even deeper issues involving the maternal psychological inheritance, which when deeply unconscious may take very strange forms. When we take the lid off the can of worms which such incidents represent, we often find they have no bottom, and we are in dark waters indeed.

The rapist is a common figure in women's dreams, and it is worth considering what this might mean symbolically in terms of one's own Mars. Although there is usually a Pluto component involved in rape, Ares in myth is not known for his courtship skills, and the angry dream aggressor may reflect a dissociated and furious Mars, attacking consciousness from within. The motif of the thug or the gang of delinquents is also a common theme in men's dreams, and once again this may reflect the man's own unacknowledged aggression pursuing him from the unconscious. Another Martial figure is the arsonist, for fire can be an image of suppressed rage which threatens to break out and consume the edifice of one's conscious values. Such dreams, if they are recurrent, demand attention, and point to issues around Mars, which will usually be found to be active by transit or progression.

Audience: Can a person's Mars be affected by social values and pressures?

Liz: Certainly. We are all vulnerable to collective values, and all the inner planets may be challenged, sometimes creatively and sometimes harmfully, by the moral and ethical structures of a particular society. As I have said, Mars is itself "antisocial," in that the planet reflects an instinct for self-gratification and individual survival which will inevitably collide, at some point, with the wishes of others and of the group. We all experience a certain amount of tempering of Mars, which is necessary if we are to live with other people. But the tempering may be too harsh in some social situations, and even in some cultures. An entire people may suffer from collective depression—I think, from what I have seen on my travels, that this has been the case with countries under Soviet rule. I mentioned earlier that Mars makes a bad communist, and in communist-ruled nations it is, in a sense, the Mars of an entire people which is repressed. There are of course nations which are so Martial that they justify the right to invade everybody else's turf. An untempered Mars may easily adopt the attitude that what is mine is mine and what is yours is also mine. But we could spend the next week just talking about the collective psychology of war.

We are working our way toward the example chart for this session, but there are a few more general points about Mars which I would like to cover. Firstly, I wanted to mention a wonderful workshop demonstration of Mars which I encountered many years ago. This workshop was run by an astrologer named Alexis Edwards, who brought a quantity of really delicious sweets and chocolates and so on, and put them all on a big table in the middle of the room. Then he instructed the group to get up and take whatever they wanted from the table. After everyone had eaten their sweets, an extremely funny discussion followed about the different ways in which different people procured the goodies they wanted, since this reflected in a very direct, "everyday" fashion the operation of Mars in the different signs.

One individual with Mars in Libra, for example, was overheard saying to his neighbour, "Would you mind getting that chocolate slice for me? I'm just so terribly tired, I don't think I can cope with all those people pushing to get to the table." A woman with Mars in Aries had arrived at the table before Alexis even finished giving his instructions, and had managed to pocket not one but two biscuits. A man with Mars as well as the Sun and Mercury in Virgo, who fell about laughing at the whole thing afterward, decided he would not have any sweets, because eating such things in the late morning was bad for the level of blood sugar. Someone with Mars in Cancer was observed to move with apparent indolence and nonchalance toward the table, circling around it for a while as though she really didn't mind which sweet she got, and then, when there was a brief lull, moving like lightning to grab the one she wanted.

This is an amusing and educational way to get the feeling of how we use Mars in ordinary life, and it is worth reflecting on our own behaviour patterns in all spheres where we must pursue something we want. The arena of courtship is, of course, an obvious place to go Mars-spotting, as is any committee meeting where one must find a way to get what one wants while dealing with others who are busy doing the same thing. In England we have a national institution called the queue, which is even more sacred than Canterbury Cathedral. If we have business at the bank or the shop and there are others there before us, we form a neat, polite line called a queue. Anyone who jumps the queue receives such appalling, hate-filled looks that most people would not dare to push their way in. Because we are British, it is rare to hear insults flung directly at the offender; more often someone in the queue mutters to someone else *sotto voce*, "How incredibly rude." This is meant to convey that the queue-jumper is so un-British, so utterly ignorant of civilised rules of conduct, that he or she might as well drop through a hole in the floor out of shame. In contrast, when travelling in Italy or Israel, as well as in New York, I have observed what might be called the "if there's an empty space, grab it" tactic, while in Turkey I have seen people actually throw each other out of the way to board a bus. But no one thinks of this as uncivilised or morally wrong; it is just normal, and any fool who chooses to stand in line will still be standing there three weeks later. Perhaps these things are reflections of Mars in a particular country's birth chart.

Audience: Is it more difficult for a woman to express Mars?

Liz: This is really the same issue as the Sun. Historically, the channels through which these masculine planets could be expressed were very clearly defined. A man could become a warrior, and do battle; or he could be ambitious and fight his way to power and wealth. A woman could express her fighting spirit to defend her home and family, or could channel Mars indirectly through pushing a compliant partner into obtaining what she wanted for her. Women have always been able to live Mars, but it is the channels which have been limited and circumscribed. On the other hand, mythology is full of images of warrior women like the Amazons, and some of the earliest deities of battle were not male, but female — the Egyptian Hathor and Sekhmet, the Babylonian Ishtar, the preclassical Greek Aphrodite. And history is full of powerful

Martial women like Catherine the Great and Queen Elizabeth I of England. This issue is a thorny one. The more extreme feminist viewpoint postulates that women have been "oppressed" and have been allowed no power over their own lives, slaves to their biology and their material dependence on their partners. Yet the expression of Martial feelings – passion, envy, anger, aggressive verbal attack – has always been more permissible to women, who were believed to be more emotional by temperament. I am wary of generalisations, and can only talk with any sincerity of individuals I work with now. And given the more open climate now, I feel that individuals, male or female, have the power to oppress themselves if they have a Mars problem within. I think it is more a question of expanding the channels and levels through which Mars can operate, and learning to choose those which are really self-gratifying rather than those which fit a principle or set of expectations, inner or outer.

Audience: But men dislike aggressive women.

Liz: Aggression is not a likeable quality in anyone if it is expressed in a blind, hateful way. But what is an "aggressive woman"? I am probably the wrong person to ask about this issue, because I do not have a great interest in always interpreting such issues as "sexist." If you mean that many men don't like a woman who shouts and screams abuse at them, you are probably right; but other women won't especially like her either, and who can blame them? I have known many competitive, dynamic Martial women who are liked and respected by work colleagues as well as partners and friends, because their energy is not expressed with the poisonous rage of unhealed childhood wounds poking through. The generalisation that everyone dislikes an aggressive woman at work is absurd; it depends upon the workplace, the people who work there, and the individual woman and how she deals with her colleagues. If you have a chip on your shoulder, you are likely to knock chips in everyone else's as well; but it is the unspoken blame for one's whole life, rather than a direct expression of Mars, which provokes the trouble.

In the end I must always return to the issue of Mars within the individual. There are real problems still to be confronted "out there" in terms of women's rights (such as abortion), and many of the goals and objectives of the women's movement are inarguably valid and long overdue. But we have much greater power than we think to shape our own lives, the imperfections of society notwithstanding. And I have never found that a lifetime's unconscious grievance against the parents, or projection of one's own power and aggression onto others, has ever helped any woman's cause.

Audience: What about Mars in the composite chart? Does it mean the same thing?

Liz: Yes, the principle is the same, although we need to remember that in the composite chart, the planets represent functions of the relationship rather than of an individual. So Mars is, in one sense, the fighting principle of the relationship, which serves the composite Sun, just as Mars in the individual chart serves the Sun. A relationship must survive in the world, must meet challenges and pressures from others, and must be able to actualise its goals. If we take the composite Sun to represent the essential character of the relationship, and what it most needs to express in order to fulfil its "purpose," then the pooled energies which form the composite Mars are mobilised to support that expression. For example, if the composite Sun is in Leo in the 10th, then the essence of the relationship is the creative development of both individuals, and the contribution they make as a unit to the world outside; the relationship must make its mark on the collective, and often this means the couple being involved in joint work ventures and creative projects. If the composite Mars is in the 2nd in Scorpio, then the energy that the couple spends on developing financial stability and a secure emotional base — and the quarrels they have over such issues — will serve to support this joint need to make a mark on the world.

A repressed Mars also has similar effects in a relationship to those it has in an individual. If there is an avoidance of competitive energy and aggression, both within the relationship and toward the world outside, then unconscious anger will invariably find its way out through covert means. Another way of understanding Mars, which we have discussed in the individual chart, is that it reflects the style by which we go after what we want; and the same may be said of a relationship. A composite with Mars in Aries trine

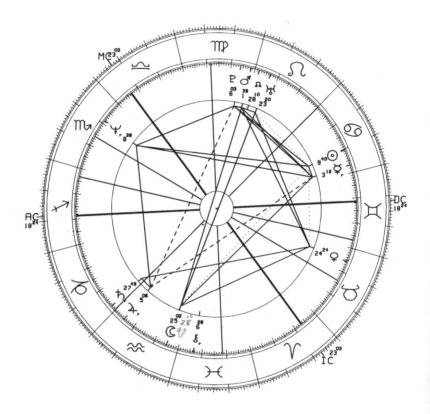

Chart 4. Diana, Princess of Wales. Born in Sandringham, England, July 1, 1961, at 7:45 P.M. BST. (52N50, 0E30) Birth data source: Buckingham Palace. Chart calculated by Astrodienst, using the Placidus house system.

Jupiter will reflect a much greater directness and openness than a composite with Mars in Pisces opposite Neptune. There are couples whom one meets at a party who are very obvious in the way they go after their joint goals, and other couples who are extremely low-key in the way they pursue their objectives. Going after what we want of course includes the objects of our sexual desire, and the sexual energy and style of the relationship will also be described by the composite Mars.

I would like now to spend some time on the signs and aspects of Mars. The general principles can be applied to both the individual and the composite chart. Other planets which form strong angles to Mars colour the manner in which we express our fighting spirit, and also reflect sides of us which either help or hinder our pursuit of our goals. If we think again of the Labours of Herakles, we might understand planets aspecting Mars to symbolise the kinds of tempering processes which we will undergo during the course of life, because any planet coupled with Mars in this way reflects a kind of Herculean labour. Some planets are comfortable for Mars to accommodate, especially Jupiter, which even in square or opposition offers an intellectual enthusiasm and philosophical dimension to the fighting spirit. But planets such as Saturn, Pluto and Chiron, even in trine, seem to suggest a very difficult labour, a hard tempering which hopefully will result in a tough, resilient quality of character rather than bitterness and resentment.

I would like you to look at the example chart for this session (see Chart 4 on page 204) as it is a good place to begin exploring the signs and aspects of Mars. Rather than beginning with a case history, I thought we could just jump in and see how far we get with an interpretation before I give you any information on Diana. Mars in this chart is 1 degree Virgo in the 8th house, conjunct Pluto, and there is also a wide conjunction to Uranus in Leo on the other side. So this Mars is sandwiched in between two outer planets. It is also sextile Mercury at the beginning of Cancer, and forms an out-of-sign opposition to the Moon in Aquarius. Finally, it is square (once again out-of-sign) with Venus. This is quite a broad array of Mars aspects, some of them harmonious and some of them obviously troublesome. Perhaps we could consider Mars in Virgo first, as well as its placement in the 8th. And it helps to keep the myths in mind, rather than falling back on flat statements such as "Mars in

Virgo is critical" or whatever. Remember the mythic images that are associated with Virgo?

Audience: Perhaps Diana might feel she needs to clean out the Augean Stables all the time.

Liz: That element is certainly part of Virgo, and you will see later that it does fit. But let's try to get a sense of how this Mars operates, as a reflection of the way in which Diana fights for her values and gets what she wants from life. Think of that 300-foot god Ares, hulking and irascible, and then dress him up in Virgoan clothes. What will he look like, and how will he behave when he comes into a room?

Audience: He might be very fastidious, very prissy.

Liz: Yes, he will be constrained by his Virgo clothes, and won't be able to just crash through the door. He will be much more self-contained and controlled and aloof, with a certain cool dignity. Mars in Virgo does not rampage about. It will move carefully, step by step, giving a quality of impeccable attention to all the details of what is going on in the environment. Whenever we think of Virgo, we should think of the virgin goddess who is not for sale, who is in absolute possession of herself. Mars in Virgo will not "sell out" in order to achieve a goal; there is a quality of integrity in the expression of one's competitive instincts, a willingness to work for what one gets. On the minus side, there is likely to be a certain lack of spontanaeity, since so much self-containment limits the expression of Mars' fiery side.

Now what about its placement in the 8th house? In what sphere of life is Mars most likely to pursue its objectives?

Audience: The 8th house is about death.

Liz: In one sense, yes; but there is a deeper and more inclusive meaning to this house of which death is only one aspect.

Audience: Sexuality.

Liz: Yes, in part. But we always need to get to the core of a house in order to understand why such disparate themes as death, sexuality and joint resources should come under the same department. The 8th house belongs to Scorpio, and it deals with that dimension of life and of the personality which is hidden beneath the surface. Where the 2nd house deals with what is visible and concrete, the 8th deals with what really runs the show from the bunker below. That is why we are so often shocked or thrown into crisis when we encounter planets in the 8th; we did not know that there was an entire realm of activity going on below the threshold of the conscious personality. Rather than defining this house as "death" or "sexuality," I am more inclined to see it as the interface where the integrated conscious personality, having developed solidity and adaptation through the first seven houses, encounters that invisible domain which it cannot control, and where the individual is subjected to experiences which change the fundamental attitude toward life because of this loss of the ego's power. In death, as in orgasm, we are not in control any longer; and the same may be said of both family complexes (which form before we even come into existence) and "joint resources" where we must pool our energy and substance with that of others.

A planet in the 8th house is therefore experienced as "other," just as one in the 7th is. Sometimes in the first half of life this "other" is projected onto a parent or a partner, especially in the emotional sphere of a relationship; but more commonly it is felt as a compulsion or explosive "pocket" inside oneself, over which one has no control. The behaviour of an 8th house planet is never initially out in the open, although experience and a willingness to look within tend to alter this. The planet seems to take us over for a while, often leaving profound changes in its wake, and we must begin to explore the underworld of the personality in order to understand what has happened to us. So the Mars function of competitiveness, aggression and battle spirit will not initially be a well-integrated side of Diana's personality. She would be likely to start out in life as a little too kind and nonaggressive, vulnerable to the manipulations of others. Mars would tend to erupt at critical moments, to her surprise as much as anyone else's, and it would take time and some inner exploration to learn to handle Martial instincts in a conscious way.

Some of the aspects of Mars tend to underline this interpretation. This is especially true of Mars in opposition to the Moon, where the aggressive instinct is in conflict with the need for security and the urge to belong. With this aspect there is usually a dilemma between self-assertion and wanting to please others, which is why it can sometimes reflect an edgy temper—one placates and placates and then all of a sudden one has simply had enough and comes out fighting, to everyone's astonishment including one's own. Here the Moon in Aquarius in the 2nd house emphasises the need to feel secure within the containment of a social group. And as we have seen, Mars energy is basically inimical to smooth collective cooperation; it is too individualistic, too much a servant of the Sun. Are there any Mars-Moon squares or oppositions in the group?

Audience: Yes, I have an opposition. It's true, I am told I have a very bad temper.

Liz: With any opposition there is a need to find a balance between the two opposing principles. One way a better balance can be achieved between Mars and the Moon is to let one's anger and need for self-assertion express in small, regular doses, rather than in one huge cataclysm. Usually one or the other end of this aspect is pushed into the unconscious (in Diana's case it would most likely be Mars because it is submerged in the 8th, and also because the Moon is her Sun sign ruler and is therefore a very powerful personality factor). You can see that some conscious effort to express the blocked end of the opposition will help the whole situation enormously. If it were the Moon which were suppressed, then the person might have no problem with expressing anger and aggression, but might deny his or her emotional needs. These would then be likely to erupt through physical symptoms, or through bouts of emotional depression or compulsive dependency.

Mars square Venus also emphasises this dilemma between self and others. If we understand Venus to reflect Diana's sense of what is beautiful and worthwhile in life, then we can assume that her values will be in conflict with her natural instinct to fight for her own ground. What do you think about Venus in Taurus in the 5th house?

Audience: There is a great need for stability in relationship.

Liz: Yes, this is a very peaceable Venus, which needs emotional stability, material security, traditional values in relationship, and a great degree of harmony and beauty in the environment. We could also look at its placement in the 5th house and infer that Diana also places great value on old-fashioned romantic love (which is threatened by the separative side of Mars) and on children as the fruit of this love. Venus is also trine Saturn, which emphasises her desire for stability and structure; and Saturn is on the cusp of the 2nd house, which accentuates it even more. There is a clear picture building up here of a basic life dilemma in Diana's chart. The Moon and Saturn root themselves deeply in the security of the 2nd house, with Saturn in its own sign of Capricorn (a highly conservative placement) trine Venus, and the Moon placed in one of Saturn's signs. All this accentuates the traditional, highly responsible, security-loving side of Diana's personality, and reflects great emotional loyalty and reliability. But she must contend with a "rogue" Mars in Virgo in the 8th, a powerful fighting spirit which will not compromise itself, flanked by two outer planets which suggest a frustration of the Martial energy by collective principles of "right" behaviour (Uranus) and the unconscious effects of a difficult family history (Pluto).

We need to consider more carefully this pair of outer planets in relation to Mars. I think I have spoken about the way in which Uranus "sublimates" other planets, pushing them into operation on the mental level while checking their more instinctual, self-centred activity. Uranus is concerned with general principles, with collective ideas which are emerging into the light and which have not yet been processed through the individual's own value system. So Uranus will interfere with Mars' essentially physical and instinctual mode of operation, demanding that Diana acts according to ideal principles rather than personal desires. This can be extremely positive, since it gives Mars a brain, which he ordinarily lacks; there is a capacity for reflection and a broader viewpoint which helps to civilise the 300-foot brute. The same thing might be said of Mars in Aquarius; this is a much more reasonable Mars, which can consider the welfare of the group. But you can also see where this might be a difficulty too, because Mars loses some of his natural fighting spirit and his capacity for spontaneous action.

I have some trouble in equating Uranus with "individuality," because although it can express in an unpredictable and disruptive way (which reflects its function of breaking down old social structures), it is concerned with new collective rather than personal ideas. The mythic image of the god Ouranos, who symbolises the ideal concept of life rather than the actuality of it, is also an image of perfectionism; this god, after all, condemned his children to the bowels of the underworld because they were made of earth, ugly and flawed. Where there is an ideal concept of perfection, whether for a person or for a society, there is no room for the individual, who will never fit a statistic and who will, thank goodness, always defy any attempt to create a perfectly functioning social organism. Uranus expresses that dimension of Aquarius which is opposed to the Sun-ruled Leo, and which will level the individual in the name of the group—even if that group is "New Age."

So although Uranus may behave in an iconoclastic fashion, it is not concerned with the individual; it is really striving to replace one social system (the cynical, outworn Saturnian one) with another social system (the improved, Promethean one where full human potential can be realised according to a new idea or philosophy). Without the civilising effects of Uranus, we would be trapped within the stagnant "that's just how it is, mate" worldliness of Saturn, and this Promethean spirit of social reform in its most positive form is evident in Diana's chart through her Moon in Aquarius opposite Uranus and her Mars conjunct Uranus. If Diana is able to make the best use of this combination of energies, she can direct her Mars toward humanitarian goals of some kind, and might enjoy work in the helping professions, or philanthropic activities which address recognised social ills. But if she cannot get the balance right, she is likely to pay for too Promethean a use of Mars with a certain amount of personal frustration, resulting in periodic bouts of anger and depression.

Audience: The conjunction of Mars with Pluto does the opposite to Mars—it pulls it down into the instinctual realm.

Liz: Yes, that is true. But Pluto is also an outer planet, and like Uranus serves the collective rather than the individual. Pluto does not reflect our personal desires; it symbolises the emotional and instinctual needs of the species, the collective, and most of all the family, which is an ancient tribal organism that passes down from generation to generation its particular methods of survival. When Mars aspects Pluto, the "tempering" or Labour of Herakles which we must face is often the family psychological inheritance, which predisposes us toward certain emotional patterns that may conflict with our own more individual will and desires. Diana will have to find a way to combine individual self-assertion with the emotional rules of behaviour she has unconsciously absorbed from her family. She cannot undo the past, nor eradicate whatever scars she might carry from it. Putting Mars together with Pluto in a creative way requires a certain amount of honest confrontation with that family background and the ways in which it has shaped her. Otherwise she may feel constantly thwarted by the survival needs of the group around her, and may project the frustrations of her childhood onto whatever family she forms in adult life. The sextile of Mars to Mercury is a great help in this situation, because it can provide the possibility of understanding and formulating her needs and feelings—a considerable asset when such powerful unconscious forces are putting Mars to the test.

Audience: Would it feel the same if Mars were in trine to Uranus and Pluto?

Liz: Yes, the same meaning would apply; but the sense of pressure would perhaps not be so great. Conjunctions are the most intense of the aspects, and there is no leeway to relax. One is compelled to have to deal with the energies head-on, right from childhood. On the other hand, the great intensity and urgency of the Mars-Uranus-Pluto reflects the possibility of tremendous character formation. If Diana can stand up to the tempering process to which life will subject her, she will be a social force to be reckoned with in the very best sense, and can make lasting contributions to the world around her.

Audience: Can we know something about Diana now? You said you would leave the case history until later.

Liz: I think you already know quite a bit about her without realising it; this is the chart of the Princess of Wales. But I wanted you to get the feeling of this Mars without the distraction of knowing her actual situation. The same interpretation would apply whatever her position in life. But you can see how Diana must deal with an incredible weight of collective inheritance and expectation, and still remain a person in her own right. Her Mars is really pinioned to collective service of some kind, and because the role of the future Queen is an archetypal one, she is a symbol as well as a human being, and must find a way to honour both. The Saturnian side of her gives her great strength, tenacity and reliability, but I think we need to appreciate what a Herculean labour she has taken on. I find it quite irritating when the press invade her privacy and pick holes in everything she does; it might do some of our British journalists a world of good to change places with her and see just what it feels like.

One of the great gifts of astrology is its capacity to let us understand something of what another person feels and experiences. This is a woman who, alongside the shy Cancerian nature, has great spirit and a need to make an independent contribution. Yet on the archetypal level her importance is really that of mothering the next king; she is no one in her own right. In the old days, the role of queen was that of a breeding vessel. She had to be virgin (and still does) so as not to sully the royal line with scandal or the embarrassment of a bastard tucked away somewhere (unlike the king, whose status was enhanced by a colourful sexual career); she had to come of good stock; and she had to produce an heir. Otherwise, apart from charitable works, she was expected to shut up and behave in an appropriate fashion. Remember what happened to Henry VIII's wives when they could not bear a son?

We may laugh at this now, but when Diana displayed a little Sagittarian glamour and began to befriend pop singers and actors, the press made a meal of it. Why should she not? But the archetypal background runs deep and strong within any collective, and it is an archaic, primitive, truly Plutonian force which demands that our figureheads—be they kings or presidents—remain within the confines of their symbolic roles. Diana accepted her role voluntarily—no one coerced her to marry Prince Charles—and on some level she must have anticipated, at least in part, what she was invoking in the process. Perhaps it was that Moon in Aquarius in the 2nd house, and Saturn in Capricorn trine Venus in Taurus, which drew her to the greatest stability she could possibly find (the King of England does not divorce)—not to mention her Sun in the 7th house with its dream of a radiant, powerful marriage partner. The Sun is also trine Neptune in the 10th, which suggests an element of self-sacrifice, a longing to give up her own individuality in the name of a deeper or higher collective need. Yet she would inevitably have a hard task before her, given the natal aspects and house placement of Mars, and I believe she has done extremely well considering the degree of anger and frustration she must have felt, particularly at the outset. She no doubt expected something out of a fairy tale, since the realism of her strong Saturn would not have been able to balance the romanticism of the Sun in Cancer trine Neptune until the time of its return at 29 years of age; and the tempering process to which her Mars has been subjected was probably very painful and difficult for her. Yet she has matured into a woman of great style, self-possession and quiet tenacity, and is certainly not merely a breeding vessel.

Audience: Could you comment on the synastry aspect of Charles' Saturn conjuncting Diana's Mars-Pluto?

Liz: I would like to discuss this later, when Howard and I will talk about Venus and Mars, for we will use the charts of the Prince and Princess of Wales as examples   (see discussion p. 263 and Charts 5 and 6, pages 264–265). But in general, synastry aspects seem to reflect one of the ways in which we learn to express the planets within our own charts, because if we are not fully conscious of something in ourselves, we will generally find our way into relationships which activate what we are not acknowledging. Sometimes this has a very fated feel, as is the case when unexpressed planets are triggered between parent and child. If the aggressive instinct is operating in an unconscious way, there is a great likelihood that we will be attracted to those whose planets make powerful aspects to our Mars, not least because they make us feel vital and alive – even if that planet is Saturn or Chiron and we wind up battling it out with them. We discover that we know how to fight by having to fight. In traditional synastry, hard aspects to Mars between two lovers' charts are very exciting and often sexually arousing, because there is a close relationship between the fighting spirit and the excitement of sexual challenge and conquest. One of the components of an ongoing attraction is the element of conflict, which ensures that one never wholly possesses the other person.

Audience: Is this true even of Neptune in one person's chart hitting Mars in the other?

Liz: Yes, very much so. Neptune-Mars contacts in synastry can be tremendously erotic. Neptune will excite Mars through its vulnerability (Mars loves championing the helpless) and its magical elusiveness, although there can also be a great deal of anger generated in the Mars person because the Neptune person keeps changing shape all the time. How can our Herakles cope with fighting a fog? There is no such labour as "The Battle with the Invisible Miasma" in his mythology, and he is ill-equipped to cope with Neptune's subtleties, being strong but not very good at reading double messages. Neptune can work up not only passion but considerable aggression in the Mars person, who experiences Neptune as indirect, chaotic and even deceptive and undermining. If you are unaware of your Mars, and have been living an apparently aggression-free existence, you may suddenly find yourself slamming doors and shouting, "For God's sake, come out with it, what do you really want?" while your Neptunian partner looks hurt and vulnerable and misunderstood.

Neptune is, like Uranus and Pluto, an outer planet, and describes that collective longing to return to fusion with the source of life. In a natal chart, an aspect between Neptune and Mars may suggest that Mars' tempering – its Herculean labour – will be to integrate this yearning for the Paradise Garden, which blunts Mars' fighting instrument and leaves it confused and impotent, with the more personal instinct to fight and win. Neptune whispers to Mars, "If you are too aggressive and selfish, no one will love you, and then you will be lonely and bereft, and you'll never get back into Eden again." This is of course true up to a point, but we must be prepared to leave Eden occasionally if we are to feel in any way potent and in charge of our own life. Neptune may swamp Mars, and all the natural aggression must then express itself in a fashion which is not recognisably angry – hence the Mars-Neptune reputation for addiction to drugs and alcohol. Obviously not everyone with a Mars-Neptune aspect is an alcoholic, but there is nevertheless usually a need to be conscious of one's feelings of anger, lest they run underground and surface as highly manipulative forms of covert destructiveness. There is considerably more rage in drug and alcohol addiction, as well as in certain characteristic Mars-Neptune illnesses (such as "post-viral fatigue"), than we might wish to admit. If you doubt this, just ask the other members of the family, who must usually carry all the unconscious anger themselves, and are made to feel horribly guilty about it. Think of what it might be like to be the wife of a chronic alcoholic, and you will get the picture. With Mars-Neptune, others are often undermined, humiliated, and coerced to look after the afflicted person, although he or she may never express anything identified as rage. Mars-Neptune can be a master at passive aggression.

Yet this aspect can also be tremendously creative. Because of Neptune's extreme sensitivity to unconscious collective needs and feelings, the fighting and actualising spirit of Mars can bring the imaginative realm into incarnation, and the individual may possess a unique gift at anticipating collective fashion and "reading" the audience. Mars-Neptune is sometimes associated with theatre and dance, and other creative media where direct audience participation is part of the dynamic. An actor's gift is not simply the ability to memorise lines and utilise technique to create an on-stage character. A good actor can feel others' responses on the gut level, and knows when he or she has touched some deep chord; and there is great power to manipulate collective emotion in an almost magical way. One knows when one has lost the concentration of the audience, or when the chap in the third row, fifth seat from the right has got bored and is surreptitiously reading his newspaper. A creative blend of Mars-Neptune can retain this delicate emotional contact with the collective while at the same time going for the Oscar in a perfectly overt way.

It would be interesting now to move on to Mars in aspect with its two most inimical bedfellows, Saturn and Chiron. If you can keep in mind the theme of wounding in relation to Chiron, and the feeling that somehow the wound will never quite heal, what do you think might be a possible interpretation of Mars-Chiron?

Audience: Physical wounding?

Liz: Sometimes, yes, although I think there need to be other additional factors, such as trouble in the 6th house, before one could make that interpretation. But there may have been an illness or accident early in life which places some kind of limit on one's energy or capacity for self-assertion on the physical level. Chiron's wounding may also be concrete but not concerned with the body itself—for example, a childhood spent in great poverty, or the experience of violence or abuse from a parent or sibling. These things can leave deep scars on the physical expression of the Mars function without leaving an actual body wound. Chiron's "incurable" pain often reflects the memory of a time when one was impotent and one's will was thwarted or subject to another's control; and even if one is successful and able to express one's goals freely in later life, there is often bitterness which does not quite go away. Also, there may be a deep fear of ever being in a situation where one might be controlled again, so Chiron may overcompensate, just as Saturn does, by becoming very controlling oneself.

I have noticed that Mars-Chiron often reflects a workaholic, because the sphere of worldly achievement may be an area where the person feels potent and in control, while in emotional and sexual matters there is always the danger of being vulnerable to another person's will or aggression. Sometimes Chiron's wound to Mars is felt on a direct sexual level, and can reflect some manipulation or humiliation of one's sexual feelings in childhood. Here, too, Chiron may overcompensate and become a kind of sexual technician, a highly skilled lover who habitually chooses more vulnerable or inexperienced partners in order to avoid any threat of hurt or humiliation. This can apply to a woman as well as a man. Chiron often compensates with a form of skill or knowledge, where intelligence is used to plug all the potential gaps through which any future injury might come.

Saturn and Chiron share this dynamic of compensating for feelings of inadequacy or wounding, and this is often the most productive and creative dimension of both planets. What we learn in a desperate effort to protect ourselves may become a true gift, and the compensation is often partly successful—although the original vulnerability never quite goes away. So Mars-Chiron can achieve a high level of competitive skill and sophisticated fighting power, fuelled by the chronic (albeit unconscious) fear that if one lets up for a moment, one will be pushed back into the same old hurt place. If one ever does stop pushing, one must inevitably face those lost, wounded feelings; but if this can be done after some achievement has been made, facing such feelings can generate tolerance and provide a very good tempering for Mars' innate insensitivity.

I have found that a similar picture of early wounding, feelings of impotence, overcompensation, and unexpressed hurt and bitterness can also accompany strong Mars-Saturn aspects. But there is usually more frustration in Mars-Saturn because of Saturn's relationship with the 10th house and collective values and structures. Often Saturn's blockage of Mars reflects a deeply embedded fear of what "they" might think, and is frequently linked with one or both parents' obsession with security or conventional moral or religious values. There is an impersonal quality to Chiron (symbolised by the "accidental" wounding of the myth) which is absent with Saturn; the latter is generally more directly parent-linked, and in adulthood there is usually a great difficulty with authority figures in the world outside because there is one inside—Freud called it the *superego*—which is forever announcing what one ought and ought not to do. Many people have referred to Mars-Saturn as the situation of trying to drive the car with the brakes on. Each time Mars tries to assert itself, the old senex goes nattering on about failure and social unacceptability. Because Saturn can so easily be projected, one may feel constantly frustrated by structures "outside."

Finding a balance between the Martial need to assert oneself, and the Saturnian need to defend oneself behind secure structures, involves first recognising that the source of frustration—although it may have a good "hook" in the external world—has its roots within. It is the negative and defeatist attitude toward obstacles, sometimes alternating with explosive compensatory ruthlessness, which generates the characteristic problems of Mars-Saturn, rather than any "fated" inability to find a creative resolution. Saturn can temper Mars with a healthy dose of realism—what we can and cannot get away with in terms of social structures, and in terms of the work necessary to achieve a goal. If this Herculean labour is accomplished, Mars-Saturn has the unique capacity to harness enormous reserves of energy for concrete ends, which is why it is so often a highly successful aspect in the worldly sense.

Perhaps we could look a bit more closely at Mars-Sun aspects, which I have mentioned already. These contacts, especially the hard angles, generate great energy, and this fiery combination must have a direct and honest outlet if the individual is not to suffer Martial attack from the world outside. The great difficulty with these two, as I have said, is that the solar principle, which is concerned with meaning and spirit, often feels debased by the crude instinctuality of Mars, and tries to disown it. In other words, one does not want to be seen as an aggressive, pushy, self-centred person. But any planet aspecting the Sun reflects an innate character structure, a property of the soul. If Mars aspects the Sun, one must be prepared to be oneself even at the risk of being labelled selfish, and live that Mars function in a clean way. This sometimes involves being a one-man or one-woman show in the outer world, which may attract the envy or resentment of others.

Do any of you have a strong Sun-Mars aspect? Do you work for other people, or are you self-employed?

Audience: I run my own business. I could not bear someone else interfering.

Liz: Exactly. Do any of you with Sun-Mars work within a structure where you must answer to others?

Audience: I work within a structure, but I have made sure I have plenty of autonomy within it.

Liz: What happens when you are obliged to follow someone else's rules or method of doing things?

Audience: There is a big collision.

Audience: I have a Sun-Mars aspect, but I also have Venus in Pisces. I work as a nurse in a hospital setting, and I'm very happy with my job.

Liz: Are you in charge of your own area, your own ward? Or must you answer all the time to superiors?

Audience: Oh, no, I couldn't bear that. I'm in charge, with staff working under me.

Liz: When Sun-Mars people come to me for a chart reading, and I find that they are working for others in a hierarchical organisation, or not working at all, I will usually suggest that they try to find a field where they can run the show and assert their own ideas — even if this means going back to school and getting further training or education. I would particularly encourage any woman with this aspect not to attempt to live all that fiery energy out at home through looking after the needs of the family; with Mars-Sun, making this one's sole focus in life is a recipe for cumulative anger and even psychosomatic symptoms such as migraine headaches or skin eruptions or stomach troubles. Or, alternatively, one winds up with a Martial partner who insists on complete control.

Audience: Is this true even of the sextile?

Liz: To a lesser extent. The sextile is a much gentler aspect, and there is not so much fiery energy trying to get loose. But even with a sextile, one needs an arena in which to assert oneself, however gently. Another way of looking at the dilemma of Sun-Mars is that one needs some place where one can always be right. Sun-Mars does not possess any innate capacity for compromise or a detached perception of others' point of view. In other words, there is usually a streak of intolerance in this aspect, which we can also see to a lesser degree with the Sun in Aries. Now, believing that one is right all the time is not necessarily a bad thing; we have to be prepared to be a little self-centred in order to see any creative project through to the end. Otherwise, all the valid arguments that others' work is just as good, that there are many ways of doing things, that one must be careful of others' feelings, and so on, will erode our energy and leave us feeling that it is not worth bothering with. No one ever won a battle by worrying about whether the enemy might be right after all. Nor can you create anything through a committee, because by the time everyone has had their say, all the originality and spark have vanished. You know the joke about the camel being a horse designed by a committee.

Audience: Is there a similar feeling to Mars in the 5th house?

Liz: Yes, it is another form of the same signature. Sun-Mars, Sun in Aries, Mars in Leo, Sun in the 1st and Mars in the 5th are all different expressions of this combination of solar and Martial energies. I would give the same suggestion to a person with Mars in the 5th – find a sphere where you can shine and be first – although it is much more powerful and a deeper issue when the two planets are in aspect. I have seen quite a few charts of people with Mars in the 5th who have "difficult" children. I always find it interesting when a child acts out a planet in one's own 5th house – as though somehow this planet needs to be expressed through our "inner" child, the side of us which is playful and creative and spontaneous and special. If we block it, then we may unconsciously project these qualities onto our children, who then feel obliged to become what we have not been able to live ourselves. The same may be said of any planet in the 5th; although sometimes fate seems to be at work with a handicapped or ill child, there is generally also an inner component which, if we can face it and work with it, takes the burden of our projections off the child, allowing it to fulfil its own destiny.

Audience: I have seen cases where Sun-Mars in a woman's chart reflects an angry or violent father.

Liz: Yes, so have I. Any aspects to the Sun in part describe the psychological inheritance from the father, just as those to the Moon in part describe the inheritance from the mother. But I feel we need to look at this situation in its proper framework, rather than simply assuming that the aspect "means" one's father will be violent. Rage in one parent generally reflects a problem in the whole family fabric, and may reflect Mars difficulties not only in the parental marriage, but in the family inheritance over many generations. The violent parent is usually acting something out for a lot of people. This does not excuse it, but it may help promote a deeper understanding of family violence, which may even serve as an antidote for the repetition of the problem. I do not believe that such issues erupting within a collective are merely the fault of one horrible person. The violent father who may be described by his child's Sun-Mars aspect will usually have inherited his feelings of impotence and frustration from his own father, and on back through the generations. Because of his complex, he will probably have chosen a wife who carries the same complex, and who suffers herself from a Mars dilemma.

The approach of family therapy, which treats the family as an organism with its own laws and unconscious mechanisms, is a far more productive one than blaming one person for all the ills. For this reason, if a client with Sun-Mars tells me that he or she had a violent father, I will try to talk a little about the problem of aggression within families (which by their nature are inimical to Martial self-assertion), for such a client will inevitably have to contend with this same internal issue in his or her own psyche. Often people do not realise that a man who is violent usually suffers from the same feelings of impotence that a more passive, victimised type does. They are mirror images of each other, hurting from the same wound. One does not need to knock other people about if one feels secure in one's potency, and violent rage is generally a blind reaction to feeling thwarted and castrated. I think I have said quite a bit on this theme already.

Ares in myth is a god who is easily goaded; he can be worked up into a foaming rage by a bit of taunting which would only raise an amused eyebrow from Hermes or Apollo. Mars can be worked up in this way by the invisible darts of unconscious emotional manipulation, and unfortunately a child with a strong Mars will often be the one who acts out the angry undercurrents of the family or group. Any planet which reflects a dominant characteristic in us is like a lightning rod, attracting the projections of those around us. In the same way a Plutonian person will often act out the family's Pluto. Alternatively, a display of violent anger may drive a Martial child into disconnecting from his or her natural aggression. Both scenarios are typical, and may be applied to the violent father as well as the child.

Audience: My father was violent, and I was the one in the family who tried to keep the peace. Maybe I was swallowing my own Mars?

Liz: Certainly you were, although very likely you could not have done anything else at the time. But you may need to explore whether this role of peacemaker has resulted in your disowning your own healthy anger and aggression in adult life, for fear of invoking further violence from others. In this seminar, Howard and I are, in a sense, taking the "side" of the inner planets, by emphasising their value and their contribution to the healthy functioning of the personality. Like the Sun, Moon, Mercury and Venus, Mars needs our inner loyalty and support, so that we can effectively defend our values in the face of opposition and can go after what we want in life. Many things, a violent parent included, may turn us against our own Martial needs. But the price we pay for disowning Mars is victimisation and impotence. The god Ares may be a little rough-looking, but he is worth cultivating all the same.

THE HENCHMAN OF THE SUN

MARS IN THE HOROSCOPE

BY HOWARD SASPORTAS

One of my main objectives today is to help you make friends with Mars. I know Liz has been emphasising the value and right use of the Mars principle as well; and it is important we do so in order to counter the bad press this planet has received in many astrological texts. The reason Mars has been so maligned probably stems from the fact that it is associated with two things about which a lot of people feel a great deal of discomfort—sex and aggression. But there is no way of getting around the fact that we are all born with Mars somewhere in our charts, which means we are all born with aggressive and sexual urges. Better to face Mars head-on and understand the positive significance of these instinctive drives, rather than deny or condemn them in ourselves. While some psychologists argue that aggression is not innate and only develops when we experience frustration getting our needs met in infancy, I believe that it is inborn—we all are equipped from birth with a certain amount of aggression. Some people come in with a more powerful aggressive drive than others (this is likely due to hereditary or constitutional factors, and possibly related to karma and past lives if you believe in reincarnation), but we all have some degree of innate aggression. Your issues around aggression will be shown, among other things, by Mars in your chart.

The sexual drive is innate and serves a vital purpose—we wouldn't be here without it. Therefore, if aggression is also an inborn component of our biological equipment, it too must have a purpose. According to Clara Thompson, we are born with a healthy, root aggression which propels us to grow and master life.

She rightfully adds that if this root aggression is blocked or suppressed, it eventually will turn negative or ugly.[3]

The realm of Mars is full of paradoxes: Mars endows us with a natural aggression which we should respect and utilise, and yet this same drive can malfunction or get out of hand and lead to deplorable acts, a host of psychosomatic ailments and even self-destructive behaviour. The unhealthy expression of aggression is unfortunately much too prevalent – all you need do is to watch the news on television to see the way people are killed, tortured and maimed everyday. I believe that if we can find constructive channels for aggressive energy and use it to serve our self-development, to unfold more of our potentials and resources and to master life in general, it is less likely to manifest negatively. If we have positive outlets for our aggressive drives and are dealing cleanly with any anger or hostility we might be feeling, we're doing our part to help reduce negative forms of aggression in the atmosphere. We may not be the ones committing murder and atrocity, but if we sit on anger and don't direct our innate aggression into constructive outlets, we are guilty of adding to the amount of violence and hostility accumulating in the air.

I'm thinking along Jungian lines now – if we deny or repress something in ourselves, other people will express it for us. There are a lot of nasty things going on in the world, which suggests to me that a lot of us don't have a good relationship with our own aggressive urges. As I say, we may not be out there raping and pillaging, but it's possible that our own unprocessed hostility and frustration and our own unchannelled root aggression is contributing to the amount of thuggery, murder and whatnot in the world. We watch television or read the newspaper and feel rightful condemnation for those perpetuating acts of violence, we're aghast at their cruelty and brutality, and naturally want to separate ourselves from such people. However, according to Jungian theory, they may be carrying our rage for us, acting as psychic vacuum cleaners who absorb and live out what is floating around in the atmosphere. And what floats around in the atmosphere is the sum total of all of our unconscious or undealt-with feelings and emo-

---

[3]Clara Thompson, *Interpersonal Psychoanalysis* (New York: Basic Books, 1964), p. 179.

tions. I think this is why many people are fascinated by violence — as distasteful as it is, violence certainly sells movies and gets high ratings on television.

Again, Jung theorised that we are both repelled and yet fascinated by our own shadow contents. So people may condemn John McEnroe for his childish rages on the court, but they're turning on the television just to see if he'll have another outburst today. Also, if we repress anger or don't find a constructive expression for our natural, root aggression, this energy will store up in the unconscious until it eventually bursts out in an uncontrollable, explosive rage. D. W. Winnicott, an English psychoanalyst and a profound psychological thinker, once wrote, "If society is in danger, it is not because of man's aggressiveness, but because of the repression of personal aggressiveness in individuals."[4]

Illness is another consequence of unused healthy aggression and repressed anger. If we need to assert ourselves and are holding back, the energy that is meant to fuel external action turns inward and can attack the body. Typical illnesses associated with unexpressed positive or negative aggression can be skin problems, stomach ailments, ulcers, sexual dysfunctions, heart disease and migraines. Also, depression often is related to blocked anger or inhibited assertion. Psychologists talk of the three "H's": hopelessness, helplessness and hostility all go together. Unexpressed assertion and unacknowledged resentment bottle up inside you. So much energy goes into holding back and restraining feeling or action that you are left drained, listless and without enthusiasm for life. When the Gestalt therapist, Fritz Perls, worked with depressed people, he used to ask them, "Who are you depressed at?"

If you are chronically ill or depressed, I would encourage you to examine closely the house Mars is placed in your chart. We don't normally think of Mars as a significator for illness or depression, but these states can be caused by an "unused" Mars. Perhaps becoming more active, expressive or assertive in that domain will unblock you, improving your health and vitality, and get you going again. For example, with Mars in the 2nd, you ought to be

---

[4]D. W. Winnicott, "Aggression in Relation to Emotional Development," in *Collected Papers* (London: Tavistock, 1958), p. 204.

Table 3. Healthy Aggression.

---

1) Healthy aggression serves as protection against predatory attack.

2) Healthy aggression is a positive impulse to comprehend and master the external world. It is a force deep inside us which provides the impetus to learn new skills.

3) Healthy aggression is the basis for achieving independence and breaking away from those who would dominate or overprotect us.

4) Healthy aggression endows us with the will to unfold more of who we are, and grow into what we are meant to become.

---

quite assertive in terms of developing your skills and resources or acquiring greater security or valued possessions. With Mars in the 3rd, you should ask yourself if you're communicating enough with others, since it may help to share your ideas and feelings more openly with those around you; maybe taking up a new study, writing more letters or treating yourself to the occasional weekend break could be the tonic to lift your spirits. Those of you with Mars in the 7th may need to be more assertive in the relationship arena. The same rationale would also apply to the houses with Aries or Scorpio on the cusp—we need to challenge ourselves in these areas, and if we aren't doing so, we become limp and therefore (consciously or unconsciously) angry and frustrated. And while you're at it, look to see what house Mars is transiting now in your chart—this could be a sphere of life currently calling for increased assertion, "oomph," and self-expression.

In the chapter on aggression in *The Dynamics of the Unconscious*, I list four positive purposes of our natural, root aggression.[5] You may be familiar with the book, but I'd quickly like to review these points with you as a prelude to discussing specific Mars aspects

---

[5]Liz Greene and Howard Sasportas, *The Dynamics of the Unconscious*, Volume 2 in *Seminars in Psychological Astrology* (York Beach, ME: Samuel Weiser, 1988).

and placements in the chart (see Table 3 on page 226). Point 1 states that healthy aggression serves as a protection against predatory attack. This is pretty obvious. If your territory is being invaded or if someone is threatening you or blocking your path of progress, it's quite appropriate to feel or express some aggression. Remember the story about the snake and the guru. A healthy snake is listening to a lecture given by a spiritual teacher who happens to be in town. The teacher is extolling the virtues of love, peace, and the philosophy of *ahimsa* (the Sanskrit word for nonviolence). Impressed, the snake has a kind of transformation, deciding never to hurt people again. Two months later the spiritual teacher is back in town. The snake, however, is now a mess, downtrodden, half-dead. So it goes up to the spiritual teacher and says, "I want my money back; I tried what you were preaching and it's nearly killed me." The teacher replies, "I didn't tell you not to hiss!" If you're feeling invaded or blocked by others, or there are people around trying to manipulate and control you, it is perfectly all right to hiss, to tell them nicely to back off.[6]

Point 2 says that our natural, root aggression provides the impetus to master the external world and learn new skills, things which are vital to our self-esteem and sense of well-being.[7] Certain English phrases aptly describe how aggression is needed to get on with life: we *attack* a problem, we *grapple* with an issue, we *contend* with or *conquer* a difficulty, and so on. If we didn't have a bit of fight in us, we would just give up when something became too challenging; we couldn't master a skill or fully develop our innate resources. It is Mars which initially propels us to take a potential and apply the effort required to turn it into a concrete reality. We are born with a basic need or urge to use our Mars to acquire new skills and realise potentials; if we are not doing this, we will feel frustrated, angry and unfulfilled. Frustration wants an outlet, and we'll end up spoiling for a fight or provoking others to act out anger for us. There are so many people in western societies today, whether due to lack of employment or a general lack of direction

---

6Piero Ferrucci, *What We May Be* (Los Angeles: Jeremy P. Tarcher, 1982; and London: Turnstone Press, 1982), p. 89.
7Many of the psychological ideas in this lecture are abstracted from Anthony Storr, *Human Aggression* (London: Penguin Books, 1982).

and purpose in life, who are suffering from a negative Mars. Any outlet to unleash their pent-up aggression will do – from mugging old ladies, getting drunk and bashing members of minorities, to football hooliganism. This kind of behaviour is rife in England right now. As I said, if we don't have a healthy outlet for Mars or our natural, root aggression, that energy turns negative. Some young offenders have been "re-formed" through Outward Bound type schemes: survival camps and expeditions where they have the chance to channel Mars into battling nature and the elements, finding the courage to scale steep rock-faces and other such challenges.

Point 3 states that healthy aggression is the basis for achieving independence and breaking away from those who would dominate or overprotect us. I've referred to the Moon and Neptune as representing fusion needs, the desire to blend and merge with others. Mars, however, gives us the courage and power to separate from mother, to find a sense of independence and autonomy. Mars helps us to break away from a too-intense bond with a caretaker, a lover or spouse, or an enmeshed family. In this sense, Mars serves as a henchman to the Sun, fuelling and giving power to the striving for individuality. The story of Hansel and Gretel comes to mind. In one version of this tale, a mother sends her children away because she simply cannot provide for them. They eventually meet the witch with the house of gingerbread, who apparently has everything Hansel and Gretel could possibly want. And yet, the villain of this piece is not the mother who sends them off into the world, but the witch with all the goodies. The witch is the dangerous one, the one who most threatens to destroy the children. The person who would overprotect you, who would provide you with everything you need and do everything for you is the person who poses the most threat to your development as an individual in your own right.[8]

I've spoken before about the relationship between closeness, dependency and anger. They form a trio. One general reason for this is that when we are close and intimate with someone, we are more likely to project our unresolved infantile complexes onto that person. In fact, I once heard of a study – I don't know if it's true and

---

[8]Anthony Storr, *Human Aggression*, p. 63.

I have no reference for it—which concluded that, statistically speaking, the person most likely to kill you is the person to whom you are closest, and the room it is most likely to happen in is the bedroom! (For me, it would be the kitchen. Don't offer to help to cook a meal with me in a small kitchen unless you are sure your Mars doesn't touch off anything in my chart.) Dependency also brings up anger. If you are dependent on someone for your happiness, if you are dependent on someone to make you feel that you are lovable and have self-worth, if you are dependent on someone for finance and security, you are more likely to be resentful and enraged when he or she lets you down for whatever reason. I've said before that the best relationships are the ones that can contain the rage and hate that inevitably will be triggered off from time to time precisely because of the love and closeness you share with the other person.

The psychologist Winnicott spoke of the "good enough mother," the mother who can accept the love the child feels for her, but who also can accept or contain the rage the child will feel toward her at times.[9] The good enough mother also is the mother who accepts that, although she loves her child, there will be times when she might want to kill the kid. The good enough therapist is the one who is still there for you the week after you have attacked him for not being good enough. We all need to learn that we can feel angry or negative toward a friend or loved one without it necessarily meaning we have to destroy that person or abolish the union; and if someone we love has times of feeling angry or hateful towards us, that doesn't have to mean the end of things. Of course, there may come a day when a relationship turns so destructive that packing your bags is the best policy.

Point 4, which is an extension of point 2, is another vitally important purpose of our natural root aggression. It simply states that healthy aggression endows us with the will to unfold more of who we are, and grow into what we are meant to become. Just as an apple seed "knows" it is meant to yield an apple and not an orange, there is a part of us—our core Self or deeper Self—which knows what we are meant to grow into or become. The core Self

---

[9]D. W. Winnicott, *Playing and Reality* (New York: Routledge Chapman & Hall, 1982), p. 11.

guides, regulates and oversees our unfoldment. Some people refer to the deeper or core Self as the transpersonal Self, because when you are acting in accord with your deeper, core Self, you automatically behave and do things which not only are right and good for you, but which also are beneficial to the larger whole of which you are a part—in this sense you have gone beyond the personal, in other words, into the realm of the transpersonal. I believe that the core Self has an active component: we need a certain amount of aggression, drive and assertion to fulfil the promise of our seed identity. The existential philosopher Paul Tillich expresses a similar belief: "Man's being is not only given to him but also demanded of him. He is responsible for it . . . man is asked to make of himself what he is supposed to become, to fulfil his destiny."[10] Tillich is saying that we have to get out there and become what we are meant to become, rather than just sitting around waiting for this to happen of its own accord.

I've been talking about Mars, in its most constructive sense, as the will of the heroic ego, the ability to stand your ground, to go after your ego needs, to honour what you believe in and value and not let other people obstruct your way. According to Jung, however, there are higher things than the ego's will to which we must bow. It would seem that there are two levels of the will: the personal will of the ego, and what might be called the will of the deeper Self or the will of the transpersonal Self. Mars symbolises the will of the ego, but it isn't always the case that what our ego wants is in line with what the deeper Self has in mind for us. What if your core Self is an apple seed, but your ego insists it would rather be an orange? You see the problem. Mars makes choices to assert the ego's will, but the big question is whether or not this is in accordance with the will of the deeper Self. What if Mars tries to run the show itself, attempting to ignore the core Self's blueprint or plan?

Isabel Hickey used to say that if you try to break a cosmic law (such as the intention of your core Self), you'll break your neck in the process. If you desire something which is not in tune with what the deeper Self has in mind for you, it is the deeper Self which will

---

[10]Paul Tillich, cited in Irvin Yalom, *Existential Psycho-Therapy* (New York: Basic Books, 1980), p. 278.

eventually, one way or another, win out. Mars may resort to pushiness or ruthlessness in order to achieve what your personal ego wants; but if this is not in accord with the aims of your deeper or transpersonal Self, you'll end up discovering that what you so avidly sought is not as satisfactory or fulfilling as you had hoped it would be. In short, it would be better all around if we could align the personal will with the will of the core Self. This may not be easy for self-centred Mars, but I believe that this is Mars' ultimate challenge or test. Some people, through prayer and meditation, actively seek to align Mars (the ego will) with God's will or the will of the deeper, transpersonal Self. Others will have to be brought to their knees before they do so; in other words, Mars may be forced to surrender to the deeper Self's will whether it likes it or not. In his book *Ego and Archetype*, the Jungian analyst Edward Edinger writes that the experience of the Self is "most likely to occur when the ego has exhausted its own resources and is aware of its essential impotence by itself." He goes on to add that, "Man's extremity is God's opportunity."[11] There's another saying, although I honestly couldn't tell you its source: *You shall know the truth, and the truth shall make you you.*

As I see it, the principles represented by both the Sun and Mars define the first stages of a process through which we can form a healthy, functional ego—an ego which is equipped to function in the world in such a way as to achieve its personal aims and desires. However, in terms of our fullest possible growth and evolution, there will come a point when the personal ego is asked to acknowledge and honour something higher than itself, to realise its role as a channel through which the will of the transpersonal Self can express itself. I briefly touched on this in my lecture on the Sun, but I'll repeat it again. While the Sun represents the process of defining our individuality and separate-self sense, it also is our link to the transpersonal or universal Self—to that part of us which feels our oneness and connection with the rest of creation. The glyph for the Sun shows the circle of wholeness encompassing the dot of individuality, and is therefore descriptive of what Jungians refer to as the ego-Self axis. Almost paradoxically, by expressing

---

[11]Edward Edinger, *Ego and Archetype* (Baltimore: Penguin, 1973; and London: Penguin Books, 1980), p. 50.

our true individuality (the Sun helped along by Mars), we are pulled into participating in some greater scheme or plan through which life's wholeness becomes evident. In his book *The Act of Will*, Roberto Assagioli, the founder of psychosynthesis, has this to say on the matter: "Just as there is a personal will, so there is a Transpersonal Will, which is an expression of the Transpersonal Self [what I also refer to as the core Self or deeper Self] and operates from the superconscious levels of the psyche. It is an action which is felt by the personal self, or 'I', as a 'pull' or 'call.' "[12]

Some astrologers believe Uranus to be a higher octave of Mercury, and Neptune a higher octave of Venus. Along these lines, it also has been said that Pluto is the higher octave of Mars. It's an interesting idea, which pertains to this discussion. We can equate Mars with the personal will, and Pluto with the will of the deeper Self. Pluto is an inexorable force which drives both personal and collective history, and for this reason there is not much you can do to countereffect Pluto's wishes. Puberty is Plutonic—a major transformation which you can't stop happening. You may not want to go through puberty—you may not want to die as a child to be reborn an adolescent—but short of killing yourself, there is not much you can do about it. Physical death also is Plutonic and there isn't a lot any of us can do about it when our time comes. Hard aspects between Mars and Pluto in the chart often indicate a battle between the personal will and the will of the deeper Self. Mars, your personal will, may really want a particular job or relationship, but Pluto—the will of your deeper Self—may think that not having that job or relationship is what you actually need. This is when Mars might turn ruthless in order to achieve its ends (and Mars-Pluto aspects are frequently associated with ruthlessness); but, as I mentioned before, even if you do succeed in fulfilling the ambitions of your personal will in this case, you'll probably find that the job or relationship wasn't "right" after all. I'll have more to say on Mars-Pluto contacts later.

I'd like to ground some of the rather "airy" input I've just given you on the purpose of our healthy, root aggression by looking more closely at how Mars operates in the chart. We'll start with an

---

[12]Roberto Assagioli, *Act of Will* (Baltimore: Penguin, 1974; and London: Wildewood House, 1974), p. 113.

overview of Mars' aspects. (See Table 4 on pages 234–235.) Liz has referred to Mars as the fighting principle for the Sun and the other inner planets. Mars trine or sextile another planet increases the power of expression of that planet, and makes it likely that you'll use this power wisely and within reason. Mars trine or sextile the ⋆ Sun means that Mars is a natural ally or true friend to your Sun. These favourable Sun-Mars aspects help you to assert and defend your individuality in a way which is not too obnoxious or overbearing (although if they form a trine in fire signs, you might still be prone to going over the top). Sun trine or sextile Mars also indicates a powerful spirit, a strong personality. With flowing Sun-Mars aspects, Mars is better able to get out there and fight for what your Sun requires to fulfil its potential. If you have Mars trine or ⋆ sextile the Moon, you're naturally inclined to stand up for your feelings; this contact gives emotional conviction, a belief that you have a right to your needs and feelings, and therefore – if other aspects don't contradict this – you should have an easier time fulfilling your emotional needs and requirements compared to someone who has difficult aspects to the Moon. A flowing Moon-Mars contact also indicates that you can assert yourself in a way which is in synch with the environment around you.

Mars trine or sextile Mercury empowers your ability to communicate and enlivens your mind. You will have the capacity to stimulate others through your words and ideas. Mars trine or sextile ⋆ Venus increases your natural charisma, attractiveness and your capacity to experience and enjoy pleasure. It also suggests that you'll strike a good balance between assertion and cooperation in relationship. Flowing Mars-Venus contacts can give a talent for expressing yourself through a creative or artistic outlet. Mars trine ⋆ or sextile Jupiter enhances your capacity to go after and achieve your Jupiterian goals in life, and a natural ability to stimulate and excite others when you share your enthusiasms and beliefs with them. Although, as with Sun trine Mars, Mars trine Jupiter in a fire sign can easily get carried away with itself, or push others a little too enthusiastically – which in England is a sure way to put people off. I'll discuss Mars trine or sextile Saturn a little later when we examine Mars-Saturn aspects in general. The same goes for Mars in aspect to the outer planets.

Table 4. Guidelines for Interpreting Mars.

MARS BY SIGN
1) Mars' sign shows the way in which you assert yourself; how you go about getting what you want.
2) The nature of the sign Mars is in shows ways you can affirm and express your individual identity, potency, and power. For instance, Mars in Gemini may do so through words and communication; Mars in Libra through relationship or asserting its ideals.
3) Mars' sign is an indication of how sexual energy is expressed and asserted.
4) Mars' sign will colour the animus image: the inner image of the masculine. You might live out this image yourself, or project it by looking for it in someone else.
MARS BY HOUSE
1) You can affirm your individual identity by showing your potency and power in the area of life designated by Mars' house placement (and the houses which have Aries or Scorpio covering them). Mars' house is where we need to develop a mastery of life and the external world.
2) Mars' house shows a sphere of life where you can feel aggressive, impatient and easily aroused to anger. If you are not in touch with or expressing your Mars energy, Mars' house position may indicate a domain which leads you into depression or illness.
3) Mars' house will show an area of life through which we often try to impress others with how sexy, "macho," or powerful we are.

I'll come to Mars conjunctions shortly, but first I want to contrast the easy aspects of Mars with squares to Mars. If you are born with Mars square a planet, you have some lessons to learn in terms of the use or expression of the planet Mars squares. Mars will add

Table 4. Guidelines for Interpreting Mars (cont.)

MARS BY ASPECT
1) Any planet aspecting Mars will influence and colour how we assert ourselves. Mars in aspect to Uranus, for instance, will heighten and intensify assertion and self-expression, while Mars-Saturn aspects can slow down or stultify assertion. In general, planets in hard aspects to Mars indicate the kinds of issues, struggles or problems we encounter when we try to assert and express our autonomy and individuality.   2) The nature of a planet aspecting Mars may indicate an area of life through which we can feel potent or affirm our identity. For instance, Mars in aspect to Neptune could indicate our gaining a sense of potency and identity by being involved with "Neptunian" things, such as music or healing.   3) Planets aspecting Mars will also colour the animus image. A woman may project this and look for it in a man. A man may try to affirm his male ego by behaving in a way which reflects the nature of any planet aspecting Mars.

force and impetus to any planet it squares, but there is a danger you will be too rash, impetuous or clumsy in the way you use or express that planet—a bit like Ares, the Greek god of war, who was considered rather manic, brutish, bloodthirsty and awkward. It is less widely known that Ares was not only a warrior, but he was originally trained as a dancer by one of his tutors, the phallic god Priapus. Dancing unites the feelings with the body. As I said ear- *lier, a flowing Mars aspect helps you express or vent your drives and feelings through the body in the form of some kind of action. Mars squares, however, imply various problems with assertion and balanced or harmonious self-expression.

We'll begin with Sun square Mars. Early on in my study of astrology, I remember reading a book which advised that anyone with Sun square Mars should never play with guns, because one could accidently go off on you. I don't know, it could happen. While I think the author of the book was maybe being a little too literal or specific (or paranoid), he probably was basing this interpretation on the fact that Sun square Mars can produce a high degree of tension in the personality. The Sun and Mars are both "masculine" or *animus* principles; if you have them in square, you may be too assertive, too impatient and impulsive, too aggressive, pushy, self-centred, auto-cratic or even violent—all the qualities associated with a "negative animus." So it will be necessary to learn to tone down your assertion and expression—otherwise you will be too much for most people and obstruct your own path of progress in the process. It's possible that you may attempt to compensate for these tendencies, by trying your best to be nice and sweet, appearing docile on the surface. If this is the case, it drives your Sun-Mars underground where it comes out in the form of passive aggression, manipulation or uncon-scious controlling behaviour; or the disowning of Sun and Mars means that you will project your negative animus and attract people into your life who are domineering, pushy and impatient, or who seem particularly prone to fits of anger or violence when in your vicinity. I've already discussed some of this with you in my lecture on the Sun, because anything aspecting the Sun usually is experi-enced first via the father. It might be interesting to isolate a few sign examples of Sun square Mars just to elaborate on how this aspect can manifest. Give me a suggestion.

Audience: How about the Sun in Aries square Mars in Cancer?

Howard: Yes, that's a juicy one. The Sun in Aries gives a naturally strong urge to self-expression, indicating a desire to lead and initi-ate, and the fiery need to be adventurous and take risks in order to fulfil your individual potentials. How helpful will Mars in Cancer be here? Probably not a great friend to the Sun, because, to begin with, you have your Sun in a fire sign and Mars—which is meant to be an ally to the Sun—in a water sign. Your Arien urge to lead, take risks, or pave the way for something new could be hindered by the indirectness and hesitancy Mars often feels in Cancer, a sign that prefers what is safe and known. You can see how the Sun in Aries trine Mars in Leo or Sagittarius would work much better in this respect. However, it is wrong to assume Mars in Cancer is a wimp. I've known many people with this placement who are extremely shrewd, because they assert with Cancerian sensitivity: they "suss out" the best way to reach someone or get around someone and this helps them to achieve their desired aims and ambitions. Mars in Cancer is meant to be a good businessperson for this reason. Also, Mars in Cancer comes into its own when the feelings are aroused and stimulated, so those with this placement can often feel quite passionate about causes, crusades, or people they either fancy or dislike. If you have the Sun in Aries square Mars in Cancer, the fiery nature of the Sun, Aries, and Mars intensifies the feelings associated with watery Cancer, and you could have times of being overly emotional and carried away by passion — which might frighten some people off. You may find a similar emotional intensity with the Sun in Leo square Mars in Scorpio, or even with the Sun in Sagittarius square Mars in Pisces, although the latter tends to be more diffused. Suggest another pair? Something in air and earth would make a nice contrast.

Audience: How about the Sun in Libra square Mars in Capricorn?

Howard: How about you telling me for a change? (Silence). No one has anything to say on this one? Okay, I'll do it. The path of individuation and self-development for those with the Sun in Libra involves attaining greater balance in one's life and personality. There are a few obvious polarities that Librans need to balance: the head and the heart (mind and feelings), realism and practicality with idealism and spirituality, and the assertion of their needs and views versus cooperation and diplomacy with others. Mars in earthy Capricorn can be dogmatic and stubborn about its beliefs and how an action should be executed, and doesn't necessarily have the intellectual detachment or perspicacity that would help Libra in its solar quest of objectivity and balance. A Libran is an idealist with an airy vision of how things should be run or organised, and Mars in Capricorn can be a stickler about how something ought to be accomplished. I've noticed that people with this square are quite frequently obsessed with perfectionism, and have rigid formulas about what is right or wrong, proper and not proper. They can be extremely fussy, overly critical or judgmental both toward themselves and others. On the plus side, this mixture of planets and signs is a recipe for great persistence and gives the determination to do a job well. If I wanted something done to high standards, I seriously would consider hiring a person with this square—although I wouldn't expect them to do it overnight. Time (Capricorn) is needed to get things just right (Libra).

I hope this gives you some idea why a square of Sun to Mars can be quite a challenging aspect. While Moon square Mars can give the same kind of emotional conviction associated with the trine or sextile, the square usually indicates fast, often uncontrollable emotional responses—a short fuse or low boiling point. People with this aspect want what they want when they want it; if they are made to wait too long, they quickly become frustrated and angry, as if the body is not very good at containing feeling. Watch out when this square is activated by a transit or progression—it's likely that their mother complex will be triggered, and they could blow up at the slightest provocation. Those with this aspect may need to learn patience, and find ways to regulate and master their emotional responses and feeling nature.

Mars square Mercury energises the mind, but it can give a sharp tongue, and make a person accident-prone, argumentative, as well as restless and fidgety. Ideas or thoughts may come faster than they can be processed, and things may be blurted out that are later regretted. This square requires greater mastery and control of the mind and speech.

Mars square Venus can give the same artistic flair and personal charisma as the trine or sextile, but if often indicates an intensely passionate nature which can wreak havoc in one's life. I've seen a number of people with this square who either act out or provoke violence in relationship. The Marquis de Sade had Mars in Aries square Venus in Cancer, and you know what he got up to—the word sadism is derived from his exploits. The underlying tension usually hinges on power issues, and although you may want to blame the other person for any difficulties which arise, the conflict is an inner one: your desire to harmonise with and please a partner is at odds with a strong urge to have things your way.

In extreme cases, some people with Mars square Jupiter are fanatical: enthusiasm goes overboard and spills into frenzy and mania; they may be well-meaning, but they often think they have a monopoly on the truth—what they believe in is what everyone should believe in. Philosophical or political arguments happen frequently, and can become quite bitter. In milder cases, it is the "I won't take no for an answer" salesperson, who manages to get a foot in the door before you even open it, or overkill artists with a real talent for putting you off the very thing they're so het up about. We'll do the other Mars squares a bit later.

Mars conjunctions are not dissimilar to the square—Mars will increase the potency and drive of any planet it conjuncts. Mars conjunct the Sun heightens the urge for authority, power and self-expression; Mars conjunct the Moon heightens feelings and emotional responses, and so on. Obviously, as with any conjunction, you'll need to consider the effects of the sign in which it is placed, and also analyse it in relation to the rest of the chart, with special attention to the kinds of aspects made to the conjunction itself. A square or opposition to any Mars conjunction is bound to exacerbate matters, and can be an extremely challenging configuration to work through or handle—but it will be vital to your happiness, success or well-being that you do so.

Oppositions to Mars often operate curiously. Many people with these oppositions seem to learn about the field of experience associated with the planet opposing Mars through fights and conflicts with other people. For instance, if you have Sun opposing Mars, you need to lock horns with or come up against another person in order to find out who you are in your own right. It probably first manifests as a battle of wills with father—he wants you to be a certain way which isn't really you, and thus you're compelled to stand up for your right to be you, defining yourself more clearly in the process. Later on, the war continues to rage with father-figures or those in authority. You may think the other person is obstinate and wilful, but I assure you that if you have Sun opposing Mars, you are no wimp yourself. Any opposition to Mars reminds me of political systems in which the opposition party helps to define the policies of the party in power, and vice versa. Those with Moon opposing Mars end up battling with or about anything related to the Moon principle—conflicts with mother and females in general, domestic disputes and skirmishes over territorial rights, and, of course, arguments over emotional needs and requirements. Fighting for recognition of their emotional needs is how they define their needs more clearly and learn to stand up for themselves. People with Mercury opposing Mars frequently find themselves embroiled in arguments with others, and this is how they clarify and differentiate their thoughts and ideas. Venus opposing Mars creates battles with partners, particularly those conflicts where your values or what you desire and hold dear is at odds with what the other person wants and values. And yet, this is how you define your value system and what gives you pleasure. People with Mars opposing Jupiter battle with others about philosophy, religion or politics, learning to stand up for themselves and giving shape to their beliefs through this process. Mahatma Gandhi, the liberator of India, had this aspect and he took on the entire British Raj. John McEnroe was blessed with a Moon-Mars conjunction opposite Jupiter forming a Grand Cross with a Sun-Mercury opposition to Pluto. It's no wonder he is renowned for his rages and disagreements with the vision and perspective (Jupiter) of umpires and the professional tennis establishment in general. I'm not keen to turn you into another McEnroe, but I actually don't think you should feel too badly if you have oppositions to Mars and find yourself embroiled in battles and conflicts with others, because this is precisely how you come to know better who you are and where you stand. Lions are meant to roar, not buzz. How many people here with a Mars opposition would say they frequently tend to lock horns with people?

Audience: I have Sun opposing Mars and I did fight with my father, and now I get embroiled with people in authority.

Audience: I have Mars opposing Venus and I have attracted some violence in relationship. And I did learn to stand up for myself as a result.

Audience: I have Mars opposing Uranus and it happens to me a lot.

Howard: Yes, I bet. I'll be speaking on Mars-Uranus aspects shortly, but let's start with variations on Mars-Saturn.

With Mars trine or sextile Saturn, you tend to know the right amount of energy or effort to put into something. Saturn stabilises, organises and acts as a focus for Mars, helping it to plan a strategy as well as giving Mars the patience and stamina to carry through to the end. Even with the harmonious aspects between these two planets, you may not be able to blend them in a positive way until you've had a certain amount of experience in life and have learned a few lessons—the hard way, by first making mistakes. The trine and sextile suggest that you will master Saturn, that you can time action well, and that you won't perennially "overdo" or "underdo" as might be the case with a conjunction or hard angle between these two planets (although the trine or sextile will still incline Mars to be slower and more cautious rather than rash and impulsive). Looking at it another way, Mars will energise Saturn, so you may be someone who stands up for law and order, who is able to turn chaos into order, and who espouses the value of discipline and hard work to get anywhere in life.

The conjunction and square pose many more problems. First of all, Saturn may deter and block Mars. You think about performing an action or you start to act and then Saturn butts in saying, "Hold on, Mars, are you ready, is it the right time, are you good enough to be doing this?" So we have what has been referred to as "driving a car with the brakes on."[13] This is the underdrive side of the Mars-Saturn dilemma. Dilemma is a good word to describe the combination of these two planets: they are so contrasting by nature that when they are brought together by a conjunction or hard angle, they are bound to create tension and conflict in the psyche. In the situation I've just been describing, Mars may be too held back by Saturn. But the reverse is also true: you may try to assert (Mars) without taking limits or law (Saturn) into consideration, and end up behind bars or with a broken neck, or simply with egg all over your face—possibly beneficial for the complexion, but not so good for your ego and self-esteem, although the ignominy would be worth it if you learned something from the experience. This is the overdrive side of the dilemma, where Mars is not showing enough respect for Saturn; and there is no doubt that Mars would benefit from the sense of timing, caution and planning Saturn has to offer it. Mars needs a little Saturn at the best of times.

The opposition between Mars and Saturn has many similarities with the square. However, as with any opposition (and very often

---

[13]Alan Oken, *The Horoscope, the Road and Its Travelers* (New York: Bantam Books, 1974), p. 248.

with conjunctions and squares as well), you may favour or identify with one end of the opposition, and, as a consequence, you will experience the disowned end as coming at you from the outside. This can work either way with Mars opposing Saturn. Let's say you side with Mars, believing you can get away with rash, overly aggressive or impulsive behaviour. You probably won't succeed, because you'll meet Saturn externally – someone or something will try to stop you. Or you can play it the other way: you side with Saturn, holding back, delaying action because of overcautiousness, or a fear of failure or inadequacy. In this case, you'll attract Mars from the outside, most likely in the form of people egging you on, pushing you into doing the thing about which you are insecure or hesitant. The point I'm really trying to make is that, no matter how much the conflict appears to be between you and external reality, the dilemma between action (Mars) and stasis (Saturn) is an internal one which you carry around within you. Only by resolving the internal clash of these archetypes, only by finding a way to make peace between Mars and Saturn inside you, will you free yourself from the problems caused by projection. It may encourage you to know that Jung did not believe that projection was wholly pathological. He stressed that a projected image is a potential locked up inside yourself, and that when there is a need for this part of you to make itself known, you will meet it through whoever or whatever you have projected it onto. If you play your cards right and recognise the projection as your own, you have taken a major step toward reowning and reintegrating what you have exported onto others. In the case where you side with Mars and project Saturn, it may help to ask yourself, "Why am I attracting so much obstruction or censure – is it because there is something in me which wants to hold back or cool it to some degree?" Or in the case where you are siding with Saturn and denying Mars, you should ask "Why are people pushing me so; is there something in me which wants to act and I'm not acknowledging it?"

Audience: What about the inconjunct between Mars and Saturn? Does it work in the same way? Will projection come into play as well?

Howard: Because of the inherent tension between the contrasting natures of Mars and Saturn, I would classify an inconjunct between these two planets as a major, challenging angle, which means (as with any difficult aspect) that projection is likely, at least until you learn better. Questions always come up about the interpretation of inconjuncts or quincunxes, so it's worth taking some time to talk about them in general. In most cases, I have found the inconjunct to be a powerful aspect, and one you should always take note of in a chart. Before you ask, I am quite liberal with the orb—I give it five degrees or so. I know that if you extend it that far, you'll overlap with some minor aspect, but from my experience doing charts for people and hearing what they have to say about their lives, I'm almost certain that inconjuncts work within this range. So if you have limited them to two or three degrees, you might look at your chart again to see if you have acquired any more inconjuncts using this wider orb—you might discover a new way to understand something going on in your psyche or in your life.

Inconjuncts have been described as "neurotic aspects," not that they make you neurotic (although they can) but because they operate erratically and very often in contradictory ways. Alan Oken confirms this by describing an inconjunct as a "seesaw" type of aspect, sometimes working harmoniously for you, and sometimes causing you a great deal of trouble.[14] This makes sense since a quincunx occurs midway between a trine and opposition—hence the alternation between its trinelike positive expression and its more challenging, oppositionlike effects. At times, the two planets brought together by inconjunct seem to work or combine together in a mutually beneficial way. For instance, if you have Mars inconjunct Saturn, there will be times when it will operate like a trine—you instinctively find the right balance or blend of assertion with steadiness and common sense. However, there will be other times when this same inconjunct will function more like an opposition, creating issues and tensions similar to the ones I mentioned a few minutes ago.

When a Mars-Saturn quincunx expresses itself in difficulties, your task is to adjust and refine how you blend or balance these two planets, until you get it right. A quincunx asks that you do

---

[14]Alan Oken, *The Horoscope, the Road and Its Travelers*, p. 206.

what you can to bring its two ends together in a constructive fashion. As I said, there will be times when this happens almost automatically as if it were a trine; and there will be times when you really mess up in terms of how you bring together the two planets involved. Venus inconjunct Jupiter, for instance, can blend to give a very positive creative and expansive streak to your nature, but it also can manifest as overindulgence or make you the kind of person who swings from one extreme to another in relationship – carried away to the heights one day, and then deeply disappointed and down in the dumps the next when your beloved has failed to live up to your overidealised expectations. Many astrologers base their interpretation of inconjuncts on the natural zodiac, in which the quincunx is considered to have an Aries-Virgo (and 1st/6th house) flavour or an Aries-Scorpio (1st/8th house) flavour – Virgo and Scorpio being the two signs that are 150 degrees from Aries, and the 6th and 8th houses the two houses 150 degrees from the 1st. Virgo and the 6th house, and Scorpio and the 8th house, intrinsically ask for adjustment, refinement and transformation – hence the idea that the way in which you bring together the two inconjuncting planets will sometimes require adjusting, refining or transforming. You can chew over all this at your leisure, but we had better move on to Mars-Uranus aspects.

Mars trine or sextile Uranus is a good aspect to have in your chart. As stated earlier, a harmonious Mars contact adds power and dynamism to the expression of the planetary principle it touches. A positive link between Mars and Uranus empowers your ability to make changes in your life, or to be an agent or catalyst of change for the collective. It gives you the ability to act on new ideas or inspirations of a Uranian nature without going over the top, and usually denotes a high degree of individuality and originality – and the knack for getting away with being that way. Somehow your "differentness" is acceptable. Flowing Mars-Uranus aspects increase your magnetism and charisma, and give a great deal of underlying strength and resilience. If you run into resistance and blocks, or feel down and depressed, it probably won't be too long before you find a way to break through or bounce back into life again.

A conjunction, square or opposition between these two planets can give the same degree of originality and inventiveness as the trine or sextile, but you may have more trouble being appreciated or accepted for being different. Uranus heightens and electrifies any planet it contacts. Combine it with Mars and you have an aspect of extremely high wattage. Obviously, this high energy and power will not be operative twenty-four hours a day—you'd burn out very quickly if that were the case. But there will be times when a Mars-Uranus square, opposition or conjunction (even a well-aspected conjunction) sends such a powerful bolt of energy through your system that you may have problems handling it well. The danger is blowing a fuse or short-circuiting. People with the conjunction or a hard angle between these two planets need to strengthen and stablise their nervous systems in some way—perhaps through yoga, meditation or regular exercise—in order to be a more solid container for the lightninglike electrical force generated by these aspects. Hard Mars-Uranus contacts (and I put the conjunction into this category) indicate people with incredibly strong powers of assertion and an incredibly strong need to assert. This is fine provided that they have a constructive outlet, project, cause or campaign into which they can channel their assertive or aggressive energy. But if their need to assert is blocked or has nowhere very interesting or exciting to go, they can become exceedingly angry, restless or depressed. Mars and Uranus are both animus-type principles; when brought together you have a double hit of "masculine" force and power. The hard angles are going to require work and conscious effort to use rightly and within healthy proportions, otherwise you might exhibit traits associated with a "negative animus"—such as violence or tyrannical, fanatical and autocratic tendencies.

Mars opposite Uranus is an interesting aspect. As with any Mars-Uranus contact, people with the opposition have a powerful need to assert themselves. They seem to thrive on finding other people with an equally powerful assertive drive with whom they can lock horns and do battle. It doesn't interest them to fight with wimps; they'll instinctively seek out or attract other Uranians with whom to fight. Just imagine two strongly Uranian individuals having it out with one another. Fireworks. And yet, as discussed before, it is precisely through a fierce battle of wills that these people affirm their potency, beliefs and identity, and discover more about who they are in their own right.

♂♃

Mars-Neptune aspects have a different flavour to them. Isabel Hickey used to refer to Mars trine or sextile Neptune as "the practical idealist." With the flowing aspects, Mars (the planet of action) works in accord with Neptune (the idealist, the healer, the visionary or artist), enabling the realisation through action of ideals, dreams, healing power and creative inspiration. The conjunction (even a well-aspected one), the square and opposition are much trickier. Assertion gets mixed up with Neptune, but in a difficult way. For starters, Neptune can be very foggy, so you may be uncertain or confused about what action to take in a situation. Or, because of Neptune's ego-dissolving qualities and its penchant for self-sacrifice, you may feel guilty about asserting your personal will, perhaps believing it is superior or more evolved to "flow with the cosmos" or adjust to what those around you want rather than demanding things your way. There is an archetypal conflict between the principles represented by these two planets. Mars desperately wants to affirm your ego identity through demonstrating your power and potency as an individual and through your efforts to master the world and make something of your life, while Neptune is urging you to blend, fuse or merge with others, to transcend or move beyond the differentiated ego's "me-in-here versus you-out-there" perspective on reality. Can you see the problem?

I believe there is a way around this dilemma. People with Mars in aspect to Neptune generally have more success at achieving their aims and ambitions if this is not done purely for the satisfaction of the personal "I." To some degree, they need to comply with Neptune's wishes to transcend the ego's separateness. For instance, let's say I have Mars square Neptune and I'm in the process of setting up a really fine restaurant. If my primary aim is to make a lot of money for myself, of if I am doing it to prove to my mother and father or to the world that I am a capable and talented person, or if I'm seeking the fame and glory that running a high-class establishment would give me, then Neptune (by nature, anti-ego) will somehow undermine my success. However, if one of my main reasons for starting the restaurant is to provide a service for others, I will have more chance of it getting off the ground. A major shift in attitude may be necessary with Mars conjunct or in hard angle to Neptune. To repeat, I would fare better if I held in the front of my mind that the restaurant would be providing people with good-quality food – then at least I'm not in business solely for the purpose of padding my ego, and Neptune would be happier about the whole endeavour. Probably nothing is 100 percent altruistic, so I would have to admit to my more personal egocentric motivations, but it helps if these are secondary to the idea of myself as a channel through which something worthwhile could be brought to people.

As a general rule, if you have a Mars-Neptune contact, and you're doing something purely for the sake of bolstering your own ego, Neptune eventually will find a way to undermine you. I've often noticed that Mars-Neptune people are better at doing things for other people rather than just for themselves. They can be very powerful when fighting for a co-worker's rights or working on an animal-liberation campaign, but if they are doing something just for their own sake, they often can't get the project going, or it fails on them in the end. A Mars-Neptune aspect asks that your identity and potency be affirmed through serving others, or by acting as a channel through which something greater than yourself can manifest.

This last point needs further elaboration. Mars-Neptune contacts can be used constructively if you serve as a channel through which the transpersonal or superconscious dimension of life reveals itself. A true artist, for example, is receptive to what has been called "the imaginal realm" or "mythic realm," the plane of existence on which archetypal and universal images, ideas and feelings circulate. Through some kind of creative outlet, people with soft or hard angles of Mars to Neptune could act as mediums through which the imaginal realm is communicated to others. By nature, true psychics, mystics and healers are open to energies beyond the boundaries set by the personal ego, and in this way they also are channels for something higher or greater than themselves to come through. Neptune approves of self-transcendence, and would be pleased if Mars was used in a sensible fashion to further this end.

People with the Mars-Neptune opposition often encounter experiences which lead them to believe that the world is out to thwart their ambitions. They try to assert themselves (Mars) but then run into "circumstances" which abort their efforts, and they then wind up feeling victimised by life. Blaming the world for one's failures is a cop-out. It's more likely that they have identified or sided with their Mars (the urge to affirm one's ego identity) at the expense of Neptune; they therefore are fated to meet Neptune externally in the guise of situations that undermine the aims of the personal "I" in order to replace all-out egocentricity with the desire to serve something greater than the self.

We've already discussed one manifestation of Mars-Pluto contacts when we compared the personal will (Mars) with the will of the core Self (Pluto). In contrast to people with a conjunction or hard angle between Mars and Pluto, someone with Mars trine or sextile Pluto will probably have an easier time aligning the personal will with the deeper Self's intentions, offering less resistance in the end to what the Self has in mind. Mars and Pluto also signify two different types of anger. Mars can be equated with "ego anger," while Pluto may express itself in what is termed "id anger." In early infancy, before the age of five or six months, we are not yet aware of ourselves as a distinct "I" separate from the universe, a state psychologists refer to as "primary narcissism." Any frustration or anger that we feel during this egoless phase is experienced as global and undifferentiated—that is, it is not just oneself, but the whole world, which is bad and angry. In the chapter on aggression in *The Dynamics of the Unconscious*, I quoted the Kleinian analyst, Hanna Segal, on this subject:

> A hungry, raging infant, screaming and kicking, fantasizes that he is actually attacking the breast, tearing and destroying it, and experiences his own screams which tear him and hurt him as the torn breast attacking him in his own inside.[15]

Pretty heavy stuff: we are frustrated with the world out there, but since we haven't yet distinguished an "I" distinct from everything else, our anger is also directed towards the self. This is what is meant by id anger: it's a very black place to be, full of intense rage and totally devoid of light or hope. Because this state is so painful and unbearable, we normally cut off from it. The early repression of id anger can make one more compliant, but it can also render

---

[15]Hanna Segal, *An Introduction to the Work of Melanie Klein* (New York: Basic Books, 1980; and London: Heinemann, 1964), p. 2.

some people dead from the neck down. I believe that most of us unconsciously harbour varying degrees of unresolved infantile rage which will resurface when activated by an appropriate trigger later on in life.

In time, we gradually form an ego or separate-self sense. Once we have established a personal "I," we can experience our anger as our own—it is no longer global or undifferentiated. This is what is meant by "ego anger," the anger we feel once an "I" is formed. Ego anger comes out when people treat us unfairly or try to block the path we feel we need to follow. So Mars represents ego anger, but Pluto is more akin to id anger. If you have a difficult Mars-Pluto contact, you may be in a situation where you start out expressing a justifiable ego anger, but then it somehow turns into id anger. Let's say you're born with Mars square Pluto. One morning, just as something is coming up to transit this aspect, you buy a new shirt at a shop. Later that day you discover it's slightly discoloured and go back to return it. You've practised your assertiveness skills and even-handedly confront the shopkeeper with your request. If she refuses, your Mars anger could degenerate into or trigger your Plutonic id anger, and before you know it, you're berserk with rage because she won't exchange the shirt or give your money back. McEnroe has Moon conjunct Mars in Gemini square Pluto in Virgo, and we've seen him slip into id anger on the court. (By the way, if you were born with Mars opposing Pluto, you have a knack for provoking id anger in others—which is really a way of getting other people to act out that part of yourself.)

Audience: What can you do if you have a Mars-Pluto aspect, and experience the kind of situation you've just been talking about?

Howard: You want a formula, I'll give you a formula. First, you must not think that you're a terrible person because you feel nasty things like rage. We are human, and by virtue of being human, we all have some degree of lust, rage, envy, greed, and so on inside us. Many people are more than happy to deny what they believe are primitive or uncivilised instincts and emotions, but how can you transform something if you deny it even exists? Accept these states as part of your human inheritance and stop thinking you are horrid and unworthy for entertaining such feelings. It is psychologically clumsy to try to transform anything you are condemning. If you start by recognising and accepting the existence of these states within you, the groundwork is then laid for dealing with them. It is not advisable, however, to directly express or unleash your Mars-Pluto rage—you could end up in jail or worse. When you experienced intense anger or frustration as an infant and you fantasised killing mother or whatever, you didn't have the biological maturity to act on these impulses. But if these infantile emotions and complexes resurface in adulthood (as they will from time to time), you are physically capable of catching a bus to the gun shop, or figuring out a way to slip poison into someone's afternoon tea. Prisons are filled with people who have been taken over by their early global id anger. They are labelled as psychopaths or sociopaths.

When you feel excessive anger, it is a good idea to find some way to discharge it muscularly—to get it out of your system in a manner that is safe for yourself and others. So you might pound a cushion, run around the block a number of times, go for a swim, clean the house, dig in the garden, play a competitive sport, etc. This is sometimes referred to as emotional hygiene and allows the energy contained in the rage to be worked through cathartically. In his book *What We May Be*, Piero Ferrucci has a chapter called "Tigers of Wrath," in which he discusses ways of transforming negative aggression.[16] You can try writing an angry letter and not mailing it. You could pick up some crayons and draw what you are feeling, which is a good way to start shifting your emotional state. You also could try rechannelling the energy contained within your rage into a constructive outlet. Do this by first picking out a project to which you wish to give more steam. Then get in touch with the vigour and vibrancy of your aggressive feelings. Realise that these feelings create a great deal of energy inside you—energy which can be redirected into the task you want to complete. The next step is to picture yourself executing your chosen project with the same degree of energy the aggressive feelings have evoked in you. Finally, come out of the exercise and take whatever practical steps are necessary to begin tackling your chore. This is what is meant by redirecting the energy contained within aggression into another

---

[16]Piero Ferrucci, *What We May Be*, ch. 7.

outlet. You can also use your rage as a starting point for psychological self-investigation. Why does a particular person or situation arouse such anger? Is it connected to some earlier experience around mother or father or a sibling? In other words, rage can take you deeper into yourself.

I could talk about Mars-Pluto aspects all day, but there is just one more point I'd like to make for now. I've observed that some people with these aspects will drive themselves very hard, as if they are compelled to use their Mars in an intense Plutonic way. They test their power, courage and prowess by undertaking risky or challenging feats—mountain climbing, spending time living alone in a tent in the woods to see how well they survive, or by engaging in dangerous, life-threatening sports. Mars also energises Pluto's desire to tear down and transform, and any Mars-Pluto contact could be directed into promoting needed social or political change.

Audience: How would Mars-Pluto aspects affect sexuality?

Howard: Yes, that's a good question. I've been so busy speaking about Mars in terms of aggression, that I haven't really said much about it in relationship to sexuality. Mars-Pluto aspects certainly intensify the sexual drive and feelings. Some people may act this out literally or compulsively. Others may be frightened by the intensity of their sexuality, and as a way of avoiding the trouble it could get them into, they deny or suppress its existence. I don't think this is very healthy, because it just bottles up and comes out in subversive ways. I'm not against transmuting or sublimating libidinal urges into other activities such as a creative medium, a spiritual quest or serving others in some fashion; but I think you should do this because you choose to, not because you are running away from facing what is inside you.

Audience: Can you say something about Mars retrograde?

Howard: Mars retrograde may inhibit the outward expression of one's assertive drive. You have the impulse to assert, but then you restrain yourself, perhaps to check again and make sure you have chosen the right course of action. Remember the Falklands War between Britain and Argentina? War was officially declared when Mars was retrograde, but nothing much happened for a while because the British warships still had to travel to the Falkland Islands. I think this took about ten days. Erin Sullivan, an astrologer living in London and teaching for our Centre there, is writing a much-needed book about retrogrades.[17] She believes that a retrograde Mars could subvert or work against what the ego is seeking to realise, or against the path of individuation suggested by the placement of the Sun in the birth chart. Her reasoning is interesting. Astronomically, you can only be born with Mars retrograde when the Sun is in what is known as the opposition zone to Mars — that is, when the Sun is in between the times it would be trining Mars. So a retrograde Mars could be inconjunct or opposite the Sun, and therefore at odds with the Sun principle. Somehow you need to find a way to bring a retrograde Mars into line with the Sun, so that your actions, or the lack of them, are not the cause of your self-undoing.

I have more input for you, but I think it would be good to change gears right now and give you an exercise on Mars, similar to the one we did on Venus. (I heard that Liz told you of a Mars exercise I had in mind, which would be to turn to the person sitting next to you and punch him or her in the face. Maybe some of you would be keen to try this, but I'm not sure everyone could handle it — this is Switzerland, after all.) So, close your eyes, take a few deep breaths, relax your mind and body, and move into a quiet, inner space. First, visualise the glyph for the planet Mars and meditate a minute on it. Let that go, and see if you can come up with any images or pictures which depict the state of your own Mars. Do this as if you are watching a movie screen and you don't know what image is going to appear next. Mars may manifest as a man, a woman, an animal or as an abstraction — just allow whatever wants to come. Once you have a mental picture of Mars, spend some time dialoguing with this image. Find out how Mars is doing, whether or not it's getting what it needs. See if there is anything you can do to make Mars feel better or happier. Also, you

---

[17]Erin Sullivan, *Retrograde Planets: Traversing the Inner Landscape* (London: Arkana Penguin, 1992).

can ask your image of Mars how it feels about you. You have three minutes or so to engage in this discussion.

Okay, now say goodbye to Mars, slowly open your eyes, and when you are ready, take a few minutes to write down what you experienced. Then turn to the person next to you and punch him or her in the face. No, just kidding! What I really want you to do is to find a partner with whom you can discuss what happened in the exercise. I'm curious to hear some of your images of Mars. Who's willing to expose themselves?

Audience: Mars was me and I was trying to fight off enemies with my fists. There were so many of them, I didn't think I would succeed, so I bent down in defeat and all of a sudden—like a wave—my enemies washed over my head and disappeared into the sea and drowned.

Howard: Where is Mars in your chart?

Audience: It's in the first house square Neptune.

Howard: Yes, it would be a Neptune aspect, wouldn't it? It's funny, you almost had to surrender in order to win. The way you bent down reminds me of the way Herakles had to kneel in the swamp before vanquishing the Hydra. It's when you gave up fighting head-on that things took a turn for the better. See if you can apply this to your current life in some way.

Audience: I had a German Shepherd dog. He was locked in behind a fence, and when I asked him what he wanted, he shouted, "I want my freedom, I want to get out of here!" I have Mars in Scorpio square Neptune.

Howard: This sounds like an important message from your unconscious. That dog is going to get much angrier if you don't free him. There is a storage tank in the psyche which can only hold so much before it explodes. Maybe you could take the dog out on a lead for a while, until he grows more accustomed to being free. Otherwise, he might run wild at first. Liz used to say that if you lock something up in the basement for a long time, it is not going to be very nice or civilised when it first gets out. One more image?

Audience: I have Mars in Pisces opposite Neptune in Virgo. I imagined that Mars was underwater, but he was complaining because he wanted to be on land. So we sailed on a ship to an island where Neptune happened to live. When they met, they didn't like each other very much. They were angry with one another.

Howard: Is it a coincidence that, so far, all of you who have spoken about this exercise have Mars-Neptune contacts? I guess doing a guided fantasy on Mars is appropriate when Neptune is in aspect to it. The fact that your Mars and your Neptune are angry with each other suggests to me that more work needs to be done on integrating these principles in your psyche. If you have two archetypes in conflict, it sometimes is worthwhile to call in a negotiator. You might try imagining Venus chairing a meeting with Mars and Neptune, and see if she is able to help them work out their differences. Thanks for sharing. Before we move on, I must tell you what I imaged for Mars—a gorilla. I've been working on my Mars for years, and I still get King Kong.

I'm feeling playful and would like to try another little Mars game with you, but first we must set the scene. Mars has a lot to do with how we move in on something or somebody, and how we physically approach another person or situation. Picture this for instance. I have just finished giving a lecture and am still on the podium gathering together my bits and pieces, and there is a man with Mars in Cancer in the group who would like to ask me a personal question about the material we've been discussing. Since Cancer is not known for its directness, he may be afraid to approach me directly. He might linger in his seat after the others have gone, then stand up and circle around me at a distance, and then come slowly at me from the side. Once upon me, he first might make a comment on the weather, and then finally risk asking me his question. It's like a little dance. At some point before he reached me, I probably would have sensed that he was working up to approach me. Had I let out a glance that said "back off," he most likely would comply, and that would be that. Now compare this with a woman with a strongly placed Mars in Aries who also would like to have a word with me after a lecture. She will probably walk briskly up to the podium and come right to the point. This is what I mean by Mars showing how we approach or go after something.

Audience: Do women use their Mars in the same way as men do?

Howard: In older, traditional astrological textbooks, you often read that a man identifies with and lives out his Mars, while looking for his Venus through a woman; and a woman would identify with her Venus, and seek men who would be an appropriate hook for her Mars. There still are people around like this. Certain men may feel it is only okay to be Mars, and not okay to behave in a Venusian way; therefore Venus is disowned and imported back into his life via a woman he finds attractive or pleasing. The reverse may be true for women, but I actually don't think it's so simple nowadays. More men are comfortable expressing both Mars and Venus for themselves, and many more women are integrating the animus rather than projecting it onto men, which means that these women are relatively comfortable acting out Mars as well as Venus. I definitely approve of these developments, because it means people are living their wholeness to a greater degree. To complicate matters further, you may come across an animus-dominated woman who has rejected her Venus in favour of Mars; if this is the case, she will be looking to import Venus through a partner, whether that be a male or a female. And you can find anima-dominated men who have rejected Mars in themselves, and therefore they are seeking another person—maybe another male, maybe a female—to "be" their Mars. Some gay men stereotypically identify with Venus and seek Mars in a lover, but other gay men identify with Mars (the "macho look") and import Venus through their male partners. A gay woman who hams up her Mars and comes over superbutch will probably be attracted to women who reflect her unlived Venus image; but there are gay women who are most at home with their Venus, and therefore seek a female lover who fits their Mars image. It's also possible to find gay people who are comfortable with both Mars and Venus in themselves. For these reasons, provided that you haven't bought wholesale into the stereotyped image of men as Mars and women as Venus, your genital sex isn't really the issue. Whatever your sex and whatever orientation you have, if you are mostly coming from your Mars, you'll seek Venus in a partner. If you side primarily with Venus, then you'll be on the lookout for Mars.

In order to stimulate your thinking about Mars in the different signs, imagine a scene set in a New York singles bar—and just to be safe, let's make it before AIDS became a wide-scale concern, say 1980. Besides indicating the manner in which we move in on or approach another person, Mars also suggests how we go about impressing other people, the attributes which we think will make us appear powerful, sexy, attractive or potent. To be clear and simple, we'll say the bar is mixed, and full of men who are trying to impress women along the lines of their own Mars sign. (Remember that a woman, too, may try to impress others with her potency and power according to her Mars sign, although I imagine that the majority of women in this situation probably would use their Venus as a way of making themselves attractive and desirable.) Right now we'll concentrate on a man's approach, but it can fit for women as well. So a man with Mars in Gemini comes up to a woman in this bar, and he wants to impress her. What's his line like?

Audience: Through talking, through showing you how clever he is.

Howard: Yes, he might try to impress you with his expertise at conversation and his wide knowledge of a variety of subjects. He might mention a book he has just finished or a film he has recently seen, giving you his studied opinion. What about someone with Mars in Aquarius?

Audience: They'll tell you about the latest new electronic gadget they have at home.

Howard: That sounds slightly obscene. I was thinking along the lines of trying to impress you with their vision, their ideals or their originality. What about Mars in Scorpio?

Audience: By being mysterious.

Howard: Yes, appearing mysterious might be their way of attracting you, or they may want to demonstrate how deep and profound they are, perhaps through giving you an instant psychoanalysis into your true nature. Or they try to impress you with how good they are sexually—"Come with me for a night you'll remember" or subtly hinting, "Come with me for a big surprise." Some of them give off signals that say, "I may be dangerous or complex, but I'm not somebody you'll easily forget."

Audience: What about Mars in an earth sign—would they try to impress you by how rich and successful they are?

Howard: Well, Mars in Taurus might think he is in there with a chance if he can demonstrate what a solid, reliable, determined guy he is. Yes, and that he is solvent. He'd probably like you to see him as an earthy type, and as good sexually as the Scorpio bloke also chatting you up. Or he just might mention a certain possession he thinks will impress you—his new car or compact disc system or something like that.

Audience: Mars in Capricorn also would like to come over as competent, capable and successful, as someone wise and mature, with whom it would be good for you to be seen.

Audience: Mars in Virgo may offer to fix your leaky faucet or put shelves up for you!

Howard: Or they may want to impress you with their acute critical judgement and discriminating powers, recommending what they consider to be the best liqueur in the bar and such. This is turning silly, but you're getting the idea. Mars in an air sign will want to come over as intelligent and clever, while Mars in an earth sign would like to be seen as practical and helpful, and well-adapted to the material world. How about Mars in Leo?

Audience: Would they try to show you how important they are?

Howard: I think they would want you to notice that they are special and unique, not like everyone else in the place. They may brag a little about their achievements or the important people they know, or try to hold your attention by telling funny or dramatic stories. How about Mars in Sagittarius?

Audience: They might try to impress you by telling you all the places they have travelled, or by inviting you to Paris for the weekend. Or they want you to see how sporty or trendy they are. Some of them might share their philosophy and belief systems as a way of inspiring you and winning you over.

Howard: Good. What about Mars in Cancer or Pisces?

Audience: Men with Mars in Cancer or Pisces may try to impress you by showing how sensitive and feeling they are. Perhaps Mars in Cancer would offer to cook a meal for you, or to care for and help you in some way.

Howard: Yes, that's possible. Or they may think that if they come over as a little sad or forlorn, you won't be able to resist mothering them. Mars in Pisces would be similar—they want to demonstrate how sympathetic they are, that if you team up with them, you'll have a shoulder to cry on and someone to stand by you in difficulties. Conversely, they may play the victim in need of rescuing. Some people find that irresistible.

You can figure out the other Mars placements yourselves. I have a chart to look at in terms of Mars, but there really isn't enough time right now. Liz and I will cover it tonight during our joint session. We only have five minutes left, and I wanted to do one more thing with you. In her book *A Woman in Your Own Right*, Anne Dickson lists a number of basic rights which she believes we all merit.[18] I've put an edited version of them on the overhead projector, and as I read you these rights, I'd like you to say them to yourselves or out loud with me. This is a Mars seminar, so it's appropriate that we should end with a firm statement of our rights as individuals.

---

[18]Anne Dickson, *A Woman in Your Own Right* (London: Quartet Books, 1982), ch. 5.

1) I have the right to state my own needs and set my own priorities. (Say that now.)

2) I have the right to be treated with respect as an intelligent, capable and equal human being. (Say this out loud or to yourself.)

3) I have the right to express my feelings. (This is the right to your Moon.)

4) I have the right to express my opinions and values. (This is the right to your Mercury and Venus.)

5) I have the right to say yes or no for myself.

6) I have the right to ask for what I want.

7) I have the right to change my mind. (I like this one—just in case you ask for the wrong thing.)

8) I have the right to make mistakes. (Some people don't give themselves this right. They make a mistake and immediately think they are terrible people for it. Come on, we are only human, we don't have to be perfect.)

9) I have the right to decline responsibility for other people's problems. (There are times you might want to help others, but there are times you'd rather be at home watching television—you have the right to say no.)

10) I have the right to deal with others without being dependent on them for approval. (This can be hard to do, because as children we believe that we have to be approved of in order to win love and ensure our survival.)

Okay, that's it for now. Let's give a big round of applause for our friend Mars.

PART FOUR

CHART
INTERPRETATION

VENUS AND MARS IN CHART INTERPRETATION

A DISCUSSION WITH EXAMPLES

BY LIZ GREENE AND HOWARD SASPORTAS

Liz: We have a double act tonight, and we thought we might start off singing "Blue Moon." Howard will do the tenor, and I'll do the alto.

Howard: I thought I was doing the alto.

Liz: I can't take you anywhere, can I? Never mind; instead of singing "Blue Moon" we are going to continue with the charts of Charles and Diana, and have a look at the synastry. (See Charts 5 & 6 on pages 264–265.) This is a very interesting approach to Venus and Mars—seeing how they interact with each other and with other planets between two charts. Perhaps we might begin by considering Charles' Venus-Neptune conjunction. Howard, I think you already covered Venus-Neptune, because I didn't have time in my session on Venus aspects.

Howard: Yes, I talked about it in relation to the case history I used for my Venus lecture.

Liz: I would like to say a little more about it now, because of its placement in the 4th house in Charles' chart. This hidden conjunction suggests some very interesting things about his character, although it is a side of him which probably the public would not recognise at first glance. Neptune, as we have seen, reflects the longing in us to lose our separateness and merge with some greater whole. It is the quest for the Paradise Garden, the return to the vanished magic of the womb, the source of life. Here it combines with Venus in its own sign, so Charles' values—what he finds

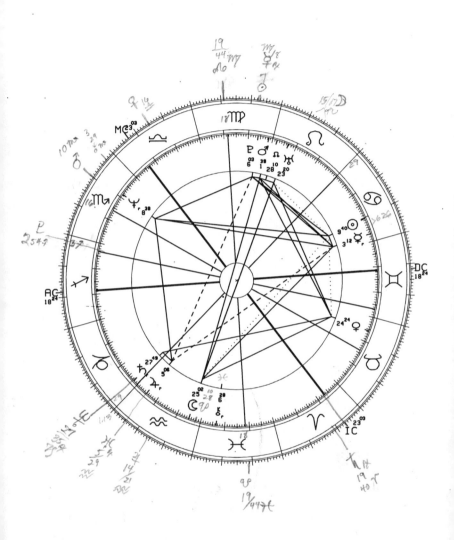

Chart 5. Diana, Princess of Wales. Born in Sandringham, England, July 1, 1961, at 7:45 P.M. BST. (52N50, 0E30) Birth data source: Buckingham Palace. Chart calculated by Astrodienst, using the Placidus house system.

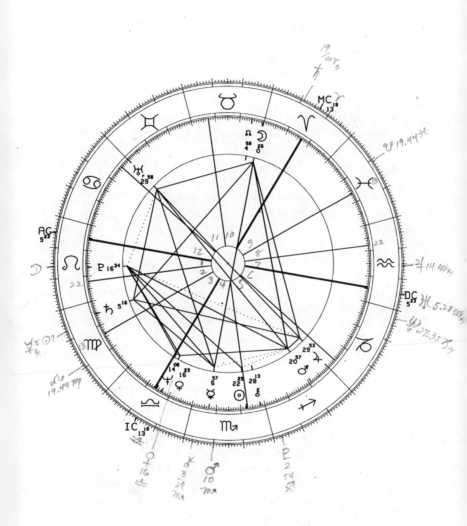

Chart 6. Charles, Prince of Wales. Born in London, England, November 14, 1948, at 9:14 P.M. GMT. (51N32, 0W08) Birth data source: Buckingham Palace. Chart calculated by Astrodienst, using the Placidus house system.

beautiful and worthwhile in life—reflect that vision of an ideal world, a Golden Age before the Saturnian Fall. Perhaps one of the places where the public might recognise this powerful conjunction is in the Prince's love of the vanished past as it is reflected in pastoral landscapes and the harmony of classical architecture. He is a seeker after beauty, and recoils from the soullessness of many modern buildings. This has earned him some enmity from the architects, but despite a certain amount of public criticism and even mockery, he remains loyal to these clearly expressed Venus-Neptune values, which also include his interest in the more mystical aspects of Jung's psychology.

Venus-Neptune has been described by various astrologers as the most romantic of all aspects. The quest for the Paradise Garden colours Charles' vision of relationship, so he would be likely, especially as a young man, to idealise love and hope for a beloved who would heal all wounds and alleviate all loneliness and make all the ills of life vanish. There is an inevitable disillusionment process which sets in with Venus-Neptune aspects, because obviously no human partner can create this perfect state of fusion. Neptune's magic depends upon fantasy and unobtainability. The only perfect partner is the one you never meet. So it seems to me there is a quality of sadness or melancholy in Charles, because he will always have a dream of love which it would be impossible for any individual woman to fulfil.

Howard: Many architects think his ideas are unrealistic and too idealistic.

Liz: Up to a point they probably are, although I have great sympathy for his protests against what he calls "carbuncles" on the landscape. But it is not really possible to recreate his Neptunian vision now. One would have to tear down half of London, and sandblast the other half. The architecture which Charles favours always belongs to a past era—Georgian, Victorian, Edwardian—and it is not economically feasible for a property developer to erect such buildings now, without the cheap labour available in past centuries.

It is generally known that Charles has found a kind of "mentor" in Sir Laurens van der Post, who is a person steeped in Jung's ideas—a writer, a visionary and an explorer. Van der Post is a Sagittarian, and I believe he has had enormous influence on Charles' thinking. I find it interesting that the Venus-Neptune conjunction is in the 4th house, which reflects the relationship with father and with roots. I think in a way Charles has looked beyond his personal father, Prince Philip, and has found a kind of spiritual father in van der Post and the Neptunian inner world of ideals and visions.

Howard: His cousin, Lord Mountbatten, was also a kind of father to him. You can see this astrologically by Mercury in the 4th ruling the 3rd house, which links the house of the father to the planet and house of relatives. I'm pretty sure that Mountbatten's death hit Charles very hard. As you were saying, Venus-Neptune can idealise people and then lose them, or be let down and disappointed.

Liz: You can see how much this Venus-Neptune conjunction tells us about the Prince of Wales. Now we need to look at Diana's chart, and see if the conjunction links up with anything there. Hopefully, we will find a connection, because this would suggest that Diana can reflect back at least some of the qualities which Charles values so highly. Can you see any cross-aspects here?

Audience: Diana's MC is in Libra, and conjuncts Charles' Venus-Neptune.

Liz: Yes, that is the main connection. The Venus-Neptune is also sextile Diana's Sagittarius Ascendant. But the contact with the MC is the more powerful aspect. What do you think this means?

Audience: Something about her appearance in the world.

Liz: The MC reflects a person's image, their presentation to the world outside. It can also be a very important factor in the physical appearance, the physical type, even more so than the Ascendant. So we can surmise that Charles finds in Diana an embodiment of that ideal beauty he seeks—the way she dresses and presents herself to the public eye, and her physical qualities.

Howard: His Venus-Neptune conjunction will be squared by Neptune for the next few years.

Liz: And then Uranus follows on its heels. Well, there may be a difficult period for him emotionally, when his relationship life seems confused and emotionally unstable. The press are like prurient bloodhounds, forever pouncing on Charles and Diana if they happen to travel anywhere independently; and like any other couple they no doubt have their difficulties and areas of incompatibility. It is possible that Charles may go through a time when he feels disillusioned – his ideal of perfection has turned out to be a mortal woman – but the transit of Uranus might also reflect a change in his attitudes, a freeing from some of the excessive idealism of Neptune. And of course both transits could reflect confusion and change in other areas – his relationship with his father, and also his values and the outer forms through which he expresses them.

Now how do you think Diana responds to her husband's Venus-Neptune at her MC?

Audience: She would feel admired.

Liz: Yes, that is one probable response. She might feel more beautiful and glamourous in his eyes, and her self-image might grow and flower. In fact it has; she has come a long way from the naive Lady Diana Spencer in terms of image and style, and I don't think this is just because the palace hairdressers have set to work on her. She has *become* that Venus-Neptune in terms of her public persona, as though he has given form to her through the projection of his own image of beauty.

Howard: Diana was born with Venus square Uranus, which makes me think that she could feel trapped at times in the relationship.

Liz: I am sure she does. Wouldn't you? It's truly life in a fishbowl, apart from whatever issues they might need to sort out between them.

Now what about her Venus, and its cross-aspects to Charles' chart? It opposes his Sun and Chiron, quite closely. Her Venus is 24 Taurus; his Sun is 22 Scorpio and Chiron 28 Scorpio. So Diana's

Venus sits right on the midpoint of his Sun and Chiron, as well as forming oppositions to them. That is a very powerful cross-aspect, especially because it involves the midpoint as well.

Audience: Isn't that a good aspect, in a way?

Liz: Everything is a good aspect, in a way. But you are right, Venus opposite the Sun in synastry is usually considered very positive, because there is a magnetic attraction. What Diana values most, what she finds beautiful and worthy in life, is embodied in Charles. There is a tension in all oppositions, but it is a tension of complements, rather than antagonists, as is the case with squares. Opposite signs are secretly the same in many ways, and Taurus and Scorpio share a deep sensuality and a great intensity and loyalty of feeling. But Diana's Venus opposing Charles' Chiron is a more difficult configuration. His Sun conjunct Chiron makes a statement about the complexity of his character; this aspect suggests to me that he is a rather lonely, intensely serious person with a feeling of woundedness around his ability to express himself. This is emphasised by the conjunction being in Scorpio. Perhaps it also infers something about his father, and a quality of isolation or woundedness which they both share, or find between them. This may be why Charles has sought "spiritual fathers" in figures like Laurens van der Post and Lord Mountbatten. The "wounded healer" quality in Charles—the sadness and isolation which has generated his deep reflectiveness and philosophical bent—is both attractive to Diana, and also perhaps disturbing or hurtful to her. She may have difficulty in understanding his seriousness and tendency to withdrawal, although she would also probably respect and admire it.

Howard: There's more. She has a close fixed T-cross involving the Moon in 25 Aquarius opposing Uranus in 23 Leo, both square Venus in 24 Taurus. So Charles' Sun in 22 Scorpio completes the empty leg of her T-cross; his Sun not only opposes her Venus but squares her Moon and Uranus as well. Anyone who has planets which fill the empty leg of your T-square will bring important tests and challenges your way. If you take the Moon to define her instinctive needs, the fact that his Sun squares it could be a problem for her—she may not be instinctively receptive or responsive to what he needs to fulfil his sense of identity? What do you think is the significance of her Uranus square his Sun?

Audience: It could lead to a breakup or major disruption.

Howard: A breakup is unlikely. But her legitimate need for space, individuality and freedom (Uranus in Leo conjunct her North Node) could be at odds with certain aspects of his nature. She also has Uranus in the 8th house, which probably indicates that she has to keep her restlessness somewhat hidden or underground.

Liz: I think Diana's rebelliousness, which is an innate quality in her—reflected by that T-cross you are referring to—is certainly triggered by the demands of her situation, and probably also by Charles' tendency not to bring his real feelings and wishes out into the open (Sun in Scorpio conjuncting Chiron). A Scorpio Sun tends to operate along quiet, intuitive lines, assuming that others will exercise the same subtle perceptions, and Scorpio can rarely be accused of adopting the "let it all hang out" attitude of discussing everything. This might be quite difficult for Diana, whose Aquarian Moon is more inclined to air things and discuss them reasonably. I keep thinking of that awful lightbulb joke—"How many Californians does it take to change a lightbulb? One to change the bulb, and five to share the experience." This has always seemed to me an archetypal American joke, reflecting the extreme side of America's Moon in Aquarius. I am not suggesting that Diana is like this—after all, she is British—but there is a very honest, open quality about the Moon in Aquarius which can find the silent depths of Scorpio quite frustrating.

Because Diana's Uranus is in the 8th, I would expect her rebellion to erupt in a very erratic, unpredictable and unconscious way. She might be perfectly calm and contented and self-contained and then suddenly, bang! she can't take it one minute more. A person with Uranus in the 8th does not walk around consciously monitoring feelings; the feelings suddenly rise to the surface and break through in a highly disruptive way, as if a bomb has gone off under the house. Planets in the 8th tend to operate in this volcanic fashion. Because Uranus squares her Moon and Venus, these emotional eruptions are likely to disturb her security needs and threaten her Taurean values. I would guess that at times she finds herself wondering how on earth she could have said or done what she just did.

Audience: Everyone is talking about Chiron, but I still don't know what it means.

Liz: I would recommend that you start with Melanie Reinhart's book *Chiron and the Healing Journey*.[19] This is an excellent analysis of the planet, or more accurately, planetoid.

Audience: I bought it, but I haven't had a chance to read it yet.

Howard: Maybe you weren't here when Liz spoke about Chiron in one of her Venus lectures. Briefly, in mythology, Chiron was known as the wounded healer. He had a wound which was incurable, and yet he was able to heal others of their wounds and pains. In the chart, Chiron shows where we are wounded, or where there is some damage, a gap or hole in us that is extremely hard to fill. Even though the wound may never heal, we can learn a great deal about life and about ourselves because of it. Liz pointed out that Charles was born with Sun conjunct Chiron in the 5th house, suggesting wounding and pain in the area of self-expression.

Audience: But what is Chiron? Where is it?

Howard: Chiron is called a planetoid, and was discovered in 1977 by the astronomer Charles Kowal. You'll find it between Saturn and Uranus in the heavens, and it has, I believe, a 52-year cycle.

Liz: The cycle is irregular, like Pluto's, and follows a similar elliptical orbit. It spends much longer in certain signs than in others.

Howard: Sometimes it orbits close to Saturn, and at other times it swings closer to Uranus.

---

[19]Melanie Reinhart, *Chiron and the Healing Journey* (New York: Penguin, 1990).

Liz: Astrologers have been watching it now for 13 years. Some speculative material was published in the early years, but since then a great deal of information has been gathered through observation of its activity in people's charts. Melanie's book is the most recent, and reflects this more empiric observation.

Howard: It really does work in interpretation. If you're not including it in your readings, you ought to get hold of an ephemeris which lists its positions. Chiron interaspects show up frequently in synastry, not just in the charts of lovers and marriage partners, but also between the charts of parents and children, and often between the charts of close friends. In some ways Chiron is like Saturn; it signifies where we have fear, damage or pain, but, if processed and understood properly, we can learn an awful lot as a result. It also says something about one's healing ability or healing powers, and is strongly placed in the charts of people who are interested in health and healing, especially in alternative or complementary approaches to medicine.

Liz: I also feel Chiron is like Saturn, although the nature of the wound is different—it is less obviously personal and parental in origin—and there is also a different way of dealing with it. Saturn compensates for and works through its sense of injury through defensiveness and through dogged practical effort. But Chiron deals with it through acquisition of knowledge, which can eventually become wisdom.

Howard: Because Chiron indicates a wound that is not able to be healed, it also teaches us about acceptance and surrendering to something that is beyond the ego's control, and this kind of surrender or acceptance can open the door to a great deal of higher understanding and insight into the meaning and purpose of one's life and of life in general. By the way, we've seen that Prince Charles has the sun conjunct Chiron in Scorpio in the 5th. Did you know that he once addressed a medical organisation and said that if he didn't have to fulfil his princely duties, he would have chosen to have trained as a doctor or a healer?

Liz: He gave a speech to the British Medical Association some years ago in which he offered his views on illness. He said that there were many people who came to their doctors with illnesses of the soul disguised as illnesses of the body. This is a wonderful description of the kind of worldview held by that Sun-Chiron in Scorpio. I am sure he would not have remained an orthodox medical practitioner; he would no doubt have taken a psychiatric qualification and then have trained at the Jung Institute.

Howard: In mythology, Chiron was the first holistic healer and educator, and served as a kind of foster parent to the semidivine children of the gods. He taught Jason how to sail, he taught Herakles astrology; Asklepios and Achilles were also under his tutelage. He made a point of giving his pupils an all-round, holistic education, teaching them how to fight, but also instructing them in ways of healing the wounds incurred in battle. Chiron symbolises a very contemporary energy or principle, and since it is conjunct Charles' Sun, he is quite in tune with some of the newest or latest trends and currents infiltrating the collective.

Liz: In the synastry between Charles and Diana, we have seen that her Venus opposes his Chiron, and that it is likely she would find this side of him quite disturbing as well as fascinating. Venus is in the sign of its dignity in Taurus, and there is something very sound and uncomplicated about it placed here. One can see this in Diana's relationship to children; she has good, solid, earthy instincts and children intuitively trust her. Since all synastry aspects form a two-way channel—each person affects the other—it is also possible that Diana disturbs Charles as well, because this sound, healthy, earthy side of her will make him aware of his own very complicated and many-sided nature. Probably he envies her for her ability to enjoy herself and take life as it is—one of the gifts of Venus in Taurus—whereas he is always digging and probing and looking for the deeper meaning and motive hidden beneath the surface of things. Venus in Taurus might enjoy dancing and partying and good food and wine, while Chiron in Scorpio sits reading Jung and Paracelsus and pondering the reason for human suffering.

So you can see that these cross-aspects are very complicated and powerful. Chiron both hurts and is hurt by the person whose planet touches it in synastry; and also it heals and is healed. But I would guess that at times it proves a bit much for Diana's Uranus, which might periodically erupt and send her off to get away from all the intensity.

Audience: Charles' Saturn conjuncts Diana's Mars and Pluto.

Liz: Yes, we are inching our way toward that one.

Audience: I have a question about the royal family, its values and what they stand for. Don't you think it might be obsolete? Prince Charles is trapped by his role, and might be happier out of it.

Liz: I am afraid I don't agree with you. But you live in Switzerland, which has always been a democracy, and which as a collective has different psychological needs. If anyone seriously suggested that the Swiss should have a royal family, you would all find it at best absurd and at worst infuriating and threatening. Britain is also a democracy. But the symbol of kingship as an ideal image of the god in man is deeply embedded in the British psyche, as it is in many other countries. It is not silly, nor obsolete, because it is archetypal; and it is part of the fabric of the nation's individuality. With a few noisy exceptions, the British love and need their royal family, because it personifies something absolutely stable and permanent in the midst of chaos, and also because every human drama, dark and light, is reflected by it, and provides a mythic enactment of an essentially religious kind. I think it is perhaps a little simplistic to believe that poor Charles is stuck in the wrong value system and would be better off out of it. His role is much subtler and more important than that, and I am sure he knows it. The values he espouses have tremendous influence on many people, and he, like his mother, the Queen, attempts to take on this responsibility with as much integrity as possible. Obviously they all fall down from time to time, because they are ordinary human beings. But although they do not govern, they have enormous psychological importance for the British people.

The apparently eccentric and overidealistic views which Charles espouses move in a different direction from the values which the Queen upholds, although they are not in collision. I think this is a very interesting development, since the two of them seem to hold together a wide spectrum of attitudes in relative harmony. Charles is also naturally very cautious and circumspect and intelligent about promulgating his views, partly because of his Moon in the 10th in Taurus trine Saturn, which, Venus-Neptune notwithstanding, gives him enough realism to know that one does not open up people's thinking by rushing about sounding like a nutter.

Howard: The Moon in the 10th also means he has to be careful not to stray too far afield from what the Queen, and the public, would approve of or condone. As you know, the 10th house is associated with career, standing before the public, and very often with the relationship with the mother. I can't believe how apt it is that Charles' Moon is 0 Taurus in the 10th, and his mother, Queen Elizabeth, has her Sun in 0 Taurus. That says it all. After all, he has inherited his title and his "profession" from her; and with the Moon conjunct his North Node in the 10th, it's absolutely right that he should be carrying on his mother's tradition.

Audience: Do you think he will be king?

Howard: I don't know. I sometimes wonder what will happen when transiting Pluto hits his Sun in a few years, which could correlate with issues to do with power, and yet that would seem too soon for the Queen to step down. I'm switching gears slightly, but my eye keeps going to that exact Jupiter-Uranus opposition across the 5th-11th house axis. This opposition is generally associated with slightly far-out ideas or a philosophy which might be considered somewhat unconventional by the establishment. I guess that goes along with his Chironian nature as well, but I wonder if his philosophy and belief system occasionally might rub his mother the wrong way—although the fact that his Uranus sextiles his Moon, and Jupiter trines it, may ease things in this respect.

Liz: With Uranus in the 11th, he collects some rather odd people around him. That might be where he causes a few shocks. But before all this came up, we were moving on to the synastry contact of Charles' Saturn on Diana's Mars-Pluto. What effect might this have?

Audience: He tries to form her, to structure her life.

Liz: Yes, I think that is one facet of it. Structure and stability are terribly important to him with Saturn in Virgo in the 2nd house, and he is also probably a creature of habit; Virgo is by nature ritualistic, and dislikes chaos. No doubt he tries to provide a solid container for her very powerful self-willed side (Mars-Pluto). At times she may feel very restricted and frustrated, because Mars-Pluto reacts strongly to any thwarting of the will, no matter how sensible the reasons; and I would guess that she can become very, very angry with him. But at the same time he keeps her "in line" in a very positive way, and can help her to learn to harness her enormous energy and use it for creative goals. He in turn may sometimes feel somewhat overwhelmed by her emotional power, especially her anger, and may react by physically withdrawing (Saturn in the 2nd) and removing himself to the country for a while. This aspect suggests that sometimes they may need to get away from each other if they find they are in a battle of wills, since both are very stubborn people.

Howard: I'm just saying this off the top of my head, but he does seem to look and dress better since they've been together. In this sense, her Mars-Pluto in Virgo may be helping him to transform his self-image or his relationship to his physical body, as shown by his 2nd house Saturn in Virgo ruling Capricorn on the cusp of his 6th.

Liz: You are right, he does look better.

Howard: This is just fantasy on my part, but I have this picture of Charles getting dressed to go out, and Diana suggesting to him what would look best.

Liz: Yes, and with his Saturn on her Mars-Pluto, he would become perverse and disagree with her choice just because she suggested it too strongly, and then she would become angry because he was so intractable, and he would feel hurt because she was trying to change him. And so on. Are we writing a soap opera?

Howard: No, it's a Mills and Boon novel.[20]

Liz: We're in the wrong business. Never mind, astrology is meatier. Anyway, Saturn reacts to Mars with a mixture of great admiration and envy masked by critical disapproval. Mars is potent in those spheres where Saturn feels shy and awkward. There are certainly issues here around physical confidence and appearance. There is also a strong sexual attraction in Mars-Saturn cross-aspects, although Saturn is often too shy to risk being openly vulnerable, and may withdraw and appear cool out of defensiveness rather than lack of passion.

Howard: Yes, I understand it the same way. Mars is where we naturally want to assert, where we naturally want to express ourselves; but Saturn is where we feel blocked and insecure. What comes naturally to her (Mars in Virgo) somehow correlates with what his Saturn in Virgo finds difficult or awkward. A similar dynamic occurs with Venus-Saturn contacts in synastry. Someone with Venus in Gemini could display a natural talent for making conversation and small talk, but a person with Saturn in Gemini may find it hard to communicate with others in this way. Therefore, as a defence, the Saturn in Gemini person might be critical or judgemental of the Venus in Gemini person's fluency.

Liz: Saturn may be deeply drawn to the other person's gift, and wish to support and shape it, but at the same time may criticise the other's apparent superficiality. This accusation of superficiality or shallowness is often expressed by the Saturn person, because Saturn has to work so very hard at the issues reflected by its sign, and takes them so very seriously; and it can be quite painful, as well as

---

[20]This is the British equivalent of a romance novel, like those published by Harlequin.

annoying, to watch someone parade about expressing with complete unselfconsciousness what one has struggled so hard to
become conscious of.

Charles' Saturn also opposes Diana's Chiron, with an orb of
only one degree. Her Chiron is in turn in her 2nd house, so there is
a very similar issue in both of them being set off by the cross-
aspect. Because Diana's Chiron is in Pisces, her sense of woundedness might revolve around a feeling of emotional insecurity and
loneliness, perhaps reflecting the instability of her earlier family
life. I am only hazarding a guess, but she may have felt helpless
and slightly victimised by whatever difficulties were occurring
between her parents; and I think it is interesting that she has
developed such a profound sympathy and concern for the ill and
the handicapped, as well as for children. She readily responds to
the helpless and to life's victims, and this I think reflects that placement of Chiron in Pisces in the 2nd.

Audience: Would this make him feel uncomfortable, because it
opposes his Saturn?

Liz: It might; but because his Saturn falls in the same house, I also
think it might potentially give them a great bond of mutual empathy, if they could express this vulnerability and insecurity to each
other.

Now what about the cross-aspects between Charles' Mars and
Diana's chart?

Audience: His Mars is right on her Ascendant.

Liz: Yes, it is a close contact, with an orb of only 2 degrees. His
Mars is also in trine Diana's Uranus, as well as sextiling her Moon.
So there seems to be a very positive response to Charles' Mars
from Diana's chart. The Ascendant is not a planet, and is the recipi-
ent of energy rather than a generator of it; an aspect from someone's planet to your Ascendant affects your sense of yourself and
how you express yourself to the world outside. So Charles,
through his vitality and energy and romantic explorer's nature
(Mars in Sagittarius in the 5th house) has great impact on Diana,

opening up her own vision and need to move beyond conventional boundaries.

Howard: I think it's fair to say that he opened up the world for her. Diana has the Sun in the 7th, a placement which suggests that she finds herself through marriage and partnership. We often think about marriage as dying as an "I" to be reborn "We," but in her case she has become a famous celebrity through it—she has come into her own through marriage. She used to be called "shy Di," but I don't think that epithet fits her any more. Now she seems to have found her power as a person in her own right, and paradoxically, this has occurred through her marriage to Charles. The public mostly love her, which would fit with her 7th house Sun trine Neptune in the 10th. Actually, that trine makes a Grand Trine with Chiron in Pisces in the 2nd—being so publicly loved and admired must have healed her in some way. Charles' Mars and Jupiter around her Ascendant also might have something to do with her finding her power through him, and the world opening up for her through their relationship.

Liz: I believe he has opened up the world for her mentally as well as on the concrete level. Probably he has expanded her mind enormously, even if she does not espouse his views, because his range of interests is so much greater than what she began with at the start of the marriage. Jupiter in Sagittarius, especially in opposition to Uranus, is really global in its concerns and its philosophy, and there is a great love of knowledge innate in Sagittarius. This potential was always there in Diana through her Ascendant, but we all develop the Ascendant slowly and with difficulty, and she needed him as the catalyst to set it off. I also think Charles both appreciates and stimulates her wilfulness, because of the trine between his Mars and her Uranus. Where his more introverted, sensitive side (Sun in Scorpio) may find it difficult to handle, the more fiery, adventurous spirit in him gets on well with Diana's rebellious quality. When he can climb out of those deep Scorpionic waters, and leave behind all the melancholy reflectiveness of the Sun-Chiron for a while, then he can just have fun with her. Probably they would get on best when they are travelling, or skiing, or working at big projects together.

Howard: Yes, I imagine there are times they play together well. Coming back to his Mars-Jupiter conjunction opposite Uranus — this is a configuration often associated with accidents. He seems to be slightly accident-prone, falling off polo horses and things like that.

Liz: Yes, and he was also involved in the tragic skiing accident which killed his friend. The accidents happen around him as well as to him. There is a very high-strung and slightly reckless element in Mars-Jupiter-Uranus, which does not always pay attention to Saturnian limits. This kind of accident-proneness does not arise from some deep-seated self-destructive impulse; it is the result of quite literally not watching where one is going. The physical coordination (Mars) can sometimes have a jerky, nervous quality (Uranus) and if one's mind is wandering off into the ethers at the critical moment (Jupiter), then one falls off one's horse.

Howard: Have you talked about Diana's background of a broken home?

Liz: Only just now, in passing, in relation to her Chiron in the 2nd house and the sense of insecurity this might reflect.

Howard: Well, it fits with the Moon-Venus-Uranus T-square, which suggests running into some disruption in childhood. In my Venus lecture, I spoke quite a bit about the inner conflict we all have between closeness needs and freedom needs, between intimacy and autonomy. It would strike me that she has a fair share of this dilemma, with the space-loving Moon in Aquarius opposite Uranus, and both square security-loving Venus in Taurus. Her parents' divorce and the upheaval it must have brought into her life reflect these aspects.

Liz: There is a rather fated feeling around the planets which fall in Diana's 8th house, especially the Uranus-Node conjunction. Planets in the 8th seem to erupt from nowhere like blows of fate, although the "nowhere" is usually the unconscious, both personal and family. Also, the nodal axis across the 2nd and 8th houses, with the North Node in the 8th, suggests that she will need to learn about life's depths and the transformative power of situations which are beyond her control. Life never follows a safe and secure ✗ route if the 8th house is strong in a birth chart, which I think the Moon conjuncting the South Node in the 2nd house might bitterly resent. Even the good and exciting things—like suddenly finding oneself Princess of Wales—have the same "Wheel of Fortune" quality. The unseen side of life will always rise up and confront Diana, requiring her to accept a dimension of reality which challenges her 2nd house Moon and Taurean Venus. She might not have chosen it voluntarily, but she will need to learn to work with it.

Now are there any further comments or questions about these two?

Audience: What about his Mercury conjunct her Neptune?

Liz: Put very simply, Diana would be likely to idealise Charles' intellect. She would see a kind of redemption in his powers of thought and reflection. Probably she has enormous admiration for his depth of mind, but at times she might also feel overwhelmed, or may expect him to find all the answers all of the time. She may exhibit a tendency to agree with everything he says, because his insight and profundity make her feel safe and contained—a touch of the Paradise Garden. On the more difficult side, Charles may become impatient with her because she seems vague or evasive to him; and Diana may feel he is too critical of her manner of expressing herself. Mercury-Neptune cross-aspects in synastry can be extremely creative, because Mercury can articulate Neptune's feelings and fantasies, while Neptune gives colour and imagination to Mercury's perceptions. The problem between them lies in Mercury's irritation with Neptune's meanderings, and Neptune's elusiveness when confronted with Mercury's precision. But in general, I think it is a very productive cross-aspect.

Howard: I think this is reinforced by a trine between her Mercury in Cancer and his Mercury in Scorpio.

Audience: Maybe she fell in love with his voice. I just love his voice.

Liz: Where is your Neptune?

Howard: Do you like my voice? I'm told I speak just like Prince Charles. Actually, Liz sounds more like Prince Charles than I do.

Liz: Well, I have a better British accent. But you would look better on a horse.

Howard: I can't play polo.

Liz: Why haven't you told me?

Audience: How would you judge the whole synastry? I think they have quite good general aspects, both with fiery signs rising and with the Suns in water.

Liz: I agree with you; I think the overall synastry is very strong and generally compatible. There are points of difficulty, such as the cross-aspect between Saturn and Mars-Pluto, which I am sure generate some quite intense sparks from time to time; but the positive contacts are strong enough to hold it together. There is always likely to be a problem with Charles' Venus-Neptune, which will inevitably seek a romantic perfection impossible to find in any love relationship; and there is always likely to be a problem with Diana's Venus-Moon-Uranus, which will inevitably want to have its cake and eat it too in the closeness versus freedom department. But the immovable structures of their situation, as well as what I believe to be the genuine love and affection between them, will provide a container for those edgy Venuses. They must find their own workable solutions for these natal aspects, and would no doubt manage much better if the press were not so incredibly certain of their right to invade others' privacy.

Audience: What do you think will happen when Pluto hits Charles' Sun?

Liz: A lot of us would like to know what will happen then. Howard mentioned this earlier. Whatever it is, it is likely to be big and irrevocable. My guess is that he will become king. But Pluto moves back and forth so slowly that there is a very large timespan in which this might occur.

Howard: When Pluto comes to Charles' Sun, it will hit Diana's T-square around the same time. Both of them are in line for major changes then, because Pluto will not only be transiting his Sun, but it will also be squaring her Moon and Uranus, and opposing her Venus. At this point, I wouldn't want to venture an interpretation of these transits.

Liz: He may take the throne at that time, but that isn't certain. It might fit the movements in her chart, however, because of its effect on the foundations of her life. Howard, do you know what degree of Capricorn falls on the Queen's Ascendant?

Howard: Queen Elizabeth is a 0 Taurus with 21 Capricorn rising.

Liz: Then Uranus and Neptune will arrive at her Ascendant around the time Pluto arrives on Charles' Sun.

Howard: Saturn is currently hanging around her Ascendant. Uranus and Neptune won't get there until 1993, and Pluto will still be around 22 Scorpio at that time.

Liz: There has always been speculation about whether the Queen might eventually abdicate.

Howard: For whatever reasons.

Audience: I wonder what might happen with Neptune squaring Charles' Venus.

Liz: Neptune is already very close, well within orb of that square. Whatever is going to "happen" is already at work. I really don't what to keep speculating about these future transits, since attempting to predict events is always very questionable and difficult; and moreover, we may not always be in a position to know what "happens" to Prince Charles since so much of his life is necessarily kept

private. Shall we move on now? Howard, you have some charts
you wanted to talk about in this session.

Howard: Yes, I have the charts of Lou and Mark, another father-son
duo (see Charts 7 and 8, pages 286–287). I only have a solar chart
for Lou (Mark's father), but I'd like to begin by looking at the
placement of the Sun in his chart. Lou was born with the Sun
square Neptune and very widely square Uranus, as well as the Sun
trine Jupiter and sextile Pluto. It's the Sun-Neptune square that
interests me. Aspect to the Sun indicate what you meet when you
move toward father in the process of separating from mother. So
what do you think Lou met through his father?

Audience: The trine to Jupiter would suggest that he saw his father
as a hero, or someone exciting to be around. But the square to
Neptune, and the wide square to Uranus, have a very different feel
to them.

Howard: Right. According to Mark's knowledge on the matter, as a
very young boy Lou was drawn to his father (Sun trine Jupiter),
but unfortunately he was killed in the First World War. This loss is
shown by the square to Neptune and the wide square to Uranus,
and also, I guess, by the sextile to Pluto. So when he was only 4 or
5, Lou lost his father, a man one imagines he had looked up to and
admired. How might this have affected Lou as a father?

Audience: Lou's ability to father could have been damaged in some
way by his father's death.

Howard: Yes, Lou's beloved father went away one day and never
came back again. This must have been felt as a crushing hurt and
disappointment for Lou, and probably made him wary of opening
himself up emotionally. As a result, fathering would not come
easily to him. Now look at Mark's chart. Like his father, he also has
a Sun-Neptune aspect, and it is connected to the 4th house because
Mark has Leo on the cusp of the 4th, the house of father. It's as if
Lou's issues around his own father were passed on to Mark. Mark
has been fairly successful in his life, and yet he still feels uneasy
and uncertain of his value and worth. I would link this to the

difficult relationship he had with Lou, a man damaged by his own experience of father.

Liz: I think it's interesting that they have both got the Sun in Aries as well. One of the main mythic themes connected with Aries is the competition of father and son, and psychologically this reflects Aries' need to have a strong father against whom one can collide in order to discover one's own potency. Father-son issues are very relevant for Aries, who in childhood seeks a father embodying enough phallic power to identify with as an ideal. Here are two Aries men neither of whom has found the potent father he was seeking.

Howard: Sacrifice is a keyword for Neptune, and when it aspects the Sun, there are sacrifices to be made around the father. Lou had to sacrifice his father to the war effort, and then Mark suffered poor fathering because of Lou's early hurt and pain around his father. Mark said that his father was and still is very distant and aloof, and the only real contact they had in Mark's growing-up years was when Lou beat him with a cane for misbehaving or not acting according to his wishes.

Liz: Lou's Venus is in Aries conjuncting Mark's Sun, and I think this is another father-son relationship in which there is a lot of love hidden away beneath all the problems of communication and expression of feeling. Lou's image of what is most beautiful and of the highest value is embodied in his son, who epitomises the Aries qualities; yet Lou cannot express his love and admiration because of his own emotional blockage.

Howard: Yes, we are back to a common theme: a father and son who feel love for one another, but complex emotional issues get in the way of the expressing of that love. When I asked Mark what he wanted from his father, he said, "I just want him to hug me."

Liz: That sounds like Marks' Venus in Pisces speaking. And look where it lands in Lou's chart.

Howard: Right on Lou's Moon-Chiron conjunction.

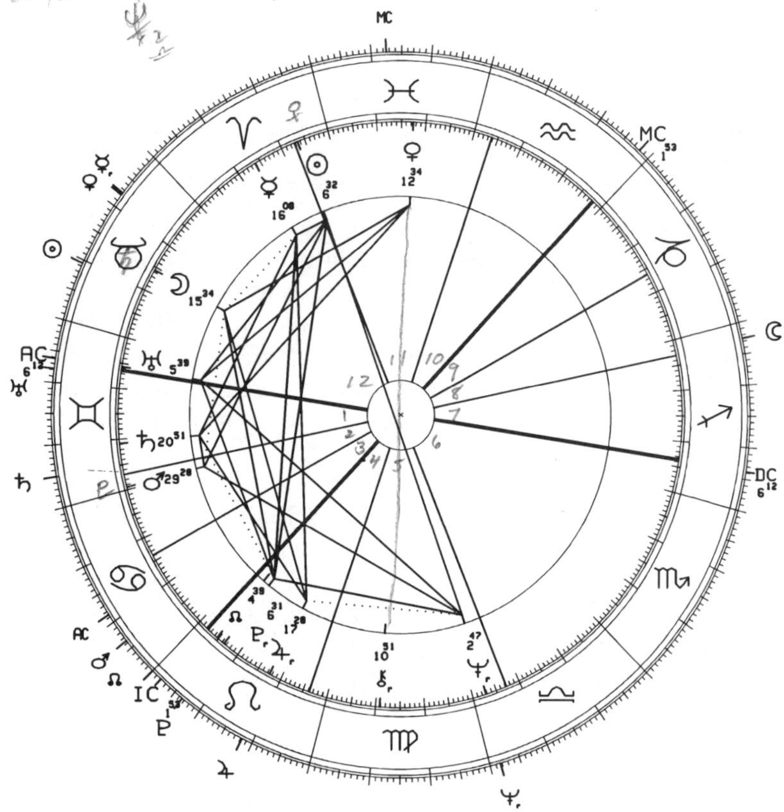

Chart 7. Mark. The birth data has been withheld for confidentiality. Chart calculated by Astrodienst, using the Placidus house system.

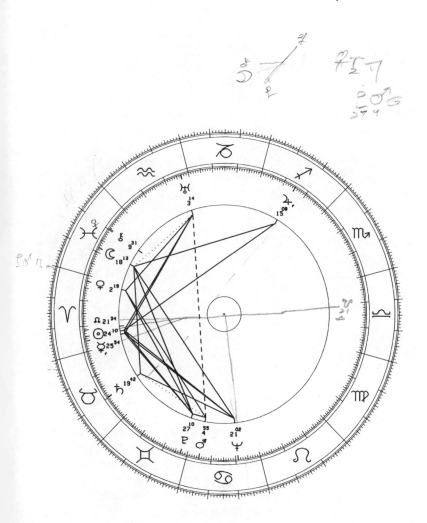

Chart 8. Lou, Mark's father. The birth data has been withheld for confidentiality. A flat chart (solar chart) has been calculated by Astrodienst, as precise birth time is unknown. House system used is Placidus.

Liz: The Venus-Moon cross-aspect is a very nice one, full of affection and fondness. Mark wants that Piscean warmth and closeness, which he deeply values, and his father certainly responds, even if at an unconscious level, because his Moon is in Pisces. But because Lou has Chiron with the Moon, he feels deeply wounded and isolated in the area of his instinctual needs and his sense of emotional security. We were both saying earlier that Chiron sometimes behaves like Saturn, and when Mark comes along with his naturally affectionate Venus in Pisces he meets a chilling response. Lou experiences his own early emotional damage, and probably feels awkward and inadequate, and reacts to Mark as though he doesn't care at all.

Howard: I want to come at this from a slightly different angle. Mark has a T-cross involving the Sun in 6 Aries, Neptune in 2 Libra, and Mars in 29 Gemini. We discussed the Mars-Neptune square this afternoon, which sometimes manifests as a desperate need or desire which seems unattainable or which you can't quite fulfil to your satisfaction. In Mark's case, the Mars-Neptune problem is linked to his Sun, the father. All his life Mark has yearned for his father's love and approval, and Lou just can't give it. Mark has tried over and over again to get his father to pat him on the back and say, "Well done, son," and to this day it has never happened. Let me tell you more about Mark's early life and upbringing. Right from a young age, Mark remembers his father as cold and remote. Then, when Mark was 12, his mother left the family—she just upped and went to New Zealand, leaving Mark alone with Lou. Mark told me that when his mother left, he took on the role of looking after his father, cooking for him, doing the housework, and so on. Mark opened up to me about this period: "After my mother disappeared, I thought, now is my chance to win my father's love. I'll mother him and care for him and look after him— I'll work hard to please him." And yet, in spite of all this effort, Mark still felt unloved and unappreciated by Lou. Then, at age 14, Mark went away to a merchant navy training school. He succeeded brilliantly in this training, and by the age of 16 or 17 was appointed "captain's boy," a much sought-after post as the captain's personal attendant. So Mark is still trying to please father, this time in the guise of captain's boy. Mark was very proud of his position at merchant navy school, and told me: "I wanted my father to praise me for my success; I desperately wanted him to congratulate me on becoming captain's boy. I would wait for him to visit me at school, hoping he would show an interest in my achievements, but he never did. When it was my birthday, he just sent me money. I wanted more than just money—he never bought me a present." In the meantime, Lou had built up a thriving business, and Mark eventually went to work for him, but to this day, he continues to feel frustrated by his father: "Even now, after working for my father for twenty years, he has never complimented me once for anything I've done." I can't be sure if this is really the case or whether it's Mark's perception of events, but there is no doubt that Mark has this gaping wound around his father which has not yet been healed or assuaged: "All I've been looking for from my father is some recognition that I am okay, but he is the kind of man who sees a half-full bottle as half-empty rather than half-full."

Liz: I would guess that Mark's description is objectively very accurate. On the one hand, with Jupiter and Pluto in the 4th house, he has such an idealised and all-powerful image of his father that Mark would always feel he wasn't a good enough son for such a shining, potent parent. With this conjunction in the house of the father, Mark has a tendency to project his own Leonine power onto his father, and then feel oppressed and humiliated by it. And Mark's Sun-Neptune predisposes him toward unrealistic expectations and subsequent disillusionment. Whenever there are planets in the 4th or 10th houses, we see our parents as archetypes rather than people, and our perception is distorted by our own psychic necessity.

Yet on the other hand, when I look at the Venus-Chiron cross-conjunction, and also at the Saturn-Moon cross-conjunction, I think Lou really has been pretty beastly in his behaviour toward Mark. Saturn can be extremely hurtful to the Moon if the Saturn person is unconscious of his or her envy and defensiveness, and the Moon, being so receptive and vulnerable, has virtually no defense, and may develop a slowly accumulating sense of depres- ⚹ sion and failure in the Saturn person's presence. And I would say the same about the Chiron-Venus contact, which, since Lou sounds so unaware of his own emotional complexities, would be likely to manifest as an abrupt rejection of Mark's value as an individual.

Howard: Mark's Mars is not only square his Sun and Neptune, but also conjunct Saturn—he has worked incredibly hard to win his father's love, but so far, all his efforts have been in vain. Mark has done well financially, he has a lovely wife, two sweet kids, a beautiful house in England and another home abroad, and yet, deep inside, he admits to still feeling incomplete and unsatisfied.

Liz: That is the stamp of an undigested Neptune—the perennial unfulfilled longing. But Mark is going to remain unsatisfied unless he can let go of his dream that his father can somehow redeem him through acceptance. I think Mark will need to "sacrifice" his father's love, and his belief that his father holds the key to his salvation, in order to find his own potency. I believe that is the deeper meaning of Neptunian sacrifice—the relinquishing of an unreal fantasy of redemption through someone or something outside oneself. If one places one's redemption in another's hands, as Mark has done with his father, then he or she will wander about forever barred from the gates of Eden, letting life slip away in an orgy of frustration and self-pity.

Howard: When I interviewed Mark, transiting Uranus was squaring his Sun, and he was going through a particularly perturbed phase with his father, as if all the feelings around his father were coming to a head.

Liz: Perhaps this is the potential time of breakthrough. Transiting Pluto has been opposing his Moon as well. I also wonder how much Mark has displaced needs which really belong to his mother—this mother who "upped and went" to New Zealand— onto his father, who is having to carry the whole parental package by himself. It is the Pluto transit to Mark's Moon that makes me wonder whether he might find a way to explore these issues and face his deeper, more unconscious feelings about his childhood. And Uranus squaring his Sun might reflect a discovery of his own identity, a release of energy and an inner separation from the father upon whom he has projected so much.

Howard: When Mark was describing how sad he felt about the whole situation with his father, I began to feel very angry toward Lou, which made me wonder where Mark's anger was in terms of all this. So I asked him if he had ever confronted Lou with his anger at not getting what he needed from him. Mark's reply is indicative of one of the typical fears of a Mars-Neptune aspect: "If I open up with my anger, I'm afraid it will flood out uncontrollably. I'm afraid I'll hurt him if I show it, and then I'd lose all chance of him becoming the father I'd like him to be. I am still hoping he'll change, that he will show me more love. Anyone as bullying or suspicious as my father must have a soft and kind side underneath. Maybe he is just afraid to show it—like Scrooge. But he's 77 now and hasn't changed yet. Maybe I'm too demanding, maybe that is putting him off." Then he asked me, "Do you think there's time left?"

Liz: There is something about Mark's fixation on his father which is very disturbing. I do not question his feeling that his father has treated him very badly indeed; but there is more in it, it goes on and on, year after year. Mark's Sun square Mars is a telling aspect in this context, just as his Sun-Neptune is. I think that Mark has a lot of trouble internalising and expressing his potency, which I associate with this square. There is something in him which does not want to be a Martial man—the nature of a square gives one the feeling that one must make a choice between two irreconcilable qualities, and if one chooses the Sun, then the "brutish," more primitive Mars attributes are pushed away from conscious expression.

The result of this difficulty in internalising Mars is that Mark remains passive in relation to his father. Lou, rather than Mark, has the power to save or destroy the relationship, and Mark is the helpless victim of Lou's behaviour. As long as his father holds this position of power, Mark does not actually have to take responsibility for his own life. He can blame his father for being a negative Mars—callous, hard, domineering, ruthless and a bully (to use his own word)—and can therefore claim that his father has blighted his life. But this spares Mark having to develop his own Mars and incorporate it into his own personality. I doubt that Lou will ever change; this is asking too much from a man of his age with a lifetime of defensive patterns. How could he change now, except on the other side of death, where Mark won't be in a position to hear about it?

So although I sympathise with Mark's pain about his father, I also feel he is avoiding something—he is avoiding his own Mars, which is after all his Sun-sign ruler, the presiding deity whose "child" he is. In order to claim his true Aries identity, he must be willing to own those Martial qualities which he projects onto Lou. Projection is a characteristic of squares, and one of the typical manifestations of Sun square Mars is that someone or something "outside" reduces one to feelings of impotence. I believe Mark must eventually stand up to his father, and express his very justifiable anger, and perhaps even walk out of his father's business and out of the old man's life. He will have to take the risk of giving up hope of his father changing, because he will never respect himself until he does.

Audience: That might free his father, too.

Liz: Indeed it might. Sometimes this happens, because the unconscious complex has both people in its grip, and if one breaks free, the other is liberated as well. But of course one cannot hope for this; one must assume that, in all likelihood, one will lose everything. This also sometimes happens, and a sacrifice is not a sacrifice if there are secret clauses saying that if one is clever, one will not have to pay after all. The emotional cleansing and renewal that comes from this positive side of Neptune cannot work unless there is a real inner relinquishing, which, to put it coldly, is what we mean by growing up. Both Lou and Mark are children in a way, playing power games; and there is a lot of spite between them. They are bound together by their complex, each behaving like little boys on the playground, shouting, "You stink!" "No, YOU stink!" "No, YOU do!" Their interlocked problem is reflected by Lou's Mars hooking into Mark's Sun-Mars-Neptune. The two Mars placements are in fact conjunct. Lou's Mars affects Mark's Sun-Neptune in the same way that Mark's Mars affects his Sun-Neptune. So it is very easy for Mark to project his Mars onto Lou—all he has to do is look at his father's Mars and say to himself, "Ah, it's all *his* fault."

Howard: It's also relevant that Lou's Pluto sits on Mark's Mars-Saturn conjunction: Lou stirs up Mark's insecurity, indecision, sense of weakness, and fear of failure. For years, Mark has been dithering about quitting his father's business and getting away from the whole scene, but he continues to work there, deadlocked, stuck in the situation. His Sun-Mars-Neptune T-square can't seem to let go of still trying to get what he wants from his father. He has done all sorts of things in the hope of pleasing Lou: "I thought I could impress my father by taking up airplane flying. After my first solo flight, I rang him to tell him of my achievement, and there was silence." Mark also reported another incident: "My wife and I worked incredibly hard to fix up this big, old house. It looked great when we finished it, and I was excited about showing my father what I had accomplished. When he came and visited, his only comment was that I hadn't done a very good job with the pillars out in front." Mark has never fully grieved for the ideal father he never had; instead, he keeps trying to turn Lou into that ideal.

Liz: But the one thing Mark has never done is to please himself. Everything is chosen with his father in mind. That is what I mean by giving away his Mars. He literally *asks* to be beaten about the head and face, and goes back each time for more. There is often a subtle masochism in Mars-Neptune, which manifests in this refusal to relinquish a hopeless dream. It is the stuff of martyrs.

You have also been describing the Moon-Saturn cross-conjunction as well. Saturn is often cool and critical toward the Moon, which crawls away feeling hurt and rejected. But I feel the key to all this is that Mark needs to relinquish his dream that his father will change so that he can get what he wants. That is also Mars-Neptune—one wants something badly (Mars) but one will not take responsibility for making it happen oneself (Neptune), because it requires being too separate, too individual.

Howard: Yes, Mark is the one who has to change. Perhaps Uranus will help bring that about.

PART FIVE

CONCLUSION

GROUP DISCUSSION

QUESTIONS AND ANSWERS

BY LIZ GREENE AND HOWARD SASPORTAS

Howard: We've set aside this session for questions and group discussion. Feel free to pick our brains in any way you wish. Ask and you shall receive—maybe.

Audience: I have a question about a chart in which all the planets are on the left side of the MC-IC axis, and I've heard it said that this means a person is self-centred. Is that true?

Liz: The weight of planets in the eastern hemisphere of a chart is certainly striking, but I would not define it as self-centred in the usual sense of "selfish." The houses on this side of the horoscope have their focus on the Ascendant, which implies an emphasis on self-development and self-motivation rather than on relationships with others (which are the concern of the Descendant and the western hemisphere of the chart). The individual with an Ascendant emphasis tends to be generally self-reliant, and is often forced by circumstances to take this attitude (although "circumstances" usually faithfully reflect one's own unconscious needs). When all the planets lie in the western section, there is more of a tendency to wait for others' cues, and to find one's motivation through relationship. I do not think this is a measure of "self-centredness," since one can be very generous and sensitive to others and yet still feel one must find one's own way in life; and equally, one can be very dependent on others yet be utterly insensitive to their reality as separate individuals. We need to be very careful with words like "self-centred." I have always liked Ambrose Bierce's definition of an egotist in *The Devil's Dictionary*. "An egotist is any person who has the audacity to think he is more important than I am."

Howard: Generally speaking, you could say that the east is more causal, and the west is more reactive. With a predominance of planets in the eastern hemisphere, you intrinsically may have more power to be causal in your life – that is, to determine what happens to you, to create your life the way you would like it to be. With a predominance of planets in the western hemisphere, you may have to adjust and deal more with what is given, therefore how you react to events and people in your life becomes the crucial and decisive factor in determining your fate, what you do with the things that come your way. Someone once said that the east allows you a choice of menu, while the west gives a set menu.

Liz: Potage, coq au vin, frites and crème caramel, and all for only 48 francs. That's wonderful, unless you happen not to like coq au vin.

Howard: You don't have to be a passive leaf blown about in the wind with many planets in the west. You have choice in terms of how you choose to react to what is given. But I don't like to make hard and fast rules about the eastern or western hemispheres. What if you have a lot of planets in the east, but you are born with Pisces rising, or Neptune in the 1st? This may alter to what extent you can determine your life. Or you may have all the planets in the western hemisphere, but be born with Sun conjunct Mars conjunct Jupiter in Leo in the 5th house, and I doubt if you will be too passive and overly adjusting to others with that configuration.

Liz: This means that if you don't like the coq au vin and there is nothing else on the menu, you can send it back and demand that it be cooked the way you like it, with a fresher coq and a different balance of wine and herbs. I am also reluctant to make hard and fast rules about these hemispheres, partly because of what you have said, Howard, and also because the progressed and transiting planets bring in new elements as they cross angles and enter new sectors of the chart. Although this won't "change" the birth chart, it can bring greater flexibility into one's life.

Howard: People also say that if you have everything in the upper hemisphere (what is actually the southern hemisphere around the

MC), then you are an extraverted public person who is meant to participate actively in society; on the other hand, everything in the lower hemisphere or around the IC may make you an introverted, private person, who needs to look inward rather than outward in life. This may be true, but in the name of wholeness, we need to develop every sign and house in our charts, not just where there are planets.

Liz: There is also a difference between "extraversion" in the sense of a basic character trait of identifying one's reality with outer things (Jung's definition) and extraversion as a need to make one's mark on society. The first may be portrayed in part by the natal signs and aspects, and the second in part by the house placements. One can be a psychological extravert (Sun conjunct Jupiter in Gemini) yet have very personal goals such as restoring the 17th-century house one inherited from one's family (Sun in the 4th). Equally, one can be a psychological introvert (Sun conjunct Saturn in Scorpio), yet be compulsively pulled into the public eye—which is the case with many actors—because of childhood pressures or a sense of obligation to the collective (Sun in the 10th).

Audience: If a planet is near the end of a house, do you read it as if it is in the adjoining house?

Howard: If a planet is within four or five degrees of the cusp of a house, I would play around with it in terms of the house it is in and the house it is close to. For instance, if you have the Sun in the 2nd but only a few degrees from the 3rd, the way to find yourself (the Sun) may be through communicating or teaching (3rd house) your values (2nd house). Or if you have Venus in the 6th but close to the 7th, you may fall in love with a co-worker. Of if you have Jupiter in the 10th but close to the 11th, your circle of friends could be expanded through your career. Be imaginative with it.

Liz: I have the idea that planets standing in one house but perched on the cusp of the next are like people perched in the doorway between two rooms. They are standing in, for example, the 9th house (suggesting that the basis of their sense of self is the quest for answers to the big questions in life) but their attention is already on the room they are about to enter, the 10th (suggesting that they need to take their worldview, their life philosophy, and transform it into some concrete contribution to society). I think we are in agreement on this one.

Audience: Can you say something about which is the best house system to use?

Howard: Excuse me, I'm going to sleep now. Wake me up in ten years.

Liz: Well, I'm afraid I shall fall asleep on this one too, so we had better set the alarm clock. Why don't you all have a group discussion amongst yourselves and wake us up if you find the right answer?

Howard: The house-division question is an endless controversy in astrology and always will be. I remember Zipporah Dobyns answering a question about which house system to use; she said that you can take a picture of a tree from many different angles, and no one view is more true or right than any of the other views. There is no right or wrong house system. It may be that one method is better for predicting events, while another is preferable for a psychological reading of a person's nature. It makes sense to try out a few until you find the one you like working with best.

Liz: I think there are a lot of conundrums like this in astrology, where you must in the end accept the fact that if it works for you, use it. But if you are looking for an absolute truth about house systems, neither of us is inclined to give it to you. We are both rather Mercurial, and inclined to try on different pairs of spectacles to look at the same view. Astrology, and people, are so much more interesting that way.

Howard: I do prefer the MC and IC to be on a house cusp, and for that reason I'm not so keen on Equal House. I just don't like to see the MC swimming around in the 9th, 10th or 11th, and I think that Liz agrees with me on this point.

Liz: Yes, I do. If you have a very precise birth time, and play about with different systems of progressing the chart (secondary progressions, "Naibod" progressions, solar arc, and so on), you will see some very striking things happening when a progressed house cusp conjuncts a planet. This has convinced me that the "quadrant" systems of house division, where the MC-IC axis forms the cusps of the 10th/4th, offer great insights which Equal House overlooks—although whether that quadrant system should be Placidus, Koch, topocentric or whatever may depend on what kind of chart interpretation you are looking for.

I feel, as Howard does, that you must try these different systems out for yourself. In England we have a great problem with birth times anyway, which is conducive to experimentation. In Switzerland, as in Scotland and America, birth times are recorded as a matter of course, and although they may be a few minutes out (allowing the doctor to cut the cord, wash the baby, and then remember to look at the clock), they are accurate enough to get into arguments about a 1-degree difference between a Placidus and a Koch cusp. But in England we are told birth times such as, "Oh, well, it was around teatime, I remember your father was about to eat a cucumber sandwich when the pains started," or, "It must have been some time in the morning because I remember saying to your grandmother that the milkman had only left one pint instead of two." So one must either be comfortably tolerant about which quadrant system to use, or one must go slowly bonkers trying to rectify charts by exotic progression systems. Now can we talk about something else?

Audience: What in a chart would indicate a narcissistic personality disorder?

Liz: Usually I have found extremely difficult issues around the Moon. Narcissism in the clinical sense reflects a deep disorder in the early bonding between mother and child. The baby is never encouraged to develop a real sense of independent psychic existence. D. W. Winnicott describes a series of typical problems between mother and child which might result in this sort of wound—the mother who alternates between overattentiveness and abrupt withdrawal, or the mother who cannot allow her child to separate because of her own dependent needs, or the mother who is so preoccupied with outside tensions and problems that she cannot bond with her infant at all. Such dilemmas may be caused by very legitimate external factors, such as serious financial crisis, or separation from the husband, or a disruptive change in environment; one cannot always point a moral finger at the "bad" mother for being "unloving." But there is generally a radical disturbance in the mirroring process which every child needs to feel safe in forming a nascent feeling of a self.

Astrologically, this kind of disturbance is in part reflected by the Moon in hard aspect to heavy planets—particularly Saturn, Chiron, Uranus, Neptune and Pluto. As a great many people have such aspects, this suggests that most of us, as I mentioned earlier, have narcissistic pockets in our personalities. It is important to remember that narcissism is the natural state of early childhood; we can speak of a "disorder" only if one becomes so stuck there that one's perception of life is primarily infantile. Difficult lunar aspects can suggest that one has got stuck. Also, powerful planets such as Uranus or Pluto in the 10th may reflect a similar dilemma, if the Moon is also in trouble. I think there is usually also some innate conflict around forming an individual identity within the child, which is often reflected by a strong Neptune; or a powerful resistance to the limits of reality, which is often reflected by an overpowerful but badly aspected Saturn. But there is no such thing as a chart which says, "Narcissistic Personality Disorder," any more than there is a chart which says, "World Dictator" or "Musical Genius." There are hints which when added together point to a possible total sum.

Howard: I'd like to say something about narcissism in general. We tend to use this word to describe an excessive interest in the self, a kind of self-worship which often is labelled as pathological. Psychologically speaking, however, there is something called primary narcissism: the feeling we have in the first six months or so of life that everything around us is an extension of who we are. According to recent psychological thought, a newborn baby needs to have this experience of being the centre of everything. In the womb, we felt as if we were one with mother and we need time after birth to adjust to the fact that she's a separate person. It's important that we have this adjustment phase in order not to feel jolted out of unity and into separateness too quickly. During the early months of life, we can't be loved or nurtured enough. If mother pampers us and centres herself around our needs, this perpetuates the feeling that everything revolves around us, and gives us time to get used to being out in the world.

Then, in the natural course of things, we are ready to give up the illusion of being the centre of the universe and acknowledge our separateness. Many books on childraising that came out in the 1940's and 1950's (like Dr. Benjamin Spock's and Truby King's) advocated something quite different: they said that right from the start, the baby should be made to adjust to the mother's routine, that the baby should be fed only according to a strict schedule and not just because it was hungry and screaming to be fed. If, in the first few months of life, we are forced to adapt continually to mother rather than the other way around, we won't have this experience of healthy primary narcissism, and we'll be left with a hole or gap, a constant yearning for that lost wholeness and Edenic sense of unity with life from which we were too quickly expelled. So later on, we run around looking for people who will centre themselves around us, or we'll compulsively look for ways to regain that sense of unity we once had in the womb and lost too soon after birth.

Conversely, a pathology develops if the phase of primary narcissism goes on too long, if mother continually overadapts to us even when we're 2 or 3 years old. If this is the case, we never learn to acknowledge our separateness, and we never develop those mechanisms needed to cope with life not being exactly as we want it to be. We expect instant fulfilment of all desires, and can't deal with frustration or with other people being different or separate from us. Healthy primary narcissism also is the basis for self-esteem. If mother adores us and centres herself around us in the beginning of our lives, we learn that we are lovable, and this is a sound basis from which to start out and grow in life. It is the deprivation of primary narcissism that can lead into secondary narcissism, which is the pathological sort – the attempt to compensate for a lack of a healthy self-image with undue self-preoccupation, almost as though we're trying to make up for the attention we didn't get in the first six or nine months or so after birth.

Liz: Because there are fashions in babyrearing, such as you describe with Dr. Spock and Truby King, it would probably be fair to suggest that entire generations can suffer from this problem of the narcissistic pursuit of a "real" self through false compensations. The so-called "me" generation (the postwar babies) has been accused of narcissism, and up to a point this is probably a just assessment – not only were Dr. Spock and Truby King in fashion, but families were still reeling from the aftermath of the Second World War, and a climate of global instability is not conducive to a mother feeling safe herself, let alone offering a sense of safety to her baby.

There is a very interesting book by Alexander Lowen, simply called *Narcissism*. He suggests, as have others, that the more pathological end of the narcissistic spectrum springs from the deep lack of an inner feeling of being real and separate; therefore, the rest of the world must exist as a part-object, not separate from the self, in order for one to feel safe. If anything intrudes upon this fantasy – for example, another person who establishes boundaries and says, "No!," then great anxiety is aroused, and considerable rage to cope with the panic. Narcissistic rage, which is usually destructively critical and "puts down" the offending party as being altogether bad or heartless, is really a cover-up for profound fear, the panic of vanishing altogether into that frightening emptiness within which is the real narcissistic wound.

Lowen also makes the point that the nature of modern life tends to generate narcissistic problems in families and therefore in society. In other words, narcissism in the pathological sense has become endemic, because it is passed down from one generation to the next (we cannot give our children what we lack within ourselves), and reflects an increasing dissociation from honest emotional relationship. It is a rather disturbing picture – a collective which is made up of psychological children, all groping about desperately seeking to find an identity through fusion with someone or something else – but I think that Lowen is probably right in many ways. We live in a culture which suffers from this problem within families, and it does not help to rush about calling other people narcissistic too glibly when we are all hurting, to a greater or lesser extent, from a collective wound.

Howard: In her book *Jealousy*, writer and journalist Nancy Friday recounts an article in *The New York Times* that listed the danger signs of a narcissistic personality disorder.[1] You were meant to read the list and check off those points that you thought applied to you. The questions it asked were things like, Do you sometimes have a grandiose sense of self-importance and uniqueness? Do you ever have fantasies of being hugely successful, powerful and brilliant? Do you crave lots of attention and admiration? Do you experience feelings of rage and humiliation in the face of defeat and criticism? There are others I can't recall just now. But honestly, I read this list and thought, yes, yes, yes, yes . . . I mean, I was just waiting for the men in white coats to come and cart me off to the asylum right there and then. It was like reading about a disease in a medical textbook and then being certain you had it. But who doesn't have some of these signs of narcissism nowadays in our highly competitive society with its frantic search for success, pleasure and personal fulfillment?

Liz: Narcissism is in the trade defined as a "borderline" condition, a broad definition of emotional problems which are bad enough to cause severe difficulties, but not bad enough to utterly incapacitate you. The men in white coats don't come for narcissists, only for astrologers. The "borderline" conflict may show in a very specific area of life, such as one's marriage, while at work one might be perfectly competent and reliable. This makes it possible to get away with a lot, since the frequent tantrums and hysterics which reflect outbursts of narcissistic rage may only occur behind closed doors at home, and no one believes the husband or lover or child who is the object of such eruptions.

Another author you should read on the theme of narcissism is Alice Miller, who ought to be required reading for anyone in the

---

[1]Nancy Friday, *Jealousy* (New York: Bantam, 1987; and London: Fontana/Collins, 1983), p. 180.

helping professions.[2] Her premise, put very bluntly, is that any person who feels compelled to work with other people's problems has a narcissistic wound; and I think she is very right about this rather controversial statement. The emotional stress and strain of counseling others is too great to justify by compassion or altruism alone; although these are usually present, we also have our own unconscious emotional investment in such work and, according to Miller, our training begins at around two days old, when we are required to mirror our mothers rather than receiving the mirroring which we so much need. This generates the dubious gift of being almost telepathically sensitive to the emotional requirements of others, with the unconscious expectation that we will be loved and acknowledged only if we continue to service the needs of others as we once serviced those of our mother. Like the actor, the doctor and the psychotherapist (and the counselling astrologer) often have a rare talent at offering what their audience most deeply needs.

Howard: And you get the secondary gain of having someone be dependent on you.

Liz: Yes, and this recreates the original early setup, where the childlike mother requires mothering from her child. And it compensates for one's own powerful dependency needs, which had to be repressed in order to look after mother. All this and we get paid, too. That's an offer no self-respecting narcissist could refuse.

Howard: Grandiosity is also related to narcissism. It's a form of exaggerated self-centredness, where you are carried away by your own sense of importance. You want the best house or car, you like to drop names of important people you know, and you expect to be the centre of attention wherever you go. Grandiosity, like narcissism, is a compensation for the lack of a healthy self-esteem. From my experience, fire signs are particularly prone to grandiosity, an

---

[2]See two good books by Alice Miller: *The Drama of the Gifted Child* (New York: Basic Books, 1983) and *For Your Own Good: Hidden Cruelty in Child Rearing & the Roots of Violence* (New York: Farrar, Straus & Giroux, 1983).

out-of-hand Aries, Leo or Sagittarius, although I've seen it in other signs as well.

Liz: This is the characteristic defence mechanism of the fire signs against feelings of helplessness and inferiority. Every element, and every sign within that element, has its own typical spectrum of modes of adaptation to life. There is a range of strengths and skills and abilities which can be expressed when one feels on top of things; and there is a range of compulsive defences when the going gets rough. If you threaten any creature it will react according to its own nature. Pick up a grasshopper and in terror it will spit foul-smelling brown liquid all over your hand. Frighten a puffer fish and it will inflate itself to four times its size. Step on a viper and it will bite you in the foot with deadly venom. Startle an opossum and it will pretend it's dead. Threaten a fire sign and it will react with a display of grandiosity.

Howard: Yes, for fire signs, inflation is a defence against feeling human and ordinary.

Audience: How about the other elements?

Liz: I have noticed that the earthy signs become obsessively ritual-istic. When earthy people are under threat, they begin nailing everything down and making lists and taking out insurance poli-cies. Because the element of earth is concerned with the material realm, it copes with anxiety by trying to take control of that realm, just as fire tries to take control of the imaginal realm through fanta-sies of superiority. Fire feels most at home in the world of myth, and when under threat it compulsively flies up into that realm. Earth feels most at home in the practical world, hence the compulsive-obsessive pattern. And it is worth remembering that our defences can also become gifts, because they are shaped from great inner need.

　　The element of water is most concerned with the realm of the feelings, and emotional fusion – a return to Eden, whether through another person or through drugs or alcohol, is the most natural defence when the watery signs are threatened. States of extreme dependency and manipulativeness are characteristic of a frightened watery sign. Air, on the other hand, disappears into the head, since the most typical line of defence for the airy signs is hyper-rationality and emotional distancing.

Howard: This reminds me of something. A few years ago I attended a psychotherapy training group, where we did an exercise that has always stuck in my mind. We formed pairs, and one person was "A" and the other "B." Person A had to say, "Please, please, please," and Person B had to respond with, "No, no, no." This went on for twenty minutes, and the exercise was intended to regress you back to a time when you really were in need and you were deprived of what you wanted. I knew the charts of many of the group members, and it was interesting to compare signs with the way different people reacted when their pleas were rejected. I'm generalising slightly, but the fire signs who were told, "No, no, no" put up with it for about three minutes and then said, "Bugger it, you aren't so great, I don't need you. If you can't give me what I want, I'll find it elsewhere from someone better." The earth signs who were told, "No, no, no" just went on pleading, "Please, please, please" for the whole time.

Liz: Yes, earth would still be at it three years later, trying to wear the other person down through sheer force of repetition.

Howard: It was interesting to see the different defences that came up in response to denial or rejection. So the fire signs' defence was, "I don't need you anyway," and the earth signs just kept trying to get what they wanted rather than accepting rejection and going through the emotions it would engender. The air signs who were told "no" started arguing with the other person, telling him or her why they should do it for them, and going into a spiel about all of us having to share this planet together so let's help each other out, or saying things like, "I did this for you once, so you should return me the favour now." In other words, when rejected, they tried to reason with the other person and find convincing arguments to change no into yes. The water signs . . .

Liz: . . . just burst into tears.

Howard: Well, yes. They got down on their knees and really begged, you know, clinging to the other person's trousers and saying, "I'll kill myself if you don't do it." Or they turned it around, and said something like, "Okay, I can cope without getting it, but is there anything you need that I can do for you?" Obviously, I'm exaggerating, but it was a lesson in the different kinds of defences different people use to avoid feeling pain and rejection. And as Liz has said, some of these defences can give rise to creative gifts as well.

Audience: Which do you consider stronger, the progressed Moon conjuncting the natal Sun, or the progressed Moon conjuncting the progressed Sun?

Liz: Haven't we been through this already? I don't think one is "stronger" or more important. But they have somewhat different levels of meaning. When the natal Sun is triggered, it pertains to one's essential character, one's essence. The core meaning of the hero's journey, the main mythic theme in life, is constellated in some way when any planet, including the progressed Moon, arrives on the natal Sun. There is often a profound sense of connectedness with "me," and a feeling of being more real and full of potentials. The progressed Sun, in contrast, is a snapshot of the hero at a certain point on his journey; it is where we have arrived at this moment in time. When the progressed Moon triggers this, it reflects a particular stage of the journey. That is why I think events are more likely to manifest under the progressed Moon–progressed Sun conjunction than the progressed Moon–natal Sun. The potential of the natal Sun is given flesh through its progressed movement, so the progressed Moon–progressed Sun conjunction can be very powerful indeed in terms of major life experiences.

Howard: In my experience with charts, I've always found the progressed New Moon—where the progressed Moon catches up with the progressed Sun—to be an extremely powerful progression. For instance, if it happens in the 11th house, the person will have a profound experience involving friends, goals, groups or organisations, either the month it is exact or slightly before. If you have a progressed New Moon in the 7th, something very important will happen in the sphere of relationships, as if a new phase is being marked. As I say, I've never seen it fail by sign or by house. If you go back to your own chart, you can check when it happened to you and you'll see what I mean.

Liz: I would also take into consideration any planets the progressed New Moon might aspect. If it triggers a natal planet, especially by hard aspect, usually not only a new phase of life is marked, but an important relationship enters one's life as well, characterised by the aspected planet. I am thinking of an example of someone I know who had the progressed New Moon land not only right on his Ascendant, but on his natal Neptune as well. This precipitated the end of his marriage, the breaking up of his enmeshed family, a new relationship, a radical change in work, and an entirely new focus—on his own self, his needs and potentials—over the following year.

Audience: I went to an astrologer when I first came to Switzerland, and I had a very strange experience with this person. He said, "Well, since your so-and-so is here, you will behave in a certain way, and you will experience such-and-such because of this placement." And so on. He gave me little bits of information which in themselves were objective and probably correct, but by the end of the reading I was frustrated and confused and I didn't really come away with anything that helped me. That experience put me off astrology for quite a while. I'd like to ask you in particular, Liz, about your way of dealing with psychological chart readings. What, for you, are the most important things to communicate to someone, particularly when the person who comes to see you is very, very disturbed?

Liz: Two things came to mind while you were speaking. I always ask clients why they have come before I make any interpretation, because my own approach is to try to use the chart to communicate what people truly want to know at the time, rather than what I think they should know according to astrological theory. For this same reason, I always have the progressed chart and the current transits in front of me, even if they have not asked for this; I feel it is important to understand what has brought them to me in the first place. I almost never "go around" the chart giving a basic interpretation—not because I think this is invalid, but because I am more interested in working with what is happening in the present, with the birth chart as a source of insight. Some people have great difficulty in saying, or even being conscious of, why they want a chart reading, and will reply, "Oh, no reason, I was just curious," or, "I wanted to see whether it really works." This kind of "curiosity" is usually a cover for anxiety (some clients expect to be told they will die within the next two weeks, or that they are really horrible people). I may see perfectly clearly that transiting Pluto is sitting on their whatnot and they are in great distress, but they may not want me to know what they are going through until they feel some trust in me and in the reading.

So one part of the answer is that I try to offer insight into whatever dilemma is confronting clients at that point in their lives. In this sense I suppose my analytic training is brought into my astrological work, because it is a kind of concentrated psychotherapy. People speak different languages, and I also feel it is important to address issues in the language which the clients speak. So if I have a hard-headed, pragmatic businessman in front of me who is going through an unfamiliar emotional crisis, I am not going to talk about reincarnation and soul evolution; that is not his language. Most people seek guidance because a crisis or crossroads is upon them and they have lost their sense of inner confidence—if they ever had one to begin with. I have found that one of the most powerful healing implements in the astrologer's hands is the chart's objective confirmation that it is all right to be oneself, that one can trust what one is, and that one is not obligated to be somebody else to please others. The astrological chart contains no intrinsic moral judgment, and I try as best I can to reflect its wholeness and neutrality back to clients.

For those who are very disturbed in a clinical sense, I will try to be extremely careful of how I put things, and will make the effort to circumlocute the charged areas, rather than increasing anxiety. Sometimes one must go in with a kind of surgical knife, because the truth about childhood issues and parental complexes can also be very healing; but this can backfire, and one must be very careful. I have found that deeply disturbed clients give off an unmistakable odour of fear, even if they are very controlled and articulate on the surface. I tend to pick this atmosphere up, and will usually try to find a door into that terror in a way which can help them face anxiety with more pragmatism and objectivity. No advice is of any practical use if the listeners are in a state of abject terror and cannot hear. Obviously, working with highly agitated people can be extremely tricky, and I have made a few bad mistakes over the years of my astrological work; but usually not the same mistake twice. Sometimes I feel that an astrological reading *per se* is of relatively no use, for some people are too much on the edge; then I will offer the support of a counsellor, and encourage the client to get into psychotherapy as quickly as possible. (I have a well-vetted list of referrals for this purpose.)

It would be very difficult to summarise what I feel my astrological work to be about, but I suppose I see it as a tool, rather than an end in itself; and I have found that most people suffer because they do not have any perspective on, or faith in, who they innately are. A chart unfolds during the course of life just as a play does, and one may be quite shocked by the entry of a character onstage whom one knew nothing about. So astrological insights, for me, are useful to help clients recognise and feel more secure on the road they are travelling anyway. The best way to develop a feeling for this kind of astrological work is to undergo psychotherapy oneself, which is why Howard and I require it as part of the Centre's Diploma Course in London. It is difficult to define the ways in which this affects one's astrological counselling, but we can have no idea of how others might feel if we have no idea what is going on inside ourselves.

All good depth psychological trainings make individual psychotherapy the core of the training, because the experience of being listened to, and given permission to be oneself, is the only way we can learn how to listen to anyone else. I have made myself quite unpopular amongst certain astrological circles by stating flatly that any counselling astrologer who has not undergone psychotherapy is malpractising. But I will stand by this statement, because without this most essential experience, we cannot apprehend the reality of the psyche and the nature and roots of others' suffering or potential for healing. Then we run the risk of becoming judgmental—spiritually superior moralists who know better than the client what is "good" or "bad" in their horoscope. Also, we do not really know what true change might be about, and how it might be accomplished, and what it may ultimately cost, if we have not undergone that process in depth ourselves.

Howard: It's so important not to be judgmental of clients, which is sometimes easier said than done, because a part of us may not like where they are coming from or how they choose to lead their lives. And yet, being judgmental will not help anyone, and clients usually pick up on it if you are. Also, people coming for readings may bring issues that stir strong feelings in you or trigger your own unresolved conflicts and tensions. These are just two reasons why psychological astrologers need a therapist, supervisor, colleague or a good friend with whom they can discuss the problems and questions a reading can raise (while maintaining the client's confidentiality) – especially a reading that has left you feeling uneasy for any reason. It's as if the issues that come up when you do different people's charts are the fuel and fodder for your own further psychological self-exploration. This is an ongoing process – you never really finish working on yourself, just as you never stop learning how to be a better astrologer.

Liz: It is indeed ongoing. I have told the following story in other seminars, and some of you may have heard it before, but it taught me an enormous amount about the issues Howard is speaking of. A number of years ago, a woman came along for a chart. From the moment that she arrived, I felt unaccountably irritated by her. There was something about the way she pressed the doorbell continuously for five seconds which set my teeth on edge. My irritation increased as she began to tell me why she wanted the reading, for it seemed that everything was always going wrong for her and it was always somebody else's fault. She was a true whiner, a professional victim. Whenever I tried to make some positive or constructive suggestion she would undermine it or reject it with a "Yes, but . . . ," which by the end of half an hour left me feeling angry and impotent. I began to think that I really couldn't be bothered to try to help her, since she was obviously in love with her suffering and would not give it up no matter how much she claimed to want help.

After an hour of this I finally lost my temper—something which is very rare indeed with clients. I said to her, "Oh, for God's sake, stop whining and whingeing. There are a great many positive decisions you could make, but you just don't want to make them, because it's easier to blame everybody else. I'm sick of listening to your endless complaints about how horrible people are and how badly life has treated you. I'm not surprised people reject you, you're the most negative, unpleasant person I've met in weeks." This was of course just what she had been waiting for—yet another horrible, unsympathetic individual who had no compassion for her suffering. She began to snivel and sob, and then whimpered, "You sound just like my mother," at which point I snapped back coldly, "And you sound just like mine!"

I listened to the echoes of what had just transpired, and thought, "Oh, dear, I think I have a problem here which I had better have a look at." I think you have got the point. In the trade, we call this transference-countertransference, and it can happen in an astrological session as easily as in ongoing psychotherapy. Some astrologers strongly resist going into therapy themselves, on the grounds that they don't "need" it. Maybe they don't in the sense of being reasonably stable and able to cope with life, but we all have blind spots and areas where we project our own issues onto others. Perhaps the resistance to therapy amongst many astrologers is related to the whole issue of narcissism which Howard and I were speaking of earlier, for this narcissistic wound is as prevalent amongst astrologers as it is amongst counselors. As an astrologer, one has considerable power and influence over others, who come consciously or unconsciously seeking not just answers but ultimate redemption. It is painful to face in oneself the same problems brought by one's clients; it is much nicer to inflate and feel vastly superior because we have access to knowledge that others have not acquired. A narcissistic wound can make us feel potent through this kind of power, whereas being in therapy ourselves reveals our ordinary humanness, from which a knowledge of astrology does not exempt us.

That is enough of that. Are there any more questions?

Audience: Can you say something about the Yod, or Finger of Fate configuration?

Howard: Did you ever see old cowboy movies, where two cattle ranchers standing some distance apart from one another lasso a little dogie between them? The planet that is at the apex of the Yod is like that baby steer—it's caught by the two other planets which are inconjuncting it and cannot act without having to take into consideration whatever those two planets represent. In general, the Yod can create a fair amount of friction and tension in your life, and you may feel fated by it. I'm thinking of a woman with Venus in Pisces forming a Finger of Fate with Pluto in Leo and Neptune in Libra. She really has had a tough time with relationships, and seemed always to get involved with people who weren't quite appropriate or right for her. In spite of the many fights and problems, she found it almost impossible to end any relationship, as if some kind of fate or compulsion kept her with a partner. Very often, it was the other person who finished it, and this woman ended up angry and hurt because she felt she had put so much into the partnership and it hadn't been appreciated or had come to nothing. The planet at the apex, in this case Venus, seems to bear the brunt of the Yod. However, as with the quincunx, sometimes the three energies brought together by a Finger of Fate can combine quite brilliantly with one another, but you also have to endure the three energies combining in such a way as to create significant troubles and tensions as well.

Because they have been sextile to one another in the heavens for so long now, it is very common to have a Yod involving Pluto and Neptune. For instance, when Pluto was in Leo sextile Neptune in Libra, planets in Pisces often were caught in the Yod. Then there was Pluto in Virgo sextile Neptune in Scorpio, so planets in Aries might be involved. With Pluto in Libra sextile Neptune in Sagittarius, Taurean planets came under fire. And now, with Pluto in Scorpio sextile Neptune in Capricorn, those people born with Gemini planets could be in line for a Yod in their charts. When a personal planet is lassoed by both Neptune and Pluto—two gods of the underworld—you can be sure there will be powerful unconscious complexes and compulsions influencing the expression of that personal planet, for better *and* for worse. Or if you believe in reincarnation, you could say that there is a great deal of karma to resolve in terms of the planet at the apex of a Yod involving Neptune and Pluto. By the way, psychologically speaking, a complex is a semi-autonomous part of the psyche which takes over and acts independently of the objective reality of a situation. So a man can be taken over by his mother complex, which will distort his perception of women with whom he gets involved. Or you can be taken over by an inferiority complex, even though it is inappropriate or unnecessary for you to feel inferior at that moment. The first step in resolving a deep-seated complex is to acknowledge its existence. This gives you a little more space and detachment from the complex, because it means that you have an "I" (a witness or an observer) which can examine and work with it to find out where it originally came from or what it is about. Lady Diana Whitmore, the founder of the Psychosynthesis and Education Trust in London, used to say that if you're a dog that bites, you bite. But if you can find a part of you which is able to disidentify from a complex or subpersonality in you, a part which can say, "I am not a dog that bites, but I *have* a dog that bites," you can then begin the process of resolving or freeing yourself from the grip of a complex—maybe you'll eventually be able to teach the dog not to bite, although it's never all that easy to teach an old complex new tricks.

Liz: I would like to comment on the nature of the quincunx, because this peculiar aspect is at the core of a Yod's effects. The quincunx produces a highly ambivalent relationship between two planets. There is enough attraction in it to sometimes generate a feeling of deep harmony, and each planet brings the best out of the other one. But then all of a sudden the harmony falls apart—rather like a relationship which sometimes feels absolutely right and beautiful but which then suddenly, for no apparent reason, degenerates into quarrelling and conflict. Then there is a period of worry and tension, where the two people cannot seem to avoid irritating each other; but just as you think the whole thing is becoming too difficult, it shifts again and everything is fine. Signs which are naturally in quincunx, such as Leo-Pisces, Aries-Virgo, or Cancer-Aquarius, have a natural fascination for each other, because each has attributes that the other completely lacks; but they are also always of different qualities (unlike signs in square or opposition, which are always both cardinal, fixed or mutable). This intrinsic differentness can be very irritating.

Howard: Yes, I talked about inconjuncts in my Mars seminar. The two planets involved often blend brilliantly. For instance, if you have Venus inconjunct Pluto there will be times when you will display depth and wisdom when it comes to understanding and handling your relationships. At other times, however, the quincunx between Venus and Pluto will give rise to intense envy, jealousy and destructive feelings toward other people. As Liz says, the quincunx aspect seems to oscillate between expressing itself positively and giving you quite a bit of trouble.

Liz: Another feature of the aspect is that the quincunx is not really strong enough to generate the kind of decisive action that a square does (where you can't stand it one minute more); but it produces too much friction to permit the reflective blending of an opposition (where indecision forces you to eventually find a compromise). There is both too much conflict, and too little. I think this is the reason why the quincunx is often associated with ill health. It symbolises tension which is not sufficiently strong to provoke direct action, but is strong enough to disturb one's equilibrium.

Howard: I remember you once compared it to a backache, which wasn't so bad that you had to stay in bed or remain home from work, but it still niggled you and created discomfort when you were out in the world. However, I believe that if it is a very close inconjunct by orb, you will feel its effects on your life quite strongly.

Liz: The quincunx turns up a great deal in synastry as well, which reflects its push-pull, attraction-repulsion quality.

Howard: Also, I would watch for planets in the heavens making a transiting inconjunct to your chart. Who here has planets in around 15 Gemini? Right now you are experiencing a transiting Yod formed by Pluto in Scorpio and Neptune in Capricorn both inconjuncting your Gemini planet. Geminis are normally very clever at skirting around difficulties, and like Hermes, they are adept at manoeuvering themselves out of or through tricky situations. But now, with Neptune and Pluto inconjuncting Gemini, people with planets in this sign may find that their usual way of sidestepping or slipping out of a problematic situation no longer works, and they are forced into facing or staying in something they would prefer to avoid. In other words, transiting Pluto and Neptune have trapped the principle represented by the Gemini planet they both have lassoed.

Audience: If there are no more questions, I'd like to tell a story about something that happened to me. About thirteen years ago, I had a very bad accident on a horse. I nearly died, but I couldn't find any hard transits affecting my chart at the time. I have a Mars-Uranus natal square, but nothing was touching this off when the accident happened. The only thing I noticed was that my progressed Ascendant was square Saturn, but I didn't think that was enough to correlate with what happened. Not being able to find a transit to describe this important event made me uncertain of the validity of astrology.

Howard: Did you check the horse's chart? Maybe it showed up there.

Audience: But the horse wasn't hurt; I was.

Liz: Perhaps the horse was projecting something.

Audience: What I wanted to tell you was that I bought Melanie Reinhart's book on Chiron, and now realise that Chiron was opposing my Saturn and squaring my progressed Ascendant, so that gave me a better picture of the mishap.

Howard: Yes, I like that, because Chiron is associated with horses — or at least with the Centaur, half-man, half-horse. I bet there were some midpoints being activated as well that you may not have seen.

Liz: I was just about to comment on midpoints. This is another area worth looking at in relation to the timing of events, inner or outer. I do not feel, as many of Ebertin's followers do, that once you have grasped midpoint pictures, you don't need to bother with anything else. Midpoints are a refinement of, rather than a substitute for, basic astrological principles. But some of the more powerful midpoints such as Sun-Moon or Venus-Mars are highly sensitive to transits and progressed planets. If a natal planet sits on a midpoint (within 1 1/2 degrees), then this midpoint is particularly important, and all three planetary energies will be triggered simultaneously. Midpoints are also especially potent if the two planets are also in aspect natally—for example, if Uranus is 15 Aries square Saturn in 9 Capricorn, the midpoint—around 27 Aquarius—is particularly sensitive because a transit over this point will trigger the Saturn-Uranus aspect by forming semisquares to both. So when you are looking at the transits at the time of your injury, as well as considering Chiron, you should check to see if anything—a transit or progressed planet, particularly the progressed Moon—was moving over an important midpoint, perhaps the Mars-Uranus midpoint which is often associated with accidents.

Audience: We talked about inner planets in hard aspect to outer planets, say, for example, Venus square Neptune, and we said that one possible manifestation would be confusion or disillusion in love. If, in synastry, someone else's outer planet, say Neptune itself, contacted that Venus harmoniously, would that ease it a bit?

Liz: No, I don't think a harmonious synastry aspect can spare you from the process of a transiting square in your own chart. A trine from someone else's Neptune to your Venus would create a feeling of almost mystical togetherness in the relationship, since Neptune will idealise Venus and be extremely responsive to its needs, while Venus will appreciate and value Neptune's vulnerability and romanticism. That might mean that your partner could appreciate your feelings, and can give emotional support during a difficult transit. But the square from transiting Neptune to your Venus is your own issue, and you will still have to confront dilemmas around your values and your sense of self-worth. Of course it is easier to go through something if you feel empathy from your partner. But on the other hand, your partner may act out the transiting Neptune, and the harmonious aspect in the synastry may exacerbate rather than lessen the atmosphere of confusion and helplessness which is so often coincident with Neptune transits.

Howard: Yes, that's what I was thinking. You have a better chance of working out your Venus-Neptune problems with people who have planets forming a harmonious angle to your Venus compared with somebody whose planets make hard aspects to it. They'll understand you better or offer you a new perspective on your Venus, although, as Liz says, it doesn't magically make your Venus problems go away.

Liz: Some people enhance our self-confidence, and some wear it down. This is reflected by the nature of the cross-aspects between the charts. It may not be an issue of whether two people love each other, but of what they invoke in each other; and if someone's Saturn, for example, opposes your Moon, he or she may love you deeply but somehow may keep being cool and critical just when you need reassurance the most. Of course such dilemmas improve if people are willing to look at it and work on it. And synastry aspects may not be directly relevant to a particular transit which is affecting your chart, other than indicating basic harmony or conflict between the personalities. But with close cross-aspects between two charts, the same transit will usually trigger both, and the personal challenge also becomes a challenge within the relationship. If your Venus is 16 Taurus, for example, trine someone's Neptune in 16 Virgo, then transiting Neptune in 16 Aquarius will form a quincunx to his or her Neptune at the same time it squares your Venus.

Howard: I've noticed something over the years. If you have a difficult aspect, such as Mars square Jupiter or Venus square Neptune, you can learn quite a bit from people who have these same planets in trine or sextile. A Mars trine Jupiter person who naturally finds the right amount of assertion to put into something can be a model or teacher for someone with the square between these planets. Also, those of you with trines or sextiles may come to a greater appreciation of what these aspects represent in you, after you've met someone who is struggling with the same planets in square or opposition.

Liz: I think we have a tendency to be attracted to people who have the same or a similar colouration around a particular planet. If you have Venus-Neptune, you will naturally feel an affinity with some-one else who has Venus-Neptune, or Venus in Pisces, or Venus in the 12th house. This is a common pattern in synastry, even if the two natal planets do not actually aspect each other across the chart. If you have Sun-Saturn, you will very likely be drawn to other people with this aspect, or with the Sun in Capricorn, because there is a kind of mutual recognition; you are both grappling with the same fundamental issues in life, and share the same inner landscape.

Audience: Does the progressed Moon affect synastry?

Liz: In a very striking way. I think you saw in the charts of the Prince and Princess of Wales that Prince Charles' progressed Moon had reached Diana's Sun at the time of their marriage. This is a typical example. When a relationship comes into being, we will usually find that one or more progressed planets and angles in one chart are touching off either the natal or progressed planets and angles in the other chart. Our feeling of compatibility with another person depends not only on the natal placements, but on the pro-gressed ones as well, since that is who we are at the present moment. Often the progressed Moon is forming powerful aspects to the other person's chart.

The state of a relationship changes all the time, and this is reflected both by the movements in the composite chart and by the constantly shifting relationships between both people's progressed and natal placements. If you meet someone and fall in love while your progressed Moon in on his Venus, you may be very disturbed when, three months later, your progressed Moon arrives in oppo-sition to his Saturn. Then you may wander about for a month muttering, "But he's changed! He used to be so loving, and now he's cold and critical!" If you can sit tight, or go away on a month's holiday, you will find that these transient emotional states pass. And the movement of your progressed Moon across another per-son's chart is a reflection of that gradual coming to know the other which is an inevitable development in any relationship. Sometimes these progressed lunar aspects, such as your progressed Moon square someone else's Uranus, coincide with a time of real crisis or breakup, but there are usually more powerful factors at work besides the progressed Moon at such times.

Audience: You said this also applied to the composite chart. Can you progress that?

Liz: Certainly. You can also examine the transits moving across it, and even work out the transits across its midpoints, although it may sound a bit odd to sit playing about with the midpoints of midpoints. However, they do work. Progressing a composite chart is tedious (unless you use a computer) but simple in principle. The composite chart is a series of midpoints between each pair of Suns, Moons and so on, including Ascendant and house cusps. If you do the same for the progressed charts of the two individuals, lo and behold, you have a progressed composite chart, which is the series of midpoints between each pair of progressed Suns, progressed Moons and so on. You will find that the progressed composite Moon moves at roughly the same rate of speed as the two individual progressed Moons. If you are sufficiently obsessive, you can not only watch what this progressed composite Moon does to the composite planets, but also to the individual natal and progressed charts. And you can watch what your progressed Moon does to the composite. The thing is, you won't have any time left for the relationship. But it is a very useful thing to explore if the relationship has hit a difficult patch, because it offers very deep insights which can help one to handle what is going on in a better way.

Howard: Did you know that Liz has been working quite a lot with composites lately, and that she is preparing a programme to teach the computer how to read composites as she would do them? The computer is going crazy.

Liz: Better the computer than me.

Howard: You must be learning a great deal about composites if you have to teach the computer to read them your way. I find I learn a lot from teaching, but I learn even more from having to write on a topic.

Liz: I am learning an enormous amount about them. I believe the best way to explore a subject deeply is to study it with the idea in mind of communicating what one is learning. It sharpens the mind, and makes one formulate things more carefully.

Howard: And then, as you go about it, you realise all the things you don't know.

Audience: Liz, could you talk about integrating the Sun and Moon in relation to the Ascendant?

Liz: Yes, I feel that the Ascendant is a very complex and profound point in the chart, and it is directly concerned with what we call "destiny." Socrates thought that each human being had a *daimon*, a kind of spirit of destiny, which personified that individual's task in life. The Ascendant is like this *daimon*. The values it represents are not usually felt as "mine," as are those of the Sun or Moon. Yet it seems that life will require us to develop the qualities of the Ascendant, by confronting us with issues in the environment which are characteristic of those qualities. The eastern point of the chart presides over physical birth and the archetypal pattern which we meet when we leave the womb. It is our first glimpse of what is "out there," and we must somehow learn to integrate this experience because we will meet it again and again, first outside and eventually within ourselves.

For example, I have found that Capricorn rising, or Saturn conjunct the Ascendant, often reflects a difficult birth, a kind of restriction or blockage which makes the entry into life hard; and frequently the first bonding with the mother is difficult and full of limitations, because she is drugged or sick or depressed, or one may be ill or forced to lie in an incubator. This is an archetypal Saturnian experience — the painful expulsion from Eden into the cold, hard mortal world — and in a profound way it reflects an essential attitude toward the environment which the person carries throughout life. In youth, usually the individual feels obstructed by the outside world, and does not trust people very much; every effort at self-expression is accompanied by an expectation that it will be a rough road. But of course we create our own reality, and eventually Capricorn rising may come to learn that it is the psychological dimension of this Saturnian archetype – self-reliance, toughness, realism and the capacity to stand alone – which needs to be developed within, so that one does not have to keep meeting its negative concrete face in the world outside.

The process to which we are subjected by the Ascendant mobilises every resource within us, most importantly the Sun and Moon. In a strange way it can unite the qualities of the two luminaries, for we need both a sense of our own uniqueness and a healthy set of instincts to meet the challenges presented by the Ascendant. We seem to move toward the Ascendant over a lifetime, and if there is some awareness of the archetypal qualities represented by the sign, and a willingness to include them in one's value system, it seems to have a pronounced integrating effect on the whole personality. I have found that many people with some knowledge of astrology dislike their Ascendant sign, and try to argue that maybe the birth time was given wrongly. "Oh, I can't possibly have Virgo rising," they say, and find some justification for making it Leo or Libra. This is so common that I have come to the conclusion that the deeper meaning of the Ascendant is not easy to face and digest, except perhaps on a superficial level.

Howard: I've been studying astrology for twenty years, and it took me about fifteen years before I began to grasp the significance of the Ascendant. The ascending sign is the sign rising out of darkness into light just as you are emerging from the dark, hidden and undifferentiated waters of your mother's womb. Conversely, the Descendant shows what is disappearing from view as you are born, and therefore often describes what is hidden in you, those shadowy traits you disown in yourself and see in others. The nature of the rising sign seeks "em-bodiment" and fostering through what is being born at that moment in time. I've come to see the Ascendant as the path leading to the Sun. By developing the qualities of your rising sign, you pave the way for growing into your Sun sign. For instance, if you are an Aries with Capricorn rising, learning discipline and structure is the key to unlocking more of the potency and leadership qualities associated with Aries. If you are a Pisces with Libra rising, working on relationships and achieving better balance between the different facets of your psyche will enable you to express your Piscean ability to heal, soothe, comfort or uplift other people. The Ascendant also shows our relationship to the archetype of _initiation._ The rising sign not only describes something about your actual birth, but it also describes how you get things started or how you enter into any new phase of growth. For example, with Capricorn or Saturn rising, you may have had a slow, difficult birth, and more broadly, you might feel hesitant or apprehensive about any later transition or passage into a new phase of life.

Audience: I was born with 0 degrees Sagittarius rising, and I've always had the feeling I held back until Scorpio was finished. I'm also late everywhere I go.

Liz: Many people believe there is an intelligent choice about one's birth time (by the soul, or whatever one wishes to call it). I am rather pragmatic about such things. Perhaps your soul thought, "Oh, good Lord, not yet, I deserve a Sagittarius Ascendant because I did Scorpio in my last incarnation and I've had quite enough of it." I have had clients ask me if the fact that they were induced early, or born by Caesarean section, meant that they had the "wrong" Ascendant, because the "natural" birth time was interfered with. But if we believe that the soul is intelligent and powerful enough to work out a precise birth time and get mother's labour going exactly on schedule, then surely it can work its way around some poor doctor's plan to induce the birth.

On the other hand, if one does not believe in souls, then it doesn't really matter anyway, since the birth time you get is simply the one you get. It doesn't matter whether you were dragged out, squeezed out, cut out or allowed to slide out in your own good time. I have no strong investment in this; either may be true, but in the end I must simply work with the chart in front of me, however the person might have arrived in this life. However, I have noticed that 0 degrees of any sign has a kind of "Thank goodness, I made it!" feeling, as though it has just narrowly escaped the preceding one. It reflects the very first rush of the new energy, and often exaggerates the sign's qualities. Equally, 29 degrees of a sign is a kind of "final fling" and often strongly marks the person with the characteristic qualities of the sign. This is why I have some trouble thinking in terms of blended cusps as many people do, because the most typical expressions I have seen of any sign have been 0 degrees and 29 degrees.

Audience: If you have the first degree of a sign rising, or the very last degree, do you attempt to rectify the chart just to make sure the Ascendant is correct?

Liz: I generally don't do rectification, unless a particular event is so glaringly obvious by transit or progression that it cannot be missed. However, as I have just implied, the first and last degrees of any sign are often glaringly obvious when the client comes through the door, and I can usually trust my instinct. I am sure rectification is a valid method of ascertaining a birth time if one has sufficient details of the person's life, and some astrologers specialise in it; but rectification can also play terrible tricks on us, because so many transits and progressions can seem to fit a given event. Also, there is often a discrepancy between a concrete event and the time it hits the person psychologically; and the exact aspect of a powerful transit may refer to the latter rather than the former. And finally, we are back to the issue of orbs, and the movement of a heavy planet over the degree of the Ascendant is complicated not only by its retrogradation but by its triggering by smaller transits (such as Mars or a lunation). If someone is really vague about their birth time, I would rather not work with an Ascendant at all, and will stay within the limits of a "flat" chart, since I am not happy speculating about astrological factors that might or might not be there.

Audience: I would like to ask a question about twins. Very often twins are born only minutes apart, but they seem totally different in character.

Liz: I think there is a great psychological challenge with identical twins, because we all need to define and express our identities as individuals, and this is made very difficult when one grows up with someone so similar in basic temperament. In order to create self-definition, I have noticed that twins tend to "divide up" the chart. One of them unconsciously agrees to be the Venus in Capricorn trine Saturn in Taurus and the Virgo Ascendant, while the other plays the Mars conjunct Uranus in Aries. Twins often act out each other's shadows, in an effort to be different from each other. When they are separated in adulthood, they begin to round out more. Of course there is also a great mystery about people, an essence which does not seem to be wholly described by the birth chart. Your astrological "twin" could, after all, be a chicken that was born at the same moment as you, but that enigma which we call the quality of consciousness uses the basic factors in the horoscope and turns them into something very individual. There is obviously an "X" factor—call it the soul, the Self, or what you will—which works *through* the chart, rather than being *defined* by the chart, and this would also apply in the case of identical twins.

Howard: Yes, it's a kind of emotional division of labour, which I discussed in terms of the freedom-closeness dilemma in the Venus lecture. There is a photographer, Diane Arbus, who did a fascinating photographic study of twins, and she managed to capture just what Liz has been saying—very often in her pictures, one twin appears bright and smiling, and the other dark and brooding. I would encourage you to try to see an exhibition of her photos, or to get hold of a book of her collected works.

Liz: I have often thought it is not a good idea for parents to dress their identical twins in identical clothes. This might make the parents' shopping easier, but it makes it even more difficult for each twin to define his or her separateness.

Howard: In *The Case for Astrology*, the authors report some studies done in time twins—unrelated people who happened to be born at the same time and place—and they often do share striking resemblances both in looks and in life histories.[3] There was a man named Samuel Hemming who was born at the same time on the same day as King George III of England. They looked very much alike and their lives were parallel in many ways in spite of their class differences. The same day that George III took the throne, Hemmings opened his ironmonger business. They were married on the same

---

[3]John Anthony West and Jan Gerhard Toonder, *The Case for Astrology* (Baltimore: Penguin Books, 1970), appendix 2, pp. 282–284.

day, they had the same number of children of the same sex, they had similar illnesses and accidents, and they both died on the same day. Then there is the story of King Umberto I of Italy who, by a fluke, met a restaurant proprietor who turned out to be his time twin, born on the same day and at the same time in the same region. They both had wives with the same name, and both had a son with the same name. The restaurant owner accidentally shot himself while cleaning a gun, and on the same day the king was shot and killed by an assassin. There are many more cases like these, which surely cannot just be put down to coincidence.

Audience: I live in Zürich and I would like to attend your school. Is it possible to commute and do it?

Liz: I would recommend buying shares in Swissair. Most of the seminars we run through the Centre for Psychological Astrology are open to the general public, and you may attend any of these you wish. But we also have an in-depth, three-year professional training which awards both a certificate and a diploma in psychological astrology. The problem for students living abroad is that, although you might through flying back and forth from Zürich to London fulfil the requirements for the Sunday seminars, there is also a required number of hours of supervision groups. These groups are small, no more than ten people, and they usually meet on a weekday evening. If you were trying to commute, you would have to be in London on a Sunday for the seminar, and then hang about for the supervision group, which might be on a Monday evening but equally might be on a Wednesday or Thursday (we have different supervisors and their schedules vary). So you can see that this makes commuting impractical. The supervision groups, and the yearly oral assessments (which are also done in a small group format), are in many ways the most important part of the course, since the seminars are theoretical, but the smaller groups focus on putting the theory into practise.

Howard: You would be awarded a certificate of completion after doing all the required seminars and supervision groups. If you wish to receive the school's diploma, then you have to write a thesis, usually between 40 and 80 pages. By the way, we don't offer a postal course.

Audience: As time is short now, I just wanted to say thank you for this course, I have gotten so much from it.

Howard: Thank you. I enjoyed it as well.

Liz: And so did I. I would like to thank you all for your enthusiasm and interest during the course of the week.

Howard: Liz and I would also like to thank the organisers of this week's seminar. First of all Geeta, who has been in charge of the taping and who was a very amusing chauffeur. Then there's Vroni, Astrodienst's secretary, without whom the whole edifice would have collapsed. And, of course, our main man here, Alois Treindl, the founder and head of Astrodienst, who worked incredibly hard to organise all this so well.

ABOUT THE CENTRE
FOR PSYCHOLOGICAL ASTROLOGY

The Centre for Psychological Astrology provides a unique work-shop and professional training programme designed to foster the cross-fertilisation of the fields of astrology and depth, humanistic and transpersonal psychology. The programme includes two aspects. One is a series of seminars and classes, ranging from beginners' courses in astrology to advanced seminars in psychological interpretation of the horoscope. The seminars included in this volume are representative of the latter, although the same seminar is never given verbatim more than once because the content changes according to the nature of the participating group and the new research and development which is constantly occurring within the field of psychological astrology. All these seminars and classes, both beginners' and advanced, are open to the public. The second aspect of the programme is a structured, in-depth, three-year professional training which awards a Diploma in Psychological Astrology upon successful completion of the course. The main aims and objectives of the three-year professional training are:

- To provide students with a solid and broad base of knowledge both within the realm of traditional astrological symbolism and techniques, and also in the field of psychology, so that the astrological chart can be sensitively understood and interpreted in the light of modern psychological thought.

- To make available to students psychologically qualified case supervision along with training in counselling skills and techniques which would raise the standard and effectiveness of astrological consultation.

- To encourage investigation and research into the links between astrology, psychological models and therapeutic techniques, thereby contributing to and advancing the already existing body of astrological and psychological knowledge.

The in-depth professional training programme cannot be done by correspondence, as case supervision work is an integral part of the course. It will normally take three years to complete, although it is possible for the trainee to extend this period if necessary. The training includes approximately fifty seminars (either one-day or short, ongoing weekly evening classes) as well as fifty hours of case supervision groups. The classes and seminars fall broadly into two main categories: astrological symbolism and technique (history of astrology, psychological understanding of signs, planets, houses, aspects, transits, progressions, synastry, etc.), and psychological theory (history of psychology, psychological maps and pathology, mythological and archetypal symbolism, etc.). Case supervision groups meet on weekday evenings and consist of no more than twelve people in each group. All the supervisors are both trained psychotherapists and astrologers. Each student has the opportunity of presenting for discussion case material from the charts he or she is working on. At the end of the third year, a 15,000–20,000 word paper is required. this may be on any chosen subject – case material, research, etc. – under the general umbrella of psychological astrology. Many of these papers may be of publishable quality, and the Centre will undertake facilitating such material being disseminated in the astrological field.

Completion of the seminar and supervision requirements entitles the trainee to a certificate of completion. Acceptance of the thesis entitles the trainee to the Centre's Diploma in Psychological Astrology and the use of the letters D. Psych. Astrol. The successful graduate will be able to apply the principles and techniques learned during the course to his or her profession activities, either as a consultant astrologer or as a useful adjunct to other forms of psychological counselling. Career prospects are good as there is an ever-increasing demand for the services of capable astrologers and astrologically oriented therapists. In order to complete the professional training, the Centre asks that all students, for a minimum of one year, be involved in a recognized form of psychotherapy with a therapist, analyst or counsellor of his or her choice. The rationale behind this requirement is that we believe no responsible counsellor of any persuasion can hope to deal sensitively and wisely with another person's psyche unless one has some experience of his or her own.

The seminars included in this book are part of the fifty or so workshops offered by the Centre. Previous volumes in the Seminars in Psychological Astrology Series are *The Development of the Personality*, Volume 1, *The Dynamics of the Unconscious*, Volume 2, and *The Luminaries*, Volume 3. Volume 5, *Through the Looking Glass*, edited by Howard Sasportas, was transcribed from lectures given by Richard Idemon at a conference he gave with Liz Greene in Vermont in August 1985. The Centre's seminars are never repeated in precisely the same way, as the contributions and case material from each individual group vary, and as there are constant new developments and insights occurring through the ongoing work of the seminar leaders and others in the field.

Liz Greene co-founded the Centre with Howard Sasportas in 1982. Together they successfully ran the programme for ten years. The tragic death of Howard Sasportas in May 1992 has been a great blow to the whole astrological world. However, due in large part to Howard's work and effort, the structure and purpose of the Centre have over the last decade proven themselves to be sound. The school will continue to offer its unique contribution to modern astrology, now under the co-directorship of Liz Greene, a Jungian analyst, and Charles Harvey, a full-time consultant astrologer, who has taught for the Faculty of Astrological Studies since 1967 and has been President of the Astrological Association of Great Britain since 1973.

If the reader is interested in finding out more about either the public seminars or the in-depth professional training offered by the Centre, please write to The Centre for Psychological Astrology, P.O. Box 890, London, NW5 2NE, England. Your request for information should include a stamped, self-addressed envelope (for United Kingdom residents only) or an International Postal coupon to cover postage abroad.